THE LEGACY OF WAR
IN GUYANA AND THE

THE LEGACY OF WALTER RODNEY IN GUYANA AND THE CARIBBEAN

Arnold Gibbons

With an Introduction by
Wazir Mohamed

University Press of America,® Inc.
Lanham · Boulder · New York · Toronto · Plymouth, UK

Copyright © 2011 by
University Press of America,® Inc.
4501 Forbes Boulevard
Suite 200
Lanham, Maryland 20706
UPA Acquisitions Department (301) 459-3366

Estover Road
Plymouth PL6 7PY
United Kingdom

Library of Congress Control Number: 2010937551
ISBN: 978-0-7618-5413-5 (paperback : alk. paper)
eISBN: 978-0-7618-5414-2

Interior design and cover image by Lynn Franklin

DEDICATION

This book is dedicated to
Pat Rodney,

Eusi Quayana,

Andaiye,

Rupert Roopnaraine,

George Lamming

and

Rex Nettleford

CONTENTS

ACKNOWLEDGEMENTS

This book could not have been completed without the help and assistance of many people. I began research at the insistence of A. J. Seymour, the Guyana poet, who believed that Walter Rodney's name should not be forgotten. He is an important part of Guyanese history. I soon came to realize that Walter Rodney is an indelible part of 20th century history and one of its seminal thinkers; and there was no shortage of people wanting to contribute and to share opinions and experiences.

I thank Aubrey Bonnet, dean, University of California at San Bernardino; professors, David Dabydeen, University of Warwick; Jacqueline De Weever, Brooklyn College; John Downing, University of Texas; Frank Kirkland, Jaffir Kassimali, Hunter College; Rainer Tetzlaff, University of Hamburg; Clive Thomas, University of Guyana and its librarian, Yvonne Stephenson; Horace Campbell, Syracuse University; Kej and Hans Hielscher, Der Spiegel; Dieter Brauer, Deutsche Welle; Carmen Jarvis, UNESCO; Leigh Pearson, Henry Ecclestone and Minako Murakami.

Many others could, of course, be named. But that would be impractical. Walter Rodney touched many lives all over the world. Some I have met in the Caribbean and the United States, others in Europe and Africa. Each had his, her own favorite story. Mine is unfinished.

I have set out to deal with the main themes of the Rodney era without the refinement of biography or the discipline of history. It is a personal odyssey through the highways and byways of a world stage where Rodney made an impact; and Guyana, the land that gave us both birth.

My wife Maryse Kieffer-Gibbons and my son, Olivier, were always ready to share their insights.

Walter Rodney's widow, Pat, and the children, Asha, Kanini and Shaka still deeply affected by their personal tragedy, contributed much to my knowledge of his work and the man who was an inspiration to so many.

INTRODUCTION

Wazir Mohamed

June 13, 2010 will mark 30 years since Walter Rodney "the prophet of self-emancipation" was murdered in Guyana at the hands of a brutal dictator acting in cahoots with the agents of international capital. It was not the first time in the modern history of the world that a defender of the people's right to equality was silenced, nor would it be the last time. Walter Rodney's killing can be compared to that of Patrice Lumumba, the first elected Prime Minister of the Congo in 1961. It could be compared with the murder of Amilcar Cabral, leader of the African Party for the Independence and Union of Guinea and Cape Verde (PAIGC) in 1973 at the hands of Portuguese agents. It could be compared with the killing in 1983 of Maurice Bishop, Prime Minister of Free Grenada, at the hands of counter revolutionary agents of his party, the New Jewel Movement. It could also be compared with the murder in 1973 of Salvador Allende, Prime Minister of Chile, at the hands of Pinochet acting in collusion with agents of international capital. These and other leaders committed one single crime; they had a passion for real change. They drew their examples for change from the working people, and created new ways, new approaches for dealing with the unequal relationship between the ruling classes and the poor. These were change agents. They recognized the historical problem of racial, economic, social, and cultural inequality between the then called "third world" and the "first world," and dedicated their lives to change the status quo in their respective countries.

These leaders among many others were killed by agents of foreign and local capital over the period 1960 and 1990 to send a message to the working people of the former colonial world. That message being that international capital and their local agents is not prepared and will not tolerate any real demands for changes in the economic status quo of the former colonies. This accounts in part for stagnation, retrogression, and continuous deterioration today of the conditions of ordinary people in most areas of the former colonial world. The dream of self emancipation is unrealized in every part of the world. Working people across the world today are furthest than they have ever been from realizing the dream of economic, social, and cultural equality. This is true for the Caribbean, the birth place of Rodney and Bishop; as it is true in Africa, the birth place of Cabral, Lumumba, Machel, Mandela, and others. Despite majority rule and so-called political independence in Zimbabwe and South Africa, these countries are yet to deal with land reform; which if dealt with democratically could produce the answer to the structure of the historical inequality colonialism created on the continent. Like Guyana, Africa, and Latin America is yet to find solutions to deal with and turn back the historical damage of ethnic and racial divisions which threatens to consume these societies.

The recipe for ethic and racial healing in Guyana and the third world was Rodney's gift to the working people. He firmly believed in unity of the working people, and was committed to the struggle to find long term solutions to the problems of ethnic and racial division that consumes Guyana and most of the former colonial world. He was not only committed, but placed his body and soul in the struggle for a new kind of popular politics, a new political culture of respect. He belonged to a new generation of scholar activists who saw the old political games for what they were. He did not equate liberation and development with the mere replacement of expatriate rulers with local versions. His determination as a scholar-activist propelled him to argue that transformation and true human development can only be achieved through the common struggle of all peoples to recognize the necessity for a single humanity. His life's work of activism and scholarship stands as an exceptional example to anyone willing to think and act outside the box. As a scholar activist he led the way by showing how easy it was for one to switch between researching and writing to activism. This is attested to by his ability to switch from researching and writing about the devastation wrought by outside forces on African societies in "How Europe Underdeveloped Africa", and about the history of the working people of Guyana to intervening in the Pan African and Liberation Movements in Africa, the movement for racial unity and democracy in Guyana, and to his work with Rastafarians in Jamaica.

While he emphasized, promoted and defended the right of former slaves, the African peoples of the Americas, the Caribbean and Guyana to rediscover their ancestral culture, as attested to in his work "Grounding with My Brothers." He was equally concerned for the East Indian descendants of indentureship in Guyana. He was non sectarian and did not harbor any sectarian attitude. His non-sectarian attitude and approach to find solutions for all peoples in Guyana is established by the equal treatment he gave to Africans and East Indians in his last published book, "A history of the Guyanese Working People, 1881-1905." In this work he debunked the culture and popular perception among sections of the Afro-Guyanese population that East Indians in Guyana are alien. Through documentary evidence of the suffering and struggles of East Indians for survival on the plantations he demonstrates their contribution as equal partners with other groups of people to the history Guyana. His insights and analysis of the contribution of Afro and Indo Guyanese to the history of Guyana is instructive and remains as an instrument to all of us whose life goal is the creation of a united multi-racial democracy in Guyana. A Guyana for all its sons and daughters. All of us who are imbued with this common goal owes it to our ancestors, to our and to future generations to put our shoulders to the wheel and work through our scholarship and in our respective communities to create such a society. This book is one plank in that struggle, as the saying goes in Guyana "one one dutty build dam."

Wazir Mohamed
Indiana University, October 2009

Chapter One

Identity and Ideology

The break-up of Britain's Colonial Empire created dislocation and in some cases a political vacuum. In the Caribbean, the vacuum was filled variously by strong leadership. Disintegration was arrested, territories were held together, deterring alternative possibilities for restlessness, national disarray and even insurgence.

In Guyana, which had known political disorder and confusion prior to independence, leadership did not succeed to any great extent in healing wounds, but arguably, exacerbated them. The precarious imbalance in race relations and electoral politics between Africans and Indians ensured continuing conflict. Race and politics were a constant reminder and a perpetual irritant, which sapped the will of the early Burnham government. Race and its derivatives—social, economic and political power—were the benchmark of all relations. Both Africans and Indians brought to nationhood the racial animosities learned in the pre-independence period. And covert if not overt hostility debilitated energies that should have gone into productive independence. Sectional rather than national loyalties prevailed and both racial groups tested the abilities of the government, whose response was cooperative socialism, essentially self-serving rhetoric designed to appease the masses.

The establishment in 1970 of a co-operative republic suggested a mixture of motives on the part of the Burnham government; one was to tighten the hold of the Peoples National Congress, the PNC, over the country, another was to outflank the Peoples Progressive Party on the Left. Clive Thomas has suggested that additional factors were responsible for this policy shift: continuing poverty; the radicalism and militancy of a population "reflected in highly developed trade union structures."[1]

Whatever the reasons for changes in policy, co-operative socialism revealed in the passing years the ineffectiveness of changes of

form without substance. It was a slogan at best which lacked popular support. Essentially, therefore, it was an administered policy
designed to promote changes, but which lacked the ingredients necessary for change: public will, conviction and impartiality. Furthermore, the PNC government did not have legitimacy and could not
implement policy which did not have the support of an electorate
still restive after the pre-independence period. And the co-operative
movement has had a democratic history.

The co-operative movement was first mentioned in Beatrice
Potter's book of the same title, published in 1891. It was intended to
help the working class see themselves as part of a social democracy
in an England from which they had been largely excluded. The
co-operative movement was in effect an arm of democracy. If the
working class, the co-operators, could so develop their institutions,
the voluntary associations, what would the future not hold for
them. The Burnham government wanted to make the co-operative
movement the focus of national development. But that was the difficulty. The co-operative idea was never intended to be used that
way; and whether it was implemented in capitalist or communist
countries, it was always "on the periphery of these nations' economic structures."[2]

Besides, there were other problems: the idea was introduced by
the PNC, the party in power and was sold very much as its idea;
and did not appear to have had widespread backing; and in the
racial climate of post-independence, this attempt at establishing an
ideological framework for nation – building could not stand. Moreover, the co-operative idea could not be imposed on a capitalist
economy without important structural changes. As a result the
Co-operative Republic, the vehicle for co-operative socialism, came
to be seen as a vapid shell with all the appearances of sloganeering
and false premises. In addition, the uneven distribution of wealth,
which had been a feature of the country before independence,
seemed barely dented by the new arrangements; and wealth appeared concentrated in the hands of party stalwarts, a manipulative middle class and the few technocrats who returned from
abroad.

Also, the new constitutional arrangements were divisive of national interests and tended to favor the members of the PNC – this
resulted in the weakening of the other parties, some of whose members were encouraged to switch allegiances. A direct consequence of
the Co-operative Republic was the de facto disappearance of opposition parties, a restriction of the democratic impulse and the funnel-
ing of political largesse to devout followers of the party in power.
Co-operative socialism as governing ideology did not succeed in rid-

ding Guyana of factionalism, nor did it succeed as a development tool. It did not because crucial matters were not addressed before its implementation: the residue of racial hostility, and the electoral dislocation which came from proportional representation in 1968, – expedient arrangements – that left the PNC in a governing position, but without the psychological support of the whole population. Furthermore, the mechanism of political representation is incomplete without the trappings of democracy.[3] And there was a progressive deterioration of these as the governing party, the PNC, sought vainly to tackle an economic crisis from the decade after independence.

Thus, the absence of enlightened leadership or social policy around which the young nation could coalesce, left an inviting vacuum for a person of ideology and or vision. The point needs to be made here that the Caribbean as a whole has never lacked strong and dynamic leaders, who have in their separate ways and for their own purposes, left indelible imprints. But it also needs to be stressed that strong leadership is not necessarily enlightened leadership. Strong leadership in the Caribbean has been identified with personal charisma, which has often won public acceptance and approval, especially when this is identified with verbal dexterity.[4]

But there are limitations to personal charisma which can prevent restraint, constructive analysis, self-reflection and lead to excess and disastrous policy. To what extent the former President of Guyana, Forbes Burnham, overcame the inherent limitations of charisma or succumbed to them, is not the object of this book. Perhaps Burnham's charisma made it difficult for him to accept limitations, or perhaps he understood the limitations well enough, but was confident that he could override them; or again, perhaps, he did not wish to and chose to ignore them. Certainly, the malaise in which Guyana found itself as a result of uninspired leadership, inadequate planning, lack of capital, balance of payments deficits, — the usual crop of economic woes, shared by many in the Third World and not a few in the First World—and authoritarian tendencies, provided opportunity for the idealism of Walter Rodney. Also, Burnham appeared to many to have overreached himself and was therefore incapable of analysis and restraint, and had run out of ideas to deal with the mounting problems of Guyana.[5] That a Burnham, depleted of resource, prepared the way for Rodney, was the deadly paradox of Guyanese politics.

Both Burnham and Rodney were men of great intelligence: that is to say, they had the mental ability to calculate, reason, analyse and perceive relationships; they also had the aptitude to learn quickly, store and recall information, use language fluently, clas-

sify, generalize and adjust to new situations. Both could adapt to
the environment and did so. Both were men who grappled with
ideas and who were prepared to pursue these ideas wherever it took
them. For Burnham, though, the practice of law, the artful challenge of politics, sharpened intelligence to the narrowness of craft.
But Rodney's intelligence continued to grow because of the continuing demands of historical research, discovery, conflict and the eventual commitment to the union of theory and practice. At any one
period in the history of a nation one such is enough, but two living
at the same time could only provoke a conflict of wills from which
solution is scarcely possible. Only an outcome is.

That outcome was in a sense predetermined. Burnham, a
staunch member of the bourgeoisie, with roots in the teaching profession, could only conceive of power in relation to the parameters of
his class – both his own and others. Power was part of the moorings
of a background of solidity which straddled the religious and the
secular with commendable ease. In time this elite—and it was an
elite comprising men of letters, technocrats and others qualified
from European and American universities—would be expected to
assume leadership and guide the masses to the fulfilment of national objectives. A gracious noblesse oblige ensured that commitment would accompany a tradition that had been handed down by
colonialists. Everything was grist for the mill and the paraphernalia of modern government was engineered to suit lofty but slender
purposes.[6] Also, the visible trappings of office, the symbols of power,
accompanied this dominance. And to relative domestic respectability was added foreign attention, which a well-publicized but superficial attention to an ideology as controversial as socialism, assured.
Socialism of any complexion is a wine of rare vintage in the Americas and fairly guarantees that a country like Guyana will be taken
seriously by the powers that be, and for quite the wrong reasons.

Guyana like most of the independent national bourgeoisie
which has affected a role for which it had scarcely been prepared.
But unlike some of the Caribbean independent territories, it rushed
headlong into political experimentation with much flare but little
consciousness of its vulnerabilities; and these were many: the new
constitutional arrangements—proportional representation—which
had driven Dr. Jagan, the chief minister from office, had left a
residue of bitterness that had burdened the new government's early
deliberations; inadequate human resources to carry out ambitious
development plans, given the fragilities of race relations; unstable
borders with both Venezuela and Suriname, —to name a few. But
these did not give the new leadership pause and it went ahead
with that certainty born of confidence in what it perceived as its

historic mission.

C. L. R. James has said that the Caribbean middle class "is like no other in history."[7] It was—and is—caught between the masses and the upper class, variously described as planter class, colonial upper class, professional class. Education provided mobility and refuge for those who obtained it. Through education the middle class could rise to the top of their respective societies. This necessarily distances it from the masses. And while in behavior, there appeared little to distinguish the one from the other, it was a very important difference, psychologically. The middle class aspired upwards; and while critical of colonial power, it was itself a replica of that power in operation pursuing its own class interests relentlessly. Education was an important part of the socialization process and language and communication were the not so hidden dimensions that explained the differences with the masses.[8]

The middle class believed itself heir to what was left of British interests and it could exercize itself in any way it chose and support whatever movement or policy that would enhance it; and clearly national unity would. Such an opportunity came with the pre-independence movement, when middle class politicians united behind the strong pull of the national movement. When the schism took place in 1964, middle class leadership exerted itself. It was much more than an ideological split: it was more catastrophic than that. It was the severance of the unity of the middle class and the masses. Henceforth, the politics of Guyana became the reassertion of middle class hegemony. While education was the aphrodisiac of the middle class and its launching pad to power, influence and material wealth, it did not so activate Walter Rodney. Although his training assured him a place in that class, he turned his back on it; and either through the strength of his convictions or the depth of his character, or both, avoided the upward mobility syndrome. Both Burnham and Rodney emphasized in different ways the significance of class and also the role of the intellectual in the politics of developing countries.

The intellectual and a developing country

What is the role of the intellectual in a developing country? And what does it mean to have critical consciousness, is how Edward Said, put the question.[9] Is the intellectual expected to reinforce his culture, affirm orthodoxy of the political system, or social system of which he is a part? Or is he expected to chart a new direction while developing a critical intelligence, guiding as he himself is guided by the intelligence of the masses? In the first instance, the intellectual is a supporter of the establishment and the powers that be; in the latter instance, the intellectual participates in an ongoing dialectic with the people and is a catalyst through which the people change their destiny. The intellectual must at one and the same time be a part of and also distance himself from the mainspring of that culture. But his critical faculty must be rooted in it, for that gives him credibility. [10] It is what George Lamming meant by the "humanization of the Guyanese coastal landscape," referring to the work of Guyanese laborers in the building of the infrastructure of the sugar cane industry. [11] It is the intimate and therefore spiritual alliance between the intellectual and the worker, where the latter adds depth and focus to the observations of the former—essentially as two peas in a pod, separate in a way and equal, both belonging and sharing the same consciousness. Edward W. Said believes that critics are bound either "filiatively (by birth, nationality, profession), or affiliatively (by social and political conviction, economic and historical circumstances . . .)." [12] And "critical consciousness stands between the temptations." It is possible on these terms to explain the sensitivities particular to the exile who draws from both the culture of birth and the culture acquired by historical or political conditioning.

Walter Rodney was born in a colonial society, spent his early years there and was by affiliation a part of it. His earliest writings were critical of it-its racism, its poverty, and its divisions by class. His years spent at university saw him acquire a mode of explaining the underlying reasons why his country and the world's poor were in such a state. Marxism, more specifically, Marx's view of history, provided explanation and ammunition that was to steel his later criticism, and lead to political awakening. Thus, historical circumstances and instruction informed a critical perspective. He could join with Fanon in a criticism of the colonial master, but unlike Fanon he would take that criticism further and pointedly seek to raise the consciousness of his countrymen about what he considered to be the evils of unchecked power. Intellectual as martyr, vulnerable, valuable, interposing self between filiative community and the community of affiliation and seeking to interpret the social, political realities of time. But Rodney went beyond criticism. He sought to change circumstances, going beyond Fanon, who would demand clarity of ideas of both intellectuals and politicians and insist that these "must be profoundly dialectical."[13]

For Rodney the "black intellectual . . . must attach himself to the activity of the black masses."[14] This was salvation for the person of intellect who wished to make a contribution to the national struggle. Indeed, he implied that it is only in this way [activity with the masses] that the intellectual, through raised consciousness, could perform the necessary and urgent tasks of nation-building.[15] Moreover, through this activity he would be strengthened and able to challenge the myths, which interceded between the nation and its people and interfered with their self-realization. Rodney understood the dangerous role of the intellectual in a developing country and as a historian he could not have been unaware of the critical dimensions of it. He eventually became a victim of it. The intellectual became critic and critic became victim.

The intellectual in a developing country must assume a number of roles, each of which deals with the nature of the society-its progress and movement in areas which are important, such as the kind of society which it is to be, and also the kind of material progress it is to enjoy. But there is also the role of the intellectual as visionary, prescribing and delineating, mapping, creating hemispheres of existences. In this respect he becomes heir to his own conceit, or victim of his own vision. As visionary he is both architect and designer of his own stage.

This creates problems, not the least of which is that of authenticity and the terms by which authenticity is defined. It involves also no less the definition of an intellectual. In order to define authenticity, it is necessary to study his output, to study the texts that he has written and to suspend judgment until this process has been accomplished.[16] Follows then important questions such as the extent to which the knowledge accumulated reflects the work of the intellectual, and if it does then to find out if it is possible to separate the intellectual from what he has been writing about, the better to know and to understand. This is not a perfunctory exercise: it concerns the way how one treats knowledge and whether one can look at a given text and say that it represents authentic ways in which knowledge is accumulated. And this knowledge is built up in critical areas of a culture as it relates to social, political, historical and institutional matters.

Rodney as intellectual was both a part of the dominant culture and outside of it. His formative work had been in history, yet it is precisely this which enables him to go beyond the historical perspective and distance himself from the dominant culture. All this, at the same time locating and placing his work within history and the historical method.

The method of inquiry used in the study of his work is textual; that is to say, the text is the main basis upon which criticism rests—this, as distinct from, though not opposed to other worldly influences, which informed his work. These other influences belong to a more comprehensive work that includes textual criticism, personal life, political conduct and various other conventions that shaped his life.

Textual criticism

Textual criticism is its own virtue, which is not to imply that it stands alone, for the distinctions between textual criticism and other conventions of literary analysis are not clear—cut. There is a constant ebb and flow of thought and reaction to textual material that cannot be separated from the object of study. But textual criticism has its own criteria for judgment and its own concerns. For example, it seeks to expose the mysteries and hidden associations in meaning. Textual criticism involves a larger scale of reference and unlike other forms of direct social and political attributes is flexible (a text can convey more than one meaning to many different persons). It can present many different sides to its suitors; it carries its own rewards. The text is always there, even though the form and shape of criticism, the individuals who employ it and the society changes. This explains why many texts are "rediscovered" by a new age. It is not that the text has changed; it is that a new critic has revealed something hidden from less perceptive eyes. Or perhaps, new circumstances now enable the critic to reveal what was previously hidden to previous researchers—computer analysis now facilitates qualitative and creative work. Textual criticism is therefore incomplete. The critic goes over familiar and unfamiliar ground, original texts, seeking to make it alive, but invariably is unable to do so completely. The text is not easily read and is subject to interpretation; hence, meaning can sometimes be elusive. But there is a way in which the critic of the text can also bring it to life-"rediscover it"—outside of the computer and also other help aides. And that is first to represent the text studied and then afterwards to discuss it in the critic's own language, a way of representing the text which belongs to the critic alone. This new language creates and stimulates knowledge of the text and the relationship of the text to the culture of which it is a part. [17]

But textual criticism cannot exist in isolation. The critic is as much a part of his culture as he is a part of the culture of what he seeks to represent; in addition, there is his discipline which makes its own demands. The critic cannot afford to be subservient to the discipline, for that would place knowledge on a pedestal from which it might be difficult to reach and thus what must be reached might be unattainable. This places the critic in the unsurmountable paradox of needing knowledge in order that knowledge can be attained. The discipline serves as a useful methodology for obtaining knowledge; and by methodology one means the intrinsic structure of the discipline, which makes it a field of study. For example, why is history a discipline to be recorded, studied, interpreted, objectified? It is so because of the social characteristics e.g. humanity, epochs, the rise and fall of kingdoms, lives of great men, the evolution of the world etc., and above all how all this fits into the picture of human experience. History has taught certain well-defined lessons, and these constitute part of its methodology; and the student of history uses this methodology as part of the interpretation of history. A discipline thus formulates the means by which it is to be studied: as it were, aiding in its own reconstruction.

The critic is very much a student, concerned not only with the problem of knowledge, but how knowledge can be revealed about the subject by means of looking at the text. In order to do so, the critic must interpose himself between the culture and the system through which culture imposes itself. In assessing the work of Walter Rodney, I was always conscious that this was the case: I had to interpret his work by placing myself at the interstices of culture and political system, the better to understand the influence of the one on the other and how each reacted separately and together. This created certain difficulties, for there were three dimensions to the problem. First, the dominant culture of metropolitan England and its effect on Guyana, its former colonial territory, and by implication all other colonial territories, differing more in degree than kind. Second, the post-independence dominance of the Peoples National Congress, PNC, the only political party so far to rule Guyana. Third, the dominance of the capitalist system in the Western world, its effect on the non—western, non—white world and the struggles of the latter to achieve control over their affairs.

Dimensions of the problem

These were the three areas that were central to an understanding of Rodney's work and in a general way that of post-colonial historians; and the consequences of the end of active colonialism, the independence of former colonial territories, their emergence in the wider world and their struggles have also occupied other disciplines.

English colonial policy has been exhaustively chronicled by writers, who have in their several ways placed individual emphases where they chose, or where their scholarship or biases led them.[18]

This has led to an impressive array of descriptions, sentiments and opinions about the Caribbean in general.[19] But they all agree that the traffic in sugar and slaves constituted the major influences on the development of Caribbean societies. Sugar and all the paraphernalia of production—planting, reaping, harvesting, the factory process, exporting, marketing, merchandising—were examples of a capitalist process, which not only had all the ingredients of inequality of function, but also actively promoted slavery and social inequality. Social inequality was the accompaniment of the English saga from the very beginning and poor whites, convicted felons and persons who were out of favor politically, came to share the early and doubtful blessings of colonization. Poor whites in the early economy of Guyana did not fare well and when the African trade opened up untold possibilities for exploitation, they surrendered some of the more demanding tasks in sugar production.

The conditions whereby Africans were forcibly taken from their homelands across the Middle Passage and which gave rise to the infamous Slave Trade, provided cheap labor for the plantations and buttressed the capitalist-industrial system. One of the significant by-products of that system was the master-slave relationship. A no less iniquitous consequence was an active racism. Thus, social inequality promoted by a class system, which had been part of the baggage of European settlers, and racism, a by-product of the capitalist-industrial system, became the heritage of Guyanese and Caribbean history.

These two social evils have influenced all the social, economic and political institutions in Guyana since then. And the admission of indentured Indians, Chinese and Portuguese in the nineteenth century to work the sugar plantations in the aftermath of the abolition of slavery, provided additional opportunities for class differences. Fledgling political representation in Guyana, which emerged after the abolition, showed evidence of the importance of social class; and beginning with white people occupying the top rung of the ladder, social status was determined more by color than by function, possessions, and even wealth. This identifiable trait was not confined to Guyana alone, but was a marked feature in all Caribbean societies, adding to their complexity; and the profiles of Richard Sennett and Jonathan Cobb of the staple of class in American civilization, apply equally to the Caribbean.[20] English colonial influence dies hard in the Caribbean and one agrees with the view of Rex Nettleford in his introduction to M.G. Smith's influential book, that race and color, economic variables, and status make up "the textured diversity" of the region.[21] In Guyana, these factors were sharply focused by the ways in which the different racial groups responded to them. Therein lies the birth of Guyanese nationalism, precariously uneven, always delicately balanced, its complex social structure as much a challenge to its constituents as those who study it.

The second dimension was the administration of the Peoples National Congress, the only political party to rule an independent Guyana. The Peoples National Congress could be an object of study alone because of how it has managed to achieve and hold on to power. Quite apart from its obvious historical importance, such a study would be significant for understanding and explaining the dominance of personality on politics and the interplay of race and politics on national affairs. The consequences of race versus politics in Guyana, as J.E. Greene has shown in his admirable book of the same title, was the triumph of the PNC, which appeared to benefit from the institution of proportional representation and greater party discipline and mobilization. [22]

Party politics in Guyana has had a long and checkered history. Political parties had come into being in response to the uneven, unfair and unrepresentative institutions that had governed the then colonial territory of British Guiana. They represented for over one hundred years the slow and painful process towards self-actualization and eventual self-government. The pace towards eventual self-rule was slow, largely because of the intransigence of a plantocracy, which through its control of the sugar industry, and the support of its acolytes,—the church and the metropolitan colonial office—conceded only the form and not the substance of representation. One does not need to belabor the point, for Guyana shared like many other colonial territories an inequity, which affected early political maturity and growth, and this added to the disaffections of exploitation and poverty, guaranteed stagnation.

Still, political enterprise was far from lacking and both the Reform Association and the Progressive Association of the late 19th century were in the vanguard seeking electoral representation and an end to the monopoly of the planters in the affairs of the country. Piecemeal change was late in coming and then only in dribs and drabs—1850, 1891, 1909—and as late as 1928 Africans and Indians who made up a majority of the population, had no vote at all. Those who had the vote were the newly enfranchised lower middle class, who began to participate in the early trade union movement. The trade union movement was a response to the need for pressure against the Colonial Office for constitutional change; but also it was one of the measures which the working class people took to protest intolerable conditions of labor; others included, public criticism, newspaper publication and political organization. Such working

class efforts are noteworthy in that, even though there was a certain racial apprehensiveness between Africans and Indians, the beginnings of working class solidarity saw the two peoples share
common objectives. Indeed, Joseph Ruhoman, an Indian, and editor
of the *People*, vigorously supported the reform movement even as he
campaigned against living conditions which promoted squalor and
backwardness among Indians. [23] The reformist zeal, which was
part of the Popular Party, was clearly shared by working class
Guyanese, united in the face of the depredations of the Colonial
Office and the obtuseness of plantation society. Such collective part-
nerships, despite attempts to dissolve them through "divide and
rule" policies, represented in the main, the first significant political
cohesion in Guyanese politics. This is not to imply an end to friction
or grievance. Such continued and still do and are economic in scope;
that is, Africans were disturbed about unemployment when Indian
immigration began; immigrant labor ate into their profits on the
sugar estates and imported goods reduced the demand for what
they produced. The result was as Cheddi Jagan, the former chief
minister of Guyana, observed:[24] "the seeds of racial strife . . . [be-
tween Africans and Portuguese and Africans and Indians] . . . were
sown at this early date by the pattern of economic competition . . . "
Now, Africans are disturbed by the probability of loss of political
power and influence as the Indian birth rate leads inexorably
towards an Indian majority at the polls. [25]

The economic conditions, which led to precarious working class
solidarity,—precarious because it had to withstand attempts to destroy its cohesion—persisted well into the century. In fact, Britain
began to fear for the security of its Caribbean possessions when
riots broke out in 1905, followed by similar outbursts in Trinidad
and Jamaica later on. The instability of the region was underlined
on the even of World War II, when a fearful Europe plunged into its
own crisis and put its strife-torn colonies temporarily behind. [26]

World war II and political change

World War II was a catalyst for increased political representation
in Guyana. Reasons were many: structural and other grievances
continued to plague colonial relations and ex-servicemen returning
from active combat, increased the numbers of those who had obtained their first political education abroad; and added to whom
were the disaffected masses, who had remained home. Britain itself
was in the midst of change: the question of Palestine had begun to
dominate thinking, India and the African colonies too, including
those which France controlled. These factors added to the burdens

of the metropolitan countries.

In Guyana, the era of change was set in motion by the Waddington Commission, which recommended that Universal Adult Suffrage be introduced. The general elections of 1953 marked the first occasion in which a unified national party, the PPP, presented itself before an electorate. The national movement which the party embodied was significant because it included both Africans and Indians; it claimed to represent the working class, though its appeal went beyond the working class; its announced policies were socialist but well within the understanding of the British Socialist Labor Party and would not have embarrassed the latter. In retrospect, such radicalism the national movement exuded quite paled before the more trenchant demands of some contemporary societies.

The Peoples Progressive Party won the elections of 1953 and proceeded to form a government, which set about the task of actively governing. Some of its legislation reflected routine social concerns: educational reform of schools and education committees, bringing them under government supervision; establishing a proper social security system, and workmen's compensation; and agricultural reform. But the governing party never was able to get through its planned legislation. What it managed to pass in the Legislature were three Bills which, for controversy and stirring up ill-will, could not have been better chosen. The party repealed the Undesirable Publications Law, which had made it illegal for "undesirable" printed matter and films to enter Guyana; it raised the ban on West Indian intellectuals whose political stances were considered dangerous to the security of the region; [in practice this measure was a defense of free speech and free assembly] and it amended the Rice Farmers Security of Tenure Ordinance of 1945, which had placed additional burdens on farmers and less on landowners for the upkeep and maintenance of property.

Ambitious programs for social legislation were not executed, for the Constitution was suspended 133 days after the party took power. Much has been written about this period and the pros and cons of suspension need not detain us here. But what is important is that a mass movement and a popular party that rested on that consensus was destroyed. The consensus was significant in Guyana's history, for it represented a return to the period of active co-operation between Africans and Indians for a short but significant period in the history of Guyana from 1885 to 1928. That period saw the beginnings of working class solidarity in the face of the continued reaction of the planters and the British government. What followed the suspension of the Constitution of 1953 was not only the end of a democratic experiment popularly supported, but the begin-

ning of active and renewed competition by Africans and Indians.
Given also deliberate attempts by the British government to spread
such red herrings as "a Communist subversion" and "a dangerous
crisis both in public order and economic affairs," and an international mass media over-sensitive to Communist scares, is it to be
wondered at that the precarious unity of Africans and Indians collapsed? The factions into which they split were the Peoples Progressive Party, and the Peoples National Congress, which while still
espousing socialism, had joined forces with the United Force, an un-
apologetic capitalist distraction. This expedient relationship sacri-
ficed principle for political gain. But the gain was as significant as
the betrayal of principle. What had occurred was no less than the
split of the working class movement into racial factions, thus exposing the flimsy basis upon which the movement rested. It can be argued, of course, that sooner or later, with the British out of the
picture, racism would have reared its ugly head. But it is also fair to
add that had the working class nationalist party overcome that crucial test—in much the same way that it had overcome in a less
flamboyant way other tests in the course of its short history—it
would have become stronger in adversity, in opposition, and
thereby prepared itself to deal with matters of race and resolve its
own contradictions. Of the two, only Jagan, who struggled for the
leadership of the party, had prior experience in elected government.
And while it is not to be imputed that Burnham was not adequate
to the task, the followers of them both, woefully lacked the tools to
carry out their duties. [27]

The consequence of the betrayal of the working class movement
was the injection of racism in the political affairs of Guyana and all
successive elections thereafter were influenced by it. This was not
altogether unexpected, for working class solidarity had been a major celebration up to the suspension of the constitution in 1953, but
after that, there was nothing to preserve that solidarity. And ideology had at best a tenuous foothold in party strategic deliberations.
Also, the PPP party and its leaders could do nothing about the
steady and unfriendly international press, which promoted the dissolution of the movement by drawing heady associations with international communism; and some of the more outlandish tabloids
anticipated revolution. [28]

The report of the Robertson Commission of 1954 into the activities that led to the suspension of the Constitution, sealed the fate of
the working class movement by recommending an indefinite waiting period before a duly elected government could take its place.
This ended whatever hope there was of resilience within the movement. Moreover, the implication that responsible government could

not succeed as long as the Peoples Progressive Party maintained its leadership, was an invitation for others to initiate their own challenge. This, of course, naturally followed. Racism, which had until then played an insignificant part in the national political movement, was identified with political behavior. The Robertson Commission had indicated the lines to be followed by the electorate. The message was unmistakably clear that the once powerful national consensus was too high a price to pay for electoral backwardness and it would not be allowed to survive. The Robertson Commission identified "communist influence within the PPP. At the time of the elections at least six of the Party's most promising leaders . . . accepted unreservedly the 'classical' communist doctrines of Marx and Lenin." While the Commission went on to say "Mr. Burnham (Chairman of the party) was generally recognized as the leader of the socialists in the Party . . . Yet we had no doubt that the socialists in the PPP were essential democrats and that left to themselves their preference at all times would have been that the Party should pursue its constitutional objectives by straightforward and peaceful means." [29] It would not have been difficult in the charged political climate in Guyana for a frustrated electorate to reach its own conclusions as to who was its favorite son. It could get no help from its leaders who were divided—literally; Jagan was imprisoned for six months. Some of the party's supporters moved in other directions: the trade union movement, which had been one of its mainstays could not agree on whom to support. Some of its members went with Jagan, others Burnham. The elections of 1957 were a test of their legitimacy, and that of 1961 also. Jagan won both elections. Guyana was a badly divided country. Race was now the decisive factor in elections, absolutely.

Jagan's party, the PPP, was in office but not in power. Between 1957 and 1964 the opposition party, the PNC, grew restive and increasingly vitriolic and the administration of government became difficult. The PNC was joined in the 1961 elections by the United Force, a party with which in 1964 it joined a coalition. The persistence of the Jagan victory at elections – 1953, 1957 and 1961– was not unnoticed overseas. Jagan's own radicalism did not help his cause. But it was clear that he enjoyed the complete support of the Indian electorate who voted solidly for him on each occasion. It became clear that the opposition parties did not stand a chance of power as long as Jagan could count on the allegiance of Indians, who were more numerous than the Africans. The Colonial Office responded to U.S. nervousness in the area—visions of Castro loomed loud. It had been hoped that a less pronounced pattern of racial voting would emerge in the elections and contribute to the formation of coalition parties—broader-based leadership to nullify radical positions. This did not happen because the demographic division of the electorate consistently favored Indians.[30] In the opinion of the Colonial Office then, majority voting did not succeed in bringing the kind of stability required for good government. Duncan Sandys, Secretary of State for the Colonies, summed up the position: "Unfortunately, this electoral system, while providing clear parliamentary majorities has not provided strong government . . . the reason for this state of affairs is that the ruling party has alienated the confidence of the non-Indian communities . . . " [31]

The consequence of this was that the electoral system was changed to one of proportional representation that ostensibly would "make it easier for new political groupings to form on a multi-racial basis." [32] But this was a devout wish. The 1964 elections contested under the new system of proportional representation saw the return of the various parties with their loyalties hardly changed. The racial basis for political groupings remained intact. Indians voted for Jagan, Africans for Burnham and the rest for D'Aguiar, the leader of the United Force, the third party. It was indeed the coalition of Burnham and D'Aguiar that finally ended the rule of Jagan. Thus, the objectives of the British government in changing the form of the constitution to encourage greater plurality did not succeed, though it did succeed in getting rid of Jagan. [33]

The rise to power of the PNC under Burnham in 1964, with the help of the UF under D'Aguiar—an ill-conceived alliance—was doomed almost from the first day. It was an alliance whose central objective was to drive Jagan from power and this it succeeded in doing. There was little ideological basis for cooperation and Burnham's brand of socialism lived uneasily with the undisguised capitalism of d'Aguiar. And the power of the latter declined considerably in the elections of 1968, the first post-independence elections in Guyana. Burnham won an election which was known for the significance of the proxy vote and the overseas vote, which attracted enormous critical comment, because it allowed non-resident Guyanese to participate. [34]

The history of Guyana since 1968 has been the assumption of power by the PNC and the removal of other parties from serious contention in national affairs—though not quite. Walter Rodney joined the Working People's Alliance because he believed that the PNC, the party which had broken away from the PPP in 1955 after the suspension of the constitution, did not represent the working class of the country, and had in fact failed them; it was a middle class party of opportunists, which had threadbare loyalty to the masses, which since 1953, first by Britain, then by local politicians had been battered from pillar to post. The schism in the first national consensus, the PPP, which won the elections in 1953, was for Rodney a major betrayal. Working class solidarity then so much in evidence, had collapsed under the combined pressure of imperial policy and personal frailty and ambition. In consequence, voting by race became a feature of the elections of 1961, 1964 and 1968. And the virtual institutionalizing of the PNC as the dominant party thereafter, frustrated the important work of restoring working class unity. The two dimensions are synchronous—the end of working class solidarity and the rise in dominance of the PNC. The domestic policies of the PNC administration are not the subject of this book and will only be examined within the context of how they affected the work of Walter Rodney.

Rodney became increasingly frustrated by the PNC. His concern that the government was becoming associated with an autocratic leader, who wanted to bring about an end to party politics [this was virtually achieved as the PPP and the United Force had little influence after 1968]. The aimless policy that was a pale imitation of socialism. The hardship of living in difficult conditions, exacerbated by corruption, which was by no means new in developing countries. These together pushed Rodney in the direction of direct involvement in Guyana's affairs. Moreover, he did not envisage the possibility of the Burnham administration mounting an effective challenge to the capitalist system, of marshalling the nation to achieve control of its resources. A close reading of his work, especially A *History, the Guyanese Working People, 1881-1905,* suggests why.

The middle class in Guyana

The middle class which had skills and marketable talents had an ambivalent role in the history of Guyana. It had thrown in their support with the plantation elite in the late nineteenth century, and had not joined forces with the workers during the riots of 1905. It had the same role as "interlocutors valabes" in French colonial Africa, who mediated between the workers and the colonialists and were well rewarded by the latter. When it proved in its interests to join common cause, it did so without reservation. For example, even though they did not join the demonstrations and strikes in 1905, they served a useful purpose in the previous years to make the complaints of workers known to the planter hierarchy. In so far as what they did was useful, it was due to the growing concern of the workers whose own consciousness had been raised. Workers had decided to intervene in their own history, or to use Friere's words "gain con-

sciousness through conflict." It was conflict and only through conflict that political power could be gained; and it was this which was
the undying contribution of the Guyanese working class to the education of the middle class. Reading Rodney's History of the
Guyanese Working People 1881-1905, one understands why, in his
view, the Burnham administration could not successfully wage an
ongoing campaign against international capitalism: it was because
Burnham had betrayed the same capacity for ambiguity as the middle class in 1905. A closer reading suggests some comparison between 1905, when the middle class failed to come to the assistance
of the workers, and 1955 when Burnham forsook the PPP and
formed his own party, the PNC.

This, then, is the third dimension to the study of Rodney: his
championing of the working people and their elevation as the
pre-eminent class in the history of Guyana. This statement needs
qualification: for he did not ignore the middle class; indeed, he assigned them their proper place. They supported change and reform
and their initial work contributed to the growth of working class
movements. But beyond that he was unwilling to go. Having, as it
were, noted the contribution of the middle class to the working class
struggle, he could not allow them further, for their history had been
one of ambiguity and compromise. In addition, there was no need
for the working class to depend on them or indeed any other vested
interest. The working class after slavery had struggled to develop
workable institutions of its own such as friendly societies and burial societies and farmers associations. That had been proof enough
for him that they had the power through raised consciousness to
deal with the problems which confronted them. It was the working
class, therefore, that would be in the vanguard of the struggle
against capitalism. He invested in it his hopes for liberation.

The belief in the working class pure and simple fed an ideological commitment to a working class without ethnic divisions. Indeed,
the common forces against which they struggled mitigated against
any pronounced divisions between Africans and Indians. Rodney
maintained "that the case for the dominant role of racial division in
the historical sphere has been overstated."[35] Also, he did not suggest that there were no cultural differences, nor did he deny the existence of "clashes," but he believed that these stemmed from
factors such as unchecked immigration, cultural differences and
state policy that aimed at keeping the races separate and unequal,
the better to control them. More to the point, his Marxist perspective did not allow him to admit of race as a factor in working class
history. He would see race as a contradiction, as a stumbling block,
which prevented the unity of the working class. Whether Marx's

views on capital and labor led him to embrace the notion of working class unity against capitalism, or whether the weight of the evidence supports the view that working class unity existed but was placed in jeopardy by a host of factors, is not clear. The potentiality for unity is there, however. It is a fine point, but an important one; on it rests the determination of how doctrinaire a Marxist Rodney was. Did he take from Marx the methodology and the analytical tools and make them his own? Rodney mastered Marx, but did not genuflect to him. His Marxism, in our view, was tempered by the gentle currents from the humanities, which gave him a richer understanding of the doctrine and its limitations, certainly. And as a patriot, he could see the difficulties that unmitigated dogma could lead to, and as a close observer of the African scene, he saw the attempts of Nyerere to establish a workable socialism in Tanzania, and as a critic of Europe in Africa and the wider world, he would not have made the error of applying Marx undiluted to Guyana (as an extension of this thought, he would have been saddened by the absolute application of Marx to Grenada). But this rests in psychohistory, which arguably, is subjective, interpretative, and inconclusive. On such, nevertheless, I rest much of my case. I do not apologize for these liberties and I do not ask the reader to condone them.

Critical analysis would be incomplete without liberties of one sort or another, though. These are necessary to analyze and evaluate Rodney's contribution in Africa, the diaspora and the world beyond; and in the ideology of post-independence countries. In fact, the book divides itself nicely into two parts, which together comprise a significant study of the second Caribbean historian, who departed from his traditional calling, to apply a critical vision to the complex of the Caribbean.

His canvas was wide: his work embraced the Caribbean, America, Africa and the whole of the developing world. Rodney was drawn to the colonial system and eventually to the concept of imperial rule, in much the same way that the late Dr. Eric Williams, prime minister of Trinidad—through the institution of slavery and the exploitation of black people in the interests of Empire. Slavery, then, was the starting point, the critical area of challenge that nurtured, developed and finally motivated other considerations. That Rodney was black added piquancy to the matter in hand and focused his intelligence. Slavery was also important because it led back to Africa, a knowledge shared by most black people at various levels of consciousness. It became an obsession that would inform his study of Africa and the roots of the colonial process.

His research led him to discover the splendid world of African civilizations, their majesty, organization, works of art and their might, which existed before the coming of the European. Research was really the re-creation of a world, which in certain ways had been forgotten, or else confined to museums or dusty tomes in privileged libraries, separated from the people who had made that world. He considered Amos Tutola and *the Palm Wine Drinkard* as a classic in the literature of the African people; and it was precisely this art of storytelling with its emphasis on the *word* or Nommo, a symbol of the life-giving force and community spirit, that distinguishes the African community of people from the harsh individualism of European man. Of that same *Nommo,* Janheinz Jahn, the German anthropologist, said: "Thus African philosophy ascribes to the word a significance which it has also in many other cultures, but there in poetry only." [36] This suggests an African literature of uniquely African cosmology, and traditions extending to the diaspora. Rodney placed this in the appropriate context: "You have to speak to Jamaican Rasta . . . and then you will hear him tell you about the Word," [37] emphasizing that the Rastas knew about this long before it became a proper subject for academic research .

The 'discovery' of Africa was not without attendant problems. Rodney found a continent, which, in his opinion, had suffered neglect, especially "prior to and immediately after it was drawn into trade relations with Europe and the Americas." [38] *His celebrated book, How Europe Underdeveloped Africa,* sought to remedy this neglect; also, he sought to document the continuing plunder and exploitation to which Africa was exposed. This wretched state of affairs was considerably exacerbated by the intrusion of race in the imperial quest. What had begun as economic relations became one in which power based on race defined international relations: "The essence of White Power is that it is exercised over black people." [39]

Rodney could do no more in Africa where he spent two years. He did not believe that the discovery of his "roots" enabled him to do something about white power there, or to try to bring about any structural changes in Tanzania where he lived. What he did learn from Africa was that imperial relations still continued and were becoming stronger despite independence and he could do nothing beyond his professorial duties, which were demanding. Too many factors intervened between him and the society for him to come more firmly to terms with its realities. When he left Africa in 1968 for the University of the West Indies, Jamaica, he came away with a conviction that international capitalism was firmly in place, and the relations it circumscribed, and which were so distressing—race relations.

But his return to the Caribbean was not without problems. His teaching appointment at the University of the West Indies did not last long—less than a year. During that time he introduced a new course in African history and gave public lectures about what he had learned abroad. He reached out to the people who, in the words of Richard Small "had already arrived at the conception that Africa has a history and they only required the illustration of that belief." [40] The very year of his university appointment found him in Montreal attending the Congress of Black Writers, where he delivered a lecture, "African History in the Service of the Black Revolution." Two days later October 15, 1968, he was banned from re-entering Jamaica. He again returned to Africa, lecturing at the University of Dar es Salaam from 1969-72.

In 1972, *How Europe Underdeveloped Africa* was published and his reputation, which had already received critical attention since the publication of his first book, Groundings with my Brothers, now was assured. What Rodney wanted, what he had begun to strive for—and this could be seen in all his published work and in his speeches—was no less than a re-formation of the world (the French word 'formation' seems more appropriate than 'education', for the former implies re-shaping reality—an objective at once bold and courageous, and at the same time impertinent, for who would dare to want to re-shape reality, what would be the terms of reference of the individual who would assign himself such labors, how would he set about his task, where would he begin?)

He was appointed professor of history at the University of Guyana in 1974, a post that he was not to take up, for in an unprecedented move the government of Guyana rescinded the appointment. This act plunged Rodney in the uncertain waters of Guyanese politics. The university professor and scholar joined forces with the revolutionary intellectuals. Rodney believed that the intellectual had a mission to help in the social transformation of the masses. It was the same mission that exercised Fanon; and both he and Rodney had arrived at the same conclusions: that structural transformations were necessary for "The Wretched of the Earth." Unlike Fanon, however, Rodney wished to be practically involved in that transformation. It was to be the cause of his death.

He joined the Working Peoples Alliance, WPA, an organization of several different groups, which became the collective arm of his endeavors on behalf of the working people. He reached out to the working people, he helped organize, and he shared what he had learned. In constant demand as a lecturer, he went abroad not infrequently in order to support his family as both he and his family were denied the opportunity to earn their livelihood in Guyana. In

1979 the WPA set itself up as a full fledged political party with the objective of returning Guyana to the working people.

The WPA challenge to the Peoples National Congress, PNC, the ruling party, was from the outset not taken lightly by the latter. There was a bungled attempted assassination of Josh Ramsammy and an attempted kidnapping of Clive Thomas which indicated "that the government was sensitive to the possibilities of this multiracial alliance of intellectuals and working people."[41] The very year, 1979, that the WPA set itself up as a political party, Rodney was arrested along with four others, together known as "the Referendum Five," and charged with setting fire to a government building and headquarters of the PNC. Two of Rodney's colleagues were killed by the police; a reporter from the Catholic Standard, who was a bystander at a demonstration of the WPA, was stabbed to death. Events seemed to move towards a climax.

June 2, 1980, the trial of Rodney and four members of the WPA began. They were denied trial by jury. This serious abrogation of the rights of citizens was condemned by the Guyana Bar Association, and the Guyana Human Rights Association observed that "the courts have been used as an instrument of political harassment on a widespread scale."[42] Four days after the trial began the prosecutor asked for an adjournment. One week after the trial was adjourned, Rodney came to a tragic end. A device concealed in a walkie-talkie exploded in a car driven by his brother. There was no inquest into his death and though the government commissioned Scotland Yard to investigate, no details were released, adding to the uncertainty and confusion which his death provoked. Who was responsible for Rodney's death still remains a mystery; and certainly it is not the author's aim to investigate the tragic circumstances of his death. But one can not deal with it and given the nature of the challenge he posed to the government of the late President Forbes Burnham, it would be impossible to deny its complicity in what can only be described as an assassination. The government's very denial of an inquest is its indictment. That Rodney met with the ultimate penalty, forces an evaluation of the precise nature of the challenge he posed.

Two areas immediately suggest themselves. One relates to international capitalism which he believed destructive of human values and what is destructive of human values cannot be ultimately productive: slavery, colonialism, imperialism are therefore counter -productive. His reading of history supports these views and How Europe Underdeveloped Africa, is a chronicle and crusade against capitalist pillage and plunder. The book is also a corrective to the generally held myth that Africa had to await the coming of

Europe in order to develop its own resources. Indeed, development and the misrepresentation of development is the theme that joins international capitalism to development and impoverishment in the Third World.

Rodney was unequivocal on this point: "To advance they [third world countries] must overthrow capitalism; and that is why at the moment capitalism stands in the path of further human social development."[43] Capitalism is responsible for the uneven development of nations and only a planned economy, such as that in socialist countries, can provide the kind of development that is in the interests of the workers. And the workers are the center of his concern. Critical he was of theories of development that concentrate primarily on economic indices, but seldom look at other aspects of the process. The satisfaction of human needs and their harnessing in the interests of national development is his view of the development which should accompany policies of third world countries. The threat that Rodney posed was no less than revolutionary in a region that had known revolutions in the past and which is constantly seeking new ideas.

The second area is related to the first: leadership and its fidelity to workers and their institutions. Leadership that is blind, self-serving, arrogant, and opportunistic is disloyal to the people it serves This explains his hostility to the Guyana government and the administration of the Jamaica Labor Party under Prime Minister Hugh Shearer. Both had betrayed the people who had elected them—there could be no greater censure. And although Rodney firmly believed that development under socialism was superior to development under capitalism, he was wary of the pitfalls of undefined concepts such as class, imperialism and socialism. Thus, education and historical consciousness are important in these definitions; and how one defines is invariably a product of one's educational value system. It is perhaps why education and historical consciousness and how they affected the education of colonial peoples and Rodney himself is the foundation upon which the author builds his case.

Apart from that the author seeks with great humility to place Rodney as a humanist concerned with the welfare of people and their condition. In that respect, socialism was a means to an end. The significance of this work, it seems to me is self-evident, but history does not always share the subjective views of individuals; and the needs of the poor and the downtrodden have often been neglected, forgotten, or confined to the dust heap.

NOTES

1. Clive Thomas. *The Poor and the Powerless: Economic Policy and Chang in the Caribbean. New York*: Monthly Review Press, 1988, p. 252.
2. Singh, Paul. *Socialism in a plural society.* London: Fabian Society, 1972, p. 16.
3. Op.Cit, Thomas. *"State Capitalism in Guyana: an Assessment of Burnham's Co-operative Socialist Republic,"* in Ambursley, F., and Cohen, R., *Crisis in the Caribbean.* New York, Monthly Review Press, 1983, p. 46.
4. Abrahams, Roger D. *The Man-of-Words in the West Indies: Performance and the Emergence of Creole Culture.* Baltimore: The Johns Hopkins University Press, 1983
5. Guyana Human Rights Association. *Human Rights Report.* January 1980 - June 1981, Georgetown, Guyana.
6. Lutchman, Harold. *An Imperial Presidency.* unpublished paper, 1983.
7. James. C.L.R. *Spheres of Existence.* Conn. Westport: Hill & Co., 1980, p. 131.
8. Said, Edward. A. *The Word, the Text and the Critic.* Cambridge. Massachusetts: Harvard University Press, 1983, p. 25.
9. *Lamming George Cimarron. Vol. 1,* Spring 1985, p. 15
10. Rodney, Walter. *History of the Guyanese Working People 1881-1905.* Kingston and London: Heinemann Education Books, 1981.
11. Said, Edward W. Op. Cit. 1983, p. 25.
12. Fanon, Franz. *The Wretched of the Earth.* London: Penguin Books, 1967, p. 156.
13. Rodney, Walter. *The Groundings with my Brothers.* London: Bogle L'Ouverture Publications, 1969, p. 156.
14. Rodney, Walter *"Marxism as Third World Ideology."* Paper. Undated. Collection at the University of Guyana.
15. Lewis, Gordon K. *Main Currents in Caribbean Thought: The Historical Evolution of Caribbean Society in Its Ideological Aspects, 1492-1900.* Baltimore. Maryland: The Johns Hopkins University Press, 1983, p. 7.
16. Goveia, Elsa V. *A Study on the Historiography of the British West Indies to the End of the Nineteenth Century.* (Mexico City: Instituto Panamericano de Geografia e Historia, 1956), p. 167
17. Sennett, Richard & Cobb, Jonathan. *The Hidden Injuries of Class.* New York: Vintage Books, 1972.
18. Smith, M.G. Culture, *Race and Class in the Commonwealth Caribbean.* Mona. Jamaica: Department of Extra-mural Studies, University of the West Indies, 1984.
19. Greene J.E. *Race vs. Politics in Guyana.* Kingston. Jamaica: Institute of Social and Economic Research, UWI, 1974.
20. Ruhoman, Peter. *Century History of the East Indians in British Guiana, 1838—1938.* Georgetown. Guiana: 1947, p .118.
21. Jagan, Cheddi. *The West On Trial.* Berlin: Seven Seas Books, 1972, p. 40.
22. McMillan, W. *Warning from the West Indies.* London: Faber, 1936.
23. Chase, Ashton. *133 Days Towards Freedom in Guyana.* Georgetown. Government Printers: 1953.

24. *The Daily Mirror*, October 7, 1953 and the News Chronicle, of the same date, both anticipated the advent of revolution.

25. *Report* of the Robertson Commission. London. HMSO. 1954.

26. Greene. J.E. Race Op.Cit, 1974.

27. Report on the British Guiana Conference. London: HMSO, Cmnd.-2203, 1963, p. 6

28. Ibid., p. 5

29. Walter Rodney. Op.Cit., 1981.

30. Jahn, Janheinz. *Muntu*. New York: Grove Press, 1961, p. 135.

31. Walter Rodney. *The Groundings with my Brothers*. London: Bogle L'Ouverture, 1969, p. 67.

32. Rodney, Walter. Op.Cit, 1967.

33. Ibid, p. 17

34. Ibid, p. 11.

35. *Guyana: Fraudulent Election. Latin America Bureau*. London: 1984, p. 60

36. *Guyana Human Rights Association. Annual Report January 1980—June 1981, Georgetown, Guyana*, quoted by C. Y. Thomas. In *Crisis in the Caribbean*. Eds. F. Ambursley and Robin Cohen. New York: Monthly Review Press, 1983. p. 39.

37. Walter Rodney. Op. Cit, 1974. p.10.

38. Mervin Alleyne and others have written persuasively about language and development in the Caribbean. "The communicative gap between the elite and the masses poses serious communicative problems of social and political organization." (Mervyn. C. Alleyne. " A Linguistic Perspective on the Caribbean." In Sidney W. Mintz and Sally Price, eds., *Caribbean Contours*. Baltimore: The Johns Hopkins University Press, p. 175) But with the rise of popular will and expression, there is much understanding of the wider social, psychological and national implications of indigenous modes of expression. These latter have come to represent, in their separate societies, a move away from traditional English to the language of creole, which, according to Hubert Devonish, is "a separate language." In the Caribbean he believes that the structure of the creoles – "English, Dutch, French and Spanish is similar." And Edward Brathwaite is of the opinion that traditional English has evolved into Caribbean English, " nation language," chiefly oral in form and particular to the Caribbean. For a further discussion of the evolution of English, see Robert McCrum et. al., *the Story of English*. New York: Viking Press, pp. 307—319.

39. In *The Word, the Text and the Critic*. Cambridge. Massachusetts: Harvard University Press, 1981, pp. 178—225, Edward W. Said brilliantly analyses the work of Foucault, Derrida, showing how each man disposes of literary criticism from a point of view which is particularly his own, and subject to an interpretive process which is broad and flexible. This makes of textual interpretation a complex process, requiring "bewildering choices."

40. I am indebted to Edward W. Said, who illumined both criticism and the nature of criticism, exposing the dimensions of the former and the subtleties of the latter. Above and beyond the problem of knowledge and the rendering and interpretation of it, is the humanity of the critic shining through.

41. The documentation of fraudulence in the national elections in Guyana makes this supposition anything but assured. For an illuminating account of election fraud, read. *Guyana: Fraudulent Revolution*. London. Latin America Bureau: 1984.

42. For a graphic account of the machinations of the British government aided and abetted by the CIA, Guyana; Fraudulent Revolution, London, Latin Bureau, is indispensable reading.

43. The overseas vote was not new in the electoral history of Guiana. Indeed non-resident Guyanese planters voted in elections for the constituent assembly. Also, it was quite possible that the absentee ballot was more widespread than commonly thought, given the administrative conveniences which ownership and power conveyed to residents and non-residents, an alluded to by Sir C. Clementi. *A Constitutional History of British Guiana*. London: Macmillan and Co. Ltd., 1937, and quoted in J.E. Greene. *Race vs Politics in Guyana*. Jamaica: Institute of Social and Economic Research, 1974.

Chapter Two

Education and Historical
Consciousness

Education in colonial times was a preparation for a world in which the twin currents of class and race were expected to continue because they circumscribed time, place and situation. Education was dormant when it should have been active; static, and confining when it should have been expanding. The general objective were to train rather than to educate and because these objectives were narrow, human development was constricted. The colonial subject thus was imprisoned by an alien standard. A narrow elite was exposed to its limited blessings and the majority was left untouched to founder in the morass of underdevelopment. Education in colonial times was marked by neglect of human resources and skewed heavily in the direction of the maintenance of class privileges.

There were reasons for this limitation. First, colonial rulers who controlled the process of education, whose own education was in fact conditioned by ideas of their own superiority, could not conceive of any other kind of relationship; and there was no reason why they should. It brought them certain advantages. Ideas of superiority were uncommonly productive. Empires had been founded on it. They brought wealth and prosperity to the elite, which ruled the nation. Moreover, they brought comfort and affluence to all who took the trouble to learn the rules and to participate in the common destiny. It was an imprisonment that was luxurious and no one could think of it ever ending. But the colonials were castrated by the education they received. Second, they won certain advantages as a result of it. A whole system of values derived from that education, and accrued to the rulers: economic prosperity, which ensured the perpetuation of the master-worker relationship and continuing productive relations. Third, education enabled the rulers to perpetuate the myth of voluntary compliance in colonial rule. The rulers of colonial society controlled education by means of the government and agencies set up for that purpose. An administrative structure of command, that started from the metropole, be it London, Paris, or Brussels, ensured the rickety functioning of colonial programs. Education was only one of the ways in which superiority over the colonial subject was maintained, but it was an important one. It was responsible for the perpetuation of this rule. It was an eventual step in the social and economic advancement of the subject, though at the time this was not what the colonial master considered. For him education of the colonial was a means by which control could be further exercised. In fact, the exposure of the colonial to schooling and education was held to be in the interest of colonial rule, for it guaranteed a constant though limited supply of trained low-order bureaucrats, whose loyalty could be counted on, in as much as the subject would be grateful for the educational opportunities provided. For the major colonial powers, this was an act of policy that paid rich dividends, but as we shall see later, it did not augur well for the territories, when they assumed independence.

Educational policy was related to social change. Inevitably, the control of politics, economics and social structure led to pronounced changes in infrastructure in areas such as communications and social mobilization and attitudes to labor unions and attendant referents—work and leisure. In Guyana, traditional or local authority was practically non-existent and Britain had an easy time of it maintaining order and control. The Aborigines, the indigenous inhabitants, had not resisted the arrival of colonial power and even though there is record of two slave rebellions in 1763 and 1823, there was no permanent local grouping that could withstand them. Thus, the colonial power could measure out educational changes on its own terms and in conformity with its own perceived needs.

At first these needs were rudimentary and confined to the education of the children of planters and minor administrative personnel connected with slavery and sugar. Needless to say, education for slaves was not part of official policy, and whatever education was at the time obtained by slaves was attributed to personal initiative under the guidance of missionaries.

Formal instruction in the 19th century consisted of elementary and secondary education. The Governor of the territory, acting with or without advisers, assumed total charge of instruction, but in practice, he allowed some latitude to the various denominational bodies that were involved in education. Mission schools were the foundation of the educational system and as in Africa did much of the early work. These mission schools were hampered by low budgets and desperate working conditions and relied more on official patronage than is perhaps realized. The quality of the instruction at school depended on the kind of mission. For example, an evangelical mission taught both manual as well as academic skills. Anglican missions established academic schools.

In Guyana, the mission schools were run by Anglican missionaries, which underlined the importance of academic subjects over manual skills. This had an untoward consequence from the point of view of development. The middle class, which benefited from the liberal curriculum never considered manual skills as viable alternative job possibilities. Agriculture and manual professions were treated as second class prospects. Despite trying conditions the schools prospered and the need for them grew because they were able to steadily supply low rank personnel for the sugar industry.

Education in the rigid colonial society both created and emphasized class barriers. In fact, class distinctions were essential to the functioning of the colonial system. Superiority based on power, privilege and wealth inevitably imposed divisions within the colonial system. This was also the case within the governing structure. 1 Among the rulers of the plantocracy were governor, advisers, planters, overseers, clerks of the estates, foremen, field foremen and the missionaries. Slaves occupied an inferior status, if it isn't a luxury to consider them as having a status at all. Class defined status.

Slavery and the class system

The system of class was institutionalized and engrained in the system of slavery. Two kinds of system were institutionalized: the specific British system of class, which had its familiar structures based on birth, family ties and social function; and the slave system as was practiced in the colonies. There, the distance from the metropolis resulted in a system with its own distinctive formation and character.

The sugar estates had a social and administrative hierarchy, made up of the governor and council, administrators and minor officials; then came the planters, their administrative staff, comprising shipping clerks, general workers, overseers, superintendents, field overseers and so on. This complex administrative process functioned through well-greased machinery that survived the demise of slavery. The system by which class was perpetuated in Guyana could be directly attributed to the strength and resilience of these structures. When slavery was abolished social and bureaucratic structures en-

sured the perpetuation of appropriate conduct and behavior. When
independence came to Guyana, the system of class and its appropriate divisions and method of conduct had already been so much im-
planted as to be established routine, and together with ethnicity
and race, created an imbalance that posed additional problems for
its politicians.

The class system was institutionalized through successive stages in
the development of the country and each stage had its own brand of
morphology. But these stages had one thing in common: in no case
did they result in any conspicuous gains for the working class, who
were forced to endure them. The end of slavery saw the decline in
importance of the upper class who became rich from the traffic in
slaves and sugar. These did not want to be involved with the new
political arrangements. Also, social distance, which was essential
for the maintenance of privilege; and snobbery vital for the perpetuation of the mystique of power, did not permit them to make concessions of that kind. Finally, the upper class was mainly
interested in profits from the estates. Politics, so straightforward in
the days of slavery, promised a degree of complexity, that they
would find tiresome and unrewarding. The division of Guyanese society on the basis of class, between workers on the one hand and
plantation owners on the other, derived its stability, then, from the
earliest separation of the aristocracy of the plantation from the exacting tasks of slavery and reinforced in the post-slavery period.
Also, the upper class did not see their role as pivotal to the politics
of the country: they did not need to be nominated or elected to the
legislative chambers in order to hold on to economic power and commercial hegemony. They derived a certain casual satisfaction from
knowing that they could continue to control without being members
of the legislative club. [1] Even though they realized the importance
of the legislature "in moulding and controlling the policy of the government", they realized that they "have special means of influencing the government to secure attention to their views and wishes."[2]
One of these was the practice of "excluding the electives from membership of the Executive Council."

Inevitably, this lethargic approach to the country's development
dispirited political affairs. The dissolution of the managerial class,
either by slavery, departure for the metropolis, inertia, or natural
attrition, affected the social structure of the colony of Guyana. In order of rank were the white managers, who supervised the estates of
the absentee proprietors, artisans, engineers, plumbers, and other
technical support staff who performed their especial duties. Then
came the middle class, ranked by color (the lighter the shade, the

preferred) and the professional middle class who were not of the preferred shade, but who, nevertheless had appropriate social
status.

Thus, the immediate post slavery society, stratified on the basis
of narrow function, became even more so on the basis of color during
the beginning years of representative institutions. The professional
middle class naturally followed the manners of those ahead of them
on the colonial totem pole. They aspired to the values of the colonial
power, approximated a system to which they did not, could not belong. That they could not, did not discourage them; and successive
generations of this class unsuccessfully tried to narrow or bridge the
gap between the metropolis, and the colony. They aspired to the values of the colonial power, and held sacred institutions, which
dominated and ordered their lives. Indeed, this might be said to be
the plight of the colonial—the seeking after an escaping ethos.
Unfortunately, the quest, and its failure, continues to this day in
some quarters, despite political independence. Social and racial discrimination were necessary concomitants of that society and the
practice of discrimination on the whole approximated the order of
social status: whites were shown preference over mulattoes, who in
turn discriminated over the African middle class. African and
Indian workers remained at the bottom of the social hierarchy. The
practice and the conduct of political affairs were inevitably influenced by social stratification; and local politicians, whatever their
profession or color, could not be expected to be treated fairly or receive the necessary kudos for their work: "rightly or wrongly, there
is a general impression amongst all races in the colony that impartiality is more likely to be found amongst men of pure Anglo-Saxon
descent than among others."[3]

Despite the injuries of class, (and these would not be hidden) the
middle class in Guyana looked up to and felt comfortable with their
colonial masters whom they adopted and imitated with singular
zeal. Discrimination could not have been particularly pleasing, but
they were impediments to be endured in the interests of greater
compatibility; and there were rewards too, in time: pittances of
power-sharing, official recognition in the form of awards and the
conferral of respectability. They became in deed and in fact "apologists" for the British crown, of whose will they were the chosen in-
struments. Lutchman suggests that "there was no indigenous
culture into which they were born or socialized, to act as a buffer
against the influences of British values."[4] But they could not have
been unaware of other influences and certainly, the presence of native aboriginal Indians would have served as a reminder of their
own status. They had to have known of the cultural roots of Africa;

and while, arguably, it would have been difficult or impossible to develop and enlarge on this shared cultural heritage, few among them
adopted a position of restraint in so far as British values were concerned. This cultural distortion—negligence, if one wishes to be
charitable—made it difficult for future generations to break from
that tradition. The other groups in Guyana, comprising of Indians,
Chinese, Portuguese, did not find the problem as critical. Religious
practice, ceremonious observance and language made it easier for
them to insulate themselves and withstand English cultural imperialism.[5] Nath mentions how legislation had to be introduced to compel Indians to send their daughters to school. This shows the
strength of residual ethnic custom among Indians and also the ability of a vibrant culture to influence social conduct.

Social and class distinctions were therefore intact in Guyana in
the 19th century because the political structures were in place and
ran relatively smoothly, as far as those in power could see. Indeed,
as Rodney points out "the political system remained open-ended"; [6]
that is to say, those in power subscribed to elective government and
with it the principle of representative government, because that was
a way of ensuring the continuation of their privileges. ii The result
was that wealthy middle class mulattoes, who could satisfy property
or income qualifications for public office, gained valuable experience
in the practice of government.[7] Correspondingly, those who could
not satisfy these qualifications, could not exercise the franchise.
This inevitably solidified the class structure and distanced the
Guyanese working people from the Guyanese middle class at a time
when cohesion would have been mutually advantageous.

The working people were frustrated on all fronts. Africans in the
aftermath of slavery found themselves facing the herculean task of
building new societies and dealing with freedom. This caused a split
in their ranks, some going off to develop independent villages and
farming communities, others moving off to the towns in search of
employment, and creating a peasantry "engaged in proletarian relations of production: wage labor, either for cash or for kind." [8] This
made of the working people "a permanent hybrid of peasant and proletarian";[9] and they were less than passive onlookers of their fate
but active participants in rural and plantation affairs. Indeed, the
peasants in some Caribbean territories shared a certain uniqueness
in the working class movement.

One writer, in discussing the peasants of Nevis, warned against
categorization, because of the variety of interpretation. 10 And the
peasants of Nevis and those of Guyana had some attributes in common: both existed on the margins of sugar plantations, which provided them the opportunity to grow crops for consumption and

exchange. Also, in the case of Guyana, the peasants had agendas of their own: they were obsessed with establishing free villages in the post-slavery years—a by no means easy task, given the compulsions of eeking out a livelihood on the margins of sugar estates, and pooling resources to buy the land on which their communities were constructed, and setting up the necessary infrastructure for cooperation, work and administration. All this, with a determination to create communities based on free association, which incidentally, included their late oppressors, who often lived in the vicinity of those very free villages. In addition, the same peasants were involved in forming associations to learn how to participate in representative politics. In fact, with the political hierarchy intact and predictable, a state of affairs, which in other circumstances could have been discouraging, they began to mobilize themselves, and by the 1880s, hardly fifty years after emancipation, had helped form the People's Association with some of the radical middle class types. It is not too much to suggest that the peasantry, in the sense implied, [11] engaged in productive relations and were the backbone of early political life in Guyana. This is not meant to detract from the contribution of the middle class some of whose radical members were in the forefront of the popular movement for change. But it is to underscore the fact that the peasantry as a class has not received proper historical acknowledgement; some views have been patently inaccurate. For example: "Their notion of freedom was to be like their masters, with, as they thought, nothing to do but to eat and drink and enjoy themselves." [12] Another view was critical of their lack of organization in the 1905 riots. [13] But Rodney interpreted this as a maturing process, for though unprepared for protracted struggle, they responded with what they had and when these failed, resorted to riots; never did they cease to wish to discuss their grievances in a peaceable manner. [14]

The Guyanese peasant, then, was the backbone of the working people and the working class movement and this is not by any means a new phenomenon: in Mexico, the peons (1911–20) and in Cuba, the campesinos (1957–58) were committed participants in the struggle; indeed, to see the working class as separate from the peasants is to drive a wage in the working peoples movement, dividing it by function, occupation, and eventually by race. This was a superfluous and unnecessary exercise, in view of the unity and strength of their oppressors. These divisions were not peculiar to Guyana, but were intrinsic to capitalist social development elsewhere. Rodney made the point that this setback the entire working class movement in Guyana and with it the cohesion which was necessary for national solidarity.[15] When a tenuous industrialization came with the manufacturing of the sugar and bauxite industries, the separation of the peasant from the working class in the these industries became crystallized and with that, all the suspicions and antagonisms that existed between emerging social formations. Thereafter only a heightened political consciousness, derived from misery and degradation, brought them into a temporary and precarious unity. The riots of 1905 were one such and the emergence of the first national political party, the PPP, was another occasion. But the division still remains, embittered by national strife, which is the inability of the one or the other to fully understand its position and mutual dependency on the other, resulting in the hardening of attitudes and consequent frustration of the movement towards national consensus.

The division of the country by trade, occupation and race intensified as the industrial and manufacturing trades developed. Competition accompanied the growth of a gathering industrial sophistication in shipbuilding, tool and die manufacturing which was peripheral to sugar and later bauxite production. Rodney contended that it was competition, promoted essentially by production zeal, that was responsible for mutual suspicion and fear which led to racist thinking among workers. [16] That it was not discouraged by the rulers of the colony caused it to fester; and there was no reason in any case why they should have discouraged racism among workers. The historical roots of class division made it easier to accept such social cleavages elsewhere and even to promote it where it did not exist. The working class in the colonies, recently freed from slavery, could not have expected to be free from an active racism, and, later on, an equally active social class system, which was accompanied by discrimination of all kinds and at all levels.

The competition between Africans and Indians was over jobs in the sugar industry, already sensitive to the advancing competition from Cuba and the East Indies, and the manufacture of beet sugar in Europe. Also, it was over pride of place in the hierarchy of the colony. Africans were not content to see the Indians, the recent arrivals, get ahead of them, especially for the limited opportunities that did exist at the time. If neither of them was happy with the material circumstances of life, neither was yet ready to do something about it and only rarely, as in the urban riots of 1905, was there any substantial resistance to British power. As difficult circumstances persisted throughout the 19th and well into the 20th century, racial antagonism grew subliminally with the intensification of class conflict. There might have been less obvious getting together socially, and of course, less mixing, but it must be understood that lack of social accommodation did not reflect deep hostility. The Indians sheltered behind an intact culture, which enabled them to survive the unaccustomed rigors of indenture. And if they were loathe to emerge from its confinements, it was because of the solace and security that an active culture provided and imposed on its adherents.

The two major groups, Africans and Indians, understood the social arrangements and the material conditions of distress in a more basic and hence profound way than is often realized. Rodney was clearly disturbed that "scholarship on the subject [of race relations] has accepted without due scrutiny the proposition that Africans and Indians existed in mutually exclusive cultural compartments." [17] There was apparent explanation for this. Africans were disturbed by the continuing immigration of Indians to the colony. This was a threat to their jobs and the limited security they had managed to cull for themselves. The steadily declining price of sugar, and sugar plantations [18]; the value of sugar estates in the decade after emancipation was 6.1% of their pre-emancipation value, down from a high of 60%; sugar output likewise declined from a high of 71, 168 hogsheads in 1829 to 47, 200 hogsheads in 1850; the obvious favoritism with which Indians were treated [a practical application of the policy of divide and rule], ensured African hostility to immigration. Indians did not initially receive favorable treatment from the planters. The early days of immigration saw them living often in destitute and often hopeless conditions. The immigrants who had been recruited in the early days of immigration had been generally unsuitable for plantation work; and to the unfortunate conditions of their passage from India was added the squalor of the settlements, where inadequate health and housing standards prevailed.

The system of indenture, under which labor came to Guyana, permitted the immigrant to sign on for five years; and at the conclusion of the contract, was either shipped back home, or the indenture renewed for a further period of five years. The immigrant was induced through bureaucratic lethargy to renew a contract that was clearly not in his interests so to do, and the pressures to remain and serve were such as to overwhelm all but the most resolute. Money was offered as an additional encouragement and an ordinance from the Crown in 1856 made it legal for a planter to enter into agreement with an immigrant for a period of five years for payment of $50.

The Des Voeux Commission, which studied the indenture system in Guyana, declared: "The effect of later legislation has been to keep the immigrant population, as a whole, out of the free labor market."[19] More notorious was the deprivation of the Indian immigrant of his liberty to compete in the marketplace and his freedom to dictate his life. The continuing ability of the planters, unrelieved by restraint—moral or otherwise—from the legislature, to dictate the affairs of workers in 19th century Guyana is a cardinal aspect of its social history. That this treatment, which began and ended with the emancipation of slavery, was allowed to continue with indentured labor—scarcely less cruel and manipulative—showed the extent to which all labor, was subject to the dictates of the planters. Such distinctions as existed between the working classes were based on their relationship with the economic forces that controlled them, and not on any innate social, or cultural differences that they might have had. The point is worth emphasizing, for there has been a tendency to assess the violence between Africans and Indians, which came to Guyana in the pre-independence period, in terms of racial differences with all the value judgments that stem there from. Rodney was unequivocal: "The evidence of this early period does not sustain the picture of acute and absolute cultural differences coincident with race. It would be more accurate to contend that the existing aspects of cultural convergence were insufficiently developed to contribute decisively to solidarity among the working people of the two major race groups."[20] In other words, there is no evidence of racial considerations dominating relations between the two groups at all. That they were apart is unquestionably true, but they were apart because each felt the need to shelter within familiar moorings. Each group had not reached the stage where it could consider itself as belonging to a common oppressed working class.

Survival in a sugar economy that had already begun to shrink was more important than working class solidarity. (Sugar and its by-products amounted to 94% of Guyana's exports in 1866, but reached a low of 69% in 1899). For the indentured who had come under particular terms of contract—five years in the first instance and return passage guaranteed at the end—life was an increasing bondage to authority. If he failed to select an employer then he had to pay a sum of money to refund the government for the cost of his upkeep. If he lasted out his indenture, he would be given a bonus and induced to sign up for an additional five years. This re-indenture caused some misgivings, even among the colonial authorities and resulted in friction between the Colonial Office and the Guyana administration.

In 1853, the term of re-indenture was set at three years, but was changed a year later to ten years with the complicity of the Government of India, five of which was to be spent in a regular indenture and the remainder as a free laborer. Regulation of the terms of indenture was absolutely necessary for the plantations, which needed regular gangs of workers at minimal cost. At no stage was indenture of benefit to the Indians. Their employment amounted to a species of serfdom and oppressive labor laws ensured confinement to the land. Absence was punishable by fine and or imprisonment.

These stringent labor laws were matched by vagrancy laws: an immigrant who was absent for work for a period of seven consecutive days could be charged with desertion and the penalty for desertion was "to extend the period of indenture by twice the period of the desertion." Nor was there relief from these burdens through the solace of family life. Records of the Guyana Immigration department are precise: 3 women for every 100 men came in 1838 and in 1900 there were 50 to every 100 men. Immigration was under strict control and the presence of women was looked upon as a burden distracting from the more pressing demands of service to the sugar and later the rice industries.

Attempts were made later in the century to ameliorate the harsh realities of the immigration laws and the vagrancy laws, but without much success. The conspicuous decline of sugar by the end of the century—compensated in part by other export industries—made it difficult for the planters to abandon cheap and reliable labor; and even though laws to change the exacting conditions of life on the plantations were passed, they did not often succeed in being adopted in the colony. The indenture system of coolie labor was institutionalized in Guyana in much the same way that slavery had been, and with it the paraphernalia of casual observance of their rights as individuals. The strains of an economy in rising competition with other countries such as Cuba and Indonesia, and demand for beet sugar in markets which had traditionally been sugar's, prevented much in the way of reforms being fully observed. The result was that the system of re-indenture by which immigrants were induced to sign on again became a denial of their liberty. They could not compete as free laborers in the marketplace and the longer the period of indenture, the more it denied them possibilities in the labor market. As the Des Voeux Commission, which enquired into the status of indentured laborers declared "when this period is considerable, the diminution of liberty becomes considerable also." [21]

Indentured Indians who were brought to Guyana between 1838 and 1916 came to replace the slaves on the plantations, following emancipation. They came under terms of contract, which in the beginning did not specify what they had to do, resulting in a great deal of unnecessary suffering. But more importantly, it caused them to look more closely at their cultural foundations as a safeguard against a potentially hostile environment. There was little immediate contact with the Africans who were envious of their presence. But there is little research to show that such envy was based on racial considerations—a tempting frame of reference for the pluralists who "minimize the importance of class divisions and to assert the paramountcy of racial and ethnic variables." [22]

After emancipation planters sought in indentured labor and land restriction, the means of curtailing the expansion of labor beyond the sugar industry. Planters controlled the Combined Court, and the legislature and could manipulate the Governor into getting what they wanted. Clementi described the constitution as "unique in the Empire", for it put the legislature "in the control of finance by elected legislators not charged with administrative responsibility." (vii) [23] Thus the planters were able to finance the indenture system with government revenues. Also, they made sure that they themselves were not unduly taxed, most of the revenue coming from the poor working class. Between 1833 and 1847 planters share of taxes fell from 76% to 2% [24] Besides, this obvious advantage, the planters made it difficult for freed slaves to purchase the available Crown lands, by setting the price too high and beyond the reach of those inclined to buy. This affected the sugar industry, and even though prices fell in the years after emancipation, they increased in the closing years of the century.

Increase in sugar exports was due to indentured labor, among other factors; and as the number of indentured Indians increased, their wages fell. The decline of the sugar industry was due to the competition of beet sugar and also more sugar production in Cuba and the Far East; and the planters continued their short sighted policy of preventing land cultivation. This policy eventually conflicted with the discovery of gold in the interior in 1880. Some of the country's bourgeoisie and its more influential shopkeepers and merchants formed mining companies to prospect for gold. They wanted the Crown lands opened up. Their demands were in direct confrontation with the planters who wished to prevent this in order to control the supply of labor. The mining entrepreneurs claimed that they represented the poor peasants, who could not obtain the land and joined common cause with the working class. [25] Constitutional reform in 1891 brought to an end legislative control of the planters. The new emerging group represented the mining interests. The two elites, the affluent bourgeoisie and the mining interests, shared power and because their interests were necessarily still opposed, the Colonial Office could depend on each watching the other. Thus in Guyana at the turn of the century the two elites safeguarded the interests of the Colonial Office. One could say also that they took charge of the interests of the working class, which had no conspicuous voice in the management of the affairs of the colony.

The beginning of national consciousness

The interests of these two groups—bourgeoisie and mining interests—could best be understood through their designs. The mining people wanted land and cheap labor. The sugar planters also wanted cheap labor in a time of scarcity. [26] The legislature understood and acted on the interests of the planters, who, despite the rise of sugar exports from 1855 to 1884, were still in financial distress. They had overcommitted themselves to experimentation and industrial change. The late 19th century was characterized by the shedding of inefficient equipment and unproductive methods that had tooled the sugar industry during slavery; and the injection and application of new technology and methods into the productive processes. These included the application of the sciences of measurement and control; sophisticated milling equipment; use of chemicals in the manufacturing process; and a new and elaborate evaporator, which allowed cane juice to evaporate more quickly into crystallized sugar.

The industrial revolution had come to Guyana and the planters invested heavily in it, both as a means of improving the quality of the sugar and as a money-saving venture to stem the economic uncertainties. But they also received aid in the form of tax relief from the British government, which also assumed the full costs for immigration. Also, the planters were given up to ten years to reimburse the government for their share of immigration expenses. [27] The collusion of mining interests, planters and government freed agricultural workers and small farmers to expand their interests; and the rice industry, which had been a purely parochial exercise, became established as acreage from coastal lands held under lease, was released by the sugar plantations.

Economic, political and other changes, which came about as a result of the Industrial Revolution, affected the relations of workers to their environment. Inevitably, they began to explore whatever opportunities there were. The rice industry was just beginning, and stimulated other areas of development; and workers who once were restricted to the sugar industry, began to take upon themselves initiatives to transform the bleakness of their lives.

Gold digging was one such opportunity, which started the first significant movement of peoples away from the coastal regions. Many forsook the sugar estates for the interior. Planters sought to stop the flow by releasing additional land for peasant cultivation. Peasant farming in Guyana came about as a result of policies enacted in the interests of planters and miners with whom the peasants had very little to do. The rise of the peasant workers to full scale agricultural laborers, working on large scale production, was not confined to the rice industry alone. The cattle industry, the coconut, coffee industries, the livestock and dairy industries had

grown to sizeable proportions; so much so that their rapid growth
brought about a decline in imported goods.

Peasant agriculture boomed and contributed in a big way to
increased revenue, much needed because of the uneven sugar export
market. Africans and Indians were the mainstays of this agricultural plenty and enjoyed such relations as are, and have been a part
of working peoples everywhere. Also, the organization of agricultural self-sufficiency and exports foreshadowed by 60 years the emphasis on of similar policy. All workers were involved: Africans, who
were the first occupiers of the land, as well as Indians, who introduced rice. While jealousies and suspicions would have been
undoubtedly there, trading and mutual self-interest demanded
co-operation. But co-operation did not come easily. The plantation
system saw to it that the two groups which had mutual distrust
should remain so and encouraged it. Neither group was respected
outside the category of beast of burden. One analyst said pointedly.
"Slavery must still exist, though at the distance of a six months'
voyage instead of six weeks." [28]

The objective of the indenture system and slavery, which it replaced, was to have available labor, forced if necessary, but by contract if it was not. Both systems were notorious for their violence:
the slave had no legal rights that owners were bound to accept; the
indentured had legal rights, which bound both owners and indentured laborers to the contractual period; but that in itself did not imply better treatment; in fact, there is evidence of brutality as
Indians faced the harsh reality of daily life on the plantations.
"Beating and flogging occurred as a regular routine element in the
plantation discipline right into the twentieth century."[29] Assaults
from managers and overseers were frequent; they were subjected to
imprisonment without warrant and other forms of physical abuse,
including "the use of the stocks." Living conditions were atrocious.
Health and hospital facilities were totally inadequate and the hospi-
tals on some plantations doubled as jails. Tuberculosis, malaria, en-
teric fever and intestinal troubles were prevalent. Conditions were
so deplorable that "at frequent intervals the death rate exceeds the
birth-rate . . . for every one thousand East Indians introduced into
the colony under the indenture system, there now remain here only
563 souls—but a little more than half . . . " [30]

The Indians, however, were not passive to these inequities. They
rioted in 1869, and went on strike often and the Court of Policy in
1894 considered special legislation to curb incidences of attacks by
Indian immigrants "on those placed in authority over them."
National concern was sufficiently upset by their aggression, for
muskets were assigned to plantations for use in emergencies.[31] Also,

so unsettling were indentured Indian laborers that planters requested and received an enlarged police force. An 1860 plan to set up a permanent military force of 200 to control the malcontents was dropped because of disagreement as to who should fit the bill—the colonial administration or the planters.

Indenture had from its beginnings been subject to controversy. The Des Voeux Commission, which had been set up in 1871 to investigate its abuses, went beyond its terms of reference and examined some of the deep-seated reasons why indentured Indians were so abused. Noting that the obligations of the master to the indentured laborer are enforceable by laws, but the rights of the indentured laborer are his to defend, the Commission went on to say that indenture "is often spoken of as if, in principle identical with slavery."

Indenture met with opposition from both slaves and planters. It was set up because of the failure of the apprenticeship scheme: emancipated slaves were understandably reluctant to participate in a state task force; and planters too were not anxious to invest in the scheme, even though they were compensated by the Colonial Office. Under apprenticeship, ex- slaves who were over 6 years of age were required to work the plantations without payment for part of the day but received payment for the remainder of it. This period of grace was in the interest of the planters who were expected to find alternate sources of labor. The apprenticeship scheme had varying degrees of success, depending on the size of territory.

In the Caribbean islands, where available land for cultivation was limited, apprenticeship did not pose any problems for planters. But in Guyana with vast acreage of cultivable land on the coastal plain, and sugar cultivation occupying a slender percentage of it, it was tempting for the freed slave to exercise independence; and some did so. Many did not leave the plantation at all, but elected to remain, less because of a love of their former oppressors, than a desire to remain on familiar ground, which provided psychological security. [32] This consideration, although selfishly motivated, was not reciprocated by planters, who treated apprentices with unbecoming cruelty. [33]

The apprenticeship system did not last long, and was discontinued in 1838, hardly five years after its inception. By then the economic forces, which had led the way to emancipation had reasserted themselves—inadequate supply of labour and foreign competition from beet sugar, imported into European markets from subsidized German productions—at a time when the plantations in Guyana were already concentrating on extensive sugar production. And even though there was a disastrous drop in prices and another periodic downturn in the economic system in Britain, sugar managed to survive. That the sugar industry did survive was a result of acts of policy.

Indenture had saved the industry, for it brought in needed supplies of replacement labor at relatively cheap cost. A change in how the labor force was manipulated and an injection of public funds did the rest. All of this could not have been possible without a pliant legislature, which the metropole,—having taken bread from the mouths of planters through emancipation—did not wish to offend by unnecessary intervention in its affairs. Decisions agreed to by the planter-dominated legislature, enabled the sugar industry to avoid complete collapse: they were "a restrictive land policy . . . fiscal controls . . . subsidized immigration . . . and indenture." [34]

These measures by the planters against labor set the stage for their continued manipulation and domination the rest of the century and even well into the 20th century. iii Also, the planters proceeded to turn Creoles against indentured Indians, when it was in their interests so to do. The seeds of the much maligned racial conflict between Africans and Indians must be placed squarely at the door of the dominant class interests of the time. Race relations between the two people were not as acerbic as has generally been made out. They did not live close together, but occupied different sections of the plantations, in voluntary residential segregation. [35]

There was less violence and friction between the two groups than might have been expected, given differences in culture, and religion; add to that the divisions created by the planters to frustrate unity and it is remarkable that so little violence has taken place between them, notwithstanding the 1960s. [36]

Rodney's position was that the disturbances in Guyana assumed a class rather that a racial character: workers had more in common with one another than each had with the oppressors and their common affliction at the hands of the planter class imposed on them a unity which was not artificial. It was working peoples' unity without the compelling reassurance of a working class that was still in embryo. Hence, for Rodney, race was a contradiction. It was class that was singular. He supported the argument by reference to the common treatment meted out against Africans and Indians and the united front that planters as a class presented when faced with the challenges of the former group. Indeed, class solidarity was a marked feature of post-emancipation and planter solidarity was in part matched by that of the workers; but only in part. "The latter [the working people] in turn responded by continuing the struggle under radically transformed legal conditions."[37] The struggle included the first strike in Guyana history, which ran for twelve to thirteen weeks. [38]

The strike as a weapon for the redress of grievance came to be used with increasing frequency after apprenticeship ended in 1838. Workers mobilized to protest inadequate wages and despicable living conditions. Women and children were also a part of the protest movement and the severe work code introduced by planters served as fuel for their determination. Such was the hold that planters had on the metropolis that at the end of apprenticeship, new immigrants—Portuguese from Madeira, Indians and Africans—were conscripted to do the plantation work. These "bound" workers thus filled the breach vacated by freed labor, many of whom refused to work for lower wages. The introduction of these workers resulted in a movement away from the plantations by freedmen. iv It was a factor eventually responsible for the rise of peasant villages, and the growth of independent freelance workers who preferred to sell their labor to the highest bidder, —reflecting psychological rather realistic expectations. The difference in wages between plantations was infinitesimal and many workers journeyed between plantations in hopes of better wages.

African workers and non indentured Indian workers could sell their labor only at certain times: at grinding season, when harvesting, transportation and grinding were involved; replanting of young canes; and crop time. These crucial seasons, when the plantations depended on their labour, saw the planters more ready and willing to "bend" from their exalted position as arbiters of the destiny of workers. But the point needs to be emphasized that increasingly after the emancipation of slavery, and for the rest of the century, workers banded together in common interest for the sake of survival. Their effective co-operation was always anathema to the planters, particularly during the crop season; but planters were glad to re-assert their complete hegemony in the off-season; and as Rodney inferred whatever work they managed to get in the off-season "was a form of patronage which was tied to their behavior during the crop season." [39] Still, the planters had a certain freedom of manoeuver and they never did lose control of labour. Indian indentured labour and contract workers from Barbados allowed the planters some flexibility, as they sought to compensate for the loss of labour. This was, of course, synonimous with exploitation, which continued without major relief, notwithstanding constitutional changes in 1891. These changes succeeded in limiting though not eradicating the power of the planters; in fact, the 1891 constitutional change was disappointing for the many separate interests that expected to benefit from it; and the not infrequent crises of sugar on the international market, the uncertainty that this created in a dependent economy, gave the planters built-in controls in the legislature.

Nor was their control limited to the legislature. They exerted control over the workers on their plantations. The freed slave, who had set himself up in villages often had to abandon his dreams of independence and sell his labor to the plantations in order to survive. While this did not diminish the will to independence, it but delayed it; and the history of the villages and villagers, was one of the more shining testaments to emerging democracy in the nineteenth century. Rodney declared that "the elected village councils of the nineteenth century were organs of democratic expression."[40] But this did not come easily. The planters managed to rush through the legislature a series of Ordinances, which effectively blocked self-improvement of villages by cutting off financial support, enforcing rates and taxes; also, the planters sought to curtail the representative status of the workers by placing them under the supervision of a Board of Villages, responsible to the legislature. The net effect of these ordinances was the centralizing of administration and control, which facilitated disposing of village monies.

The villages never wavered in protest and demands for representation and participation in government. These demands could sometimes take a violent turn. The "Angel Gabriel" riots occurred when African villagers challenged the Portuguese monopoly on trading ships. When an African political activist, John Sayers Orr, spoke out against the economic abuse, he was arrested. This signaled general unrest, which spread to the country districts. Significant about the riots of 1856 was the participation of the urban work force, including indentured Indians and villagers who were all affected by "monopoly and high prices."[41] This example of co-operation indicated that the motives for the riots were essentially economic and that the level of racial antipathy was negligible.

That the working people suffered from general economic disability was undoubtedly true, for the Commission of Enquiry noted that "the peasants had not shared in the growing material prosperity."[42] Many indentured Indians left the plantations before their contract was up. They wandered off in search of "an overland route to India", or simply to be away from the intolerable conditions to which many were totally unaccustomed—some had previously done no agricultural work, and included Brahmins. This gave rise to vagrancy, a word which, according to Eric Williams, stereotypes their behavior without clarifying meaning.[43] Add to this the occasional outburst of cruelty, even as late as 1886, and the working people could not be said to have had a more than tolerable life: "I had to prosecute an employer for whipping an indentured immigrant to his work after he had been fifteen hours at his post."[44]

The turn of the century in Guyana marked the beginning of the end of a way of life and the emergence of another form lacking in specificity. The old order was about to change, was indeed undergoing change, but the forces that would replace it, had not yet marshalled the power to make themselves effective, though there was a whiff of that in the gathering consensus, which led to constitutional reform in 1891.

The plantocracy had long seen the handwriting on the wall: the decline of an industry as important as sugar, did not take place overnight. Price fluctuations would have indicated the tenuousness of their position, when the productivity of sugar plantations quite paled before those of Cuba, for example. And as Eric Williams indicated 45 sugar began to lose its hold over the imagination and purse strings of influential circles in the metropole because it did not seem to be a paying proposition: without adding to the incipient competitive challenges from European beet sugar, which contributed much to the demise of the industry.

The gradual breakup of sugar plantations gained steam after emancipation. Those plantations, which formerly could exist on a borderline of profit, could not face the new realities which came with emancipation. Some closed down; others took the compensation given by the Colonial Office and sold out; and yet others also seized the opportunity to recoup whatever profits they could get on an investment whose end was near. "The Dutchman was out to make his home in British Guiana, the Englishman was set on making his fortune whereafter he would return home."[46] Some few hastened the return home process by abandoning their plantations altogether, before they had made their fortunes.

These hasty transactions—sales, abandonment and turnovers— played havoc with sugar production; and coupled with the costs of paying wages to freed labor, the industry found itself in a plight. And Barkly wrote in 1849 of the "fears of Capitalists, influenced by the recollection of recent loss, which lead them to withhold all and send out instructions to break up the plantations and sell stock and machinery piecemeal in preference to risking further advances." [47] But the market showed resilience.

Technology and change

Sugar, which had virtually sounded its own death knell, temporarily recovered. This was primarily due to the influx of immigrants and the low wages paid them; also, the new owners of plantations had purchased them at low cost and inherited the infrastructure intact. But perhaps the most important reason for the resilience of the industry was the introduction of industrialization on the plantations. The use of steam in the manufacturing process, for instance, was a clear improvement on the traditional "muscovado" process, saving on costs of heating. Mechanical means of transporting cane from the mills to the furnace was also started, shortening the manufacturing process, and helping to make it economical.

These improvements reduced complete reliance on manual labour, paradoxically, when it was most available because of immigration. As could be expected the improvements in the factory led to increased savings and a decline in wages. The effects of industrialization were immediately felt in a country, which had not been prepared for it. Workers who had hitherto depended on their daily output to ensure survival, found themselves no longer needed. There was nothing to cushion them against precipitous decline in their already dismal standard of living. The labor question was also a source of contention between free laborers and indentured laborers. Free laborers took less money for task work than indentured laborers and were thus guaranteed employment. Inevitably, as the free laborers were Africans and the indentured, for the most part, Indians, this created strife between them—strife, which the planters eagerly fomented and capitalized on e.g., they did not use the labor laws to compel the indentured to work, but simply relied on cheaper labor from free workers. The absence, therefore, of any form of collective bargaining agreement made it impossible for all workers to be treated fairly. It also drove a wedge in any possible worker co-operation that might have ensued. The lack of formal association of any kind among workers, contrasted with the high degree of co-ordination of planters who, at crucial times, spoke with one voice. To make matters worse, even the representatives of the indentured workers at the Immigration Office, attributed the decline in earnings to laziness on their part.[48]

Self-denigration among workers was surpassed by the adroitness with which planters manipulated a succession of governors in the latter years of the nineteenth century. Even though reform was heavy in the air—reform, which would eventually limit their power, — they pushed through the legislature acts that limited the money they would have to spend on medicine for the workers; they also inveigled the government to agree to spend more on infrastructure on the plantations. v When a further crisis hit the sugar industry, concessions in this area were recommended by a commission set up in 1894 by the legislature to determine in what ways relief could be brought to the planters. Relief to the planters was the cry most often heard after emancipation up to the early years of the twentieth century. The planters had succeeded in making their objectives those of the colony and had convinced governors and legislators of this. And well they could, for the decline in sugar prices caused significant changes that affected all. Some unprofitable plantations were abandoned; some amalgamated with others in order to cut costs and in the interests of efficiency; and many banking establishments, which had prospered as a result of the industry, closed down and went out of operation.[49]

The Guyana of the late 19th century confronts the historian with a record of a tottering economy, unstable political institutions and a populace, restive for representative changes. Yet, this unevenness gave birth to social changes for which the emancipation of slavery was the catharsis. Such social changes did not immediately involve matters of representation,—that was to come later—they dealt with the continuation of power by those who already had it; and the maintenance of their own class interests. "There was no disguising the class nature of the Court of Policy, the Combined Court, and the College of Electors . . . and it rested upon an extremely narrow franchise."[50] It was that which the planters sought to protect.

Political power, which had been held over from the Dutch occupation of the colony, they had sought to enlarge upon and for the most part succeeded in doing so, despite periods of conflict and at times confrontation. And if the planters succeeded in the imprint of their own class interests on the colony up to 1891,—they virtually had control over public funds and could pay for their own schemes thereby—it was not without struggle.

The social changes of importance—and what interested Rodney—was how opposition to the planters came to be formed among Creoles, urban and rural workers and an effervescent middle class? In the space of a generation these had united their talents and threadbare resources and created an opposition to an entrenched class. It is a story not without historical interest, in that planter hegemony rested as much on "the constitutional parliament" of the Dutch administration and English colonial practice, that Rodney believed "ultimately attests to their compatibility with continued colonial exploitation and with the basically unaltered relations of production."[51]

The power of these entrenched interests rested in a Constitution comprised of a Court of Policy, chosen by the College of Kiezers, made up of the Governor, officials appointed by him and a Combined Court or Legislature, which saw to matters of finance and voted monies, including the salaries for various project officers. The planters kept this a carefully guarded preserve, insulating them-

selves from the "winds of change," and behind such qualifications as
made it difficult for any but the wealthy who had landed property,
from aspiring to office. The grip on representative institutions was
maintained through affiliation with moneyed interests both local
and abroad and mercantile investors. Such accumulated financial
and political power, allied to the same class interests, conspired
to prevent radical social change and forestall political ambition.
Furthermore, this reactionary bloc eagerly sought to extend its
management into new areas of polity, which developed after emancipation. For example, they showed no reluctance at the "imposition
of heavy indirect taxes on the former slave."[52] Rodney mentioned
how the planters expanded their interests deliberately into such areas as "Drainage, Sea Defense, Health" to cement control, and add
to their political influence. However, this power was not as impreg-
nable as it appeared and certain chinks existed where pressure
could be successfully applied. Planters became vulnerable when
technological changes forced a new assessment of their work roles,
which they did not gladly undertake. As a result of new technology,
which favored economies of scale, many plantations were forced to
amalgamate; and these included "family holdings", which "were being superseded by limited liability companies." [53] These changes in
themselves seem inconsequential, but they must be viewed as startling commentaries on an economy and a way of life, which had been
taken very much for granted by those whom it benefited most; and
even in decline many failed to see the writing on the wall, or if they
did, believed that chance or policy could restore the situation to normal again.

The drastic fall in prices in 1884 destroyed the sanguine beliefs
many held about sugar and its future. Long term credit dried up and
many had to sell in order to avoid bankruptcy, or turn their plantations over to companies. Many merchant banks, collapsed because
they were unable to recoup monies advanced to plantations. What
made the turn of events even more difficult was that they occurred
over a relatively short period of time; and even though a downturn
in the industry had been gradually taking place since the previous
century, it had done so in such fits and starts as to escape the attention of those involved; that is, presuming that they were alert to the
realities of change. And even at the end of the century, when the industry, arguably, faced its greatest crisis, with a sharp fall in sugar
prices, the industry showed flexibility by drastically cutting production costs, which enabled it to survive, but marginally.

The plantations in Guyana had been vulnerable because of
changes in technology and growth in other areas e.g. world trading
patterns had changed in response to new demands placed upon

them by industry and commerce and, of course, developments of new markets in agriculture elsewhere. But these overseas arrangements coincided with social changes within Guyana, and for which the emancipation of slavery was responsible i.e. the birth of political consciousness of the "Creole middle class in the towns and in the countryside." They began to campaign for a "more representative political system" at all levels, including "the village and the central government." The mood for change in the constitutional arrangements in Guyana from the middle years of the 19th century, matched the materialistic changes that had been taking place outside of Guyana, but which were reflected in the country. Thus, the planters who were in control, increasingly began to feel their positions tenuous and insecure. Not that this caused a relaxation of their grip on the colony; far from it, if anything it became more pronounced, for desperation had set in, bringing its own frantic energies. They wished at all costs to coalesce, as was indicated by a change in the constitution in 1903, to allow for shareholders of companies, which ran the plantations to sit on the Court of Policy and the Combined Court. [54]

Sugar and its products continued to be produced and were the main supports, even though, as Eric Williams has shown in Capitalism and Slavery, it had already begun to decline in importance. If the working classes were less than satisfied with the material circumstances of their life, they were not prepared to do anything about them until they were thoroughly incensed, as the 1905 riots demonstrated.

Village democracy and beyond

But power could not continue to be exercised at all levels with the same efficiency and assurance. And precisely at those points where it was seen to be vulnerable that workers, who had been gaining strength and sophistication, applied pressure. [The exercise of power rests as much on the materialistic as the psychological; and the changes that were occurring both locally and overseas blunted the psychological sense of invincibility in the planter class and correspondingly raised the stocks of their former subjects].

The initial steps towards independence in Guyana were made by the workers. It was chiefly at the village level that it was most remarkable, for it is there that the Creole, the indentured immigrant and the peasant, in separate ways, pushed the development of those institutions so necessary for nation-building— "co-operative self-government", the practice of elementary democracy, and fiscal responsibility (the more so as money was always in short supply) and contingency planning for drainage and irrigation works. In fact, it would not be too much to say that life in the villages, despite obvious privations, allowed villagers the opportunity of developing the spirit of community, which was unique among people united by common destiny, or sharing a common hazard. "To live in a village was to open up the possibility of participating in a political process which was by no means under planter control." [55]

The separation, even if only partial, ensured at the very least, a qualified independence, or perhaps, one circumscribed by the more usual concerns of relative security of tenure and preservation of life and limb. This was more than passing interest, for the colonial apparatus was not dismantled after emancipation. It may have been temporarily placed under wraps, but it could be swiftly called into action and with it all the paraphernalia of the military. The riots in Ithaca village in 1867, when villagers expressed anger over rates and taxes, showed the continuing military presence in Guyana and the swiftness with which it could be summoned into action.

That the military was ready to intervene when there was a semblance of disorder or untoward behavior, indicated the suspicion and nervousness with which colonial subjects were held. There are indications that life in Guyana, and the Caribbean was not the bed of roses imagined for the colonial power, who was always kept on tenterhooks. [Some of this has passed into Guyanese folklore. The story is told of a newly-arrived governor who set out to visit the County of Berbice. The special train, which transported him had to pass through the village of Buxton, which had earned a reputation for independence and pride. The governor decided to pass through the village without stopping in order to signal his indifference to the villagers as well as to avert any possible threat to his person. On learning of his plans, the headman of Buxton assembled all the pregnant women and had them lie in the path of the train. Naturally, the train was forced to stop and the governor eventually alighted on Buxton soil, where he was given a tumultuous welcome lasting several hours]. To the usual aggravations which accompanied rule, were added the swelling chorus of demands for social justice by those oppressed.

Quite apart from the boldness of these villagers to set themselves up on their own without a great deal of assistance,—some had even refused to work the plantations as paid labourers—they conducted their affairs in a manner which had made even the planters themselves feel redundant. This was a dangerous thing to do in practice; and the planters had ways of retaliation that discomfited the offending village councils. Also, it was the early flowering of that doctrine, which became such an integral part of 20th century colo-

nial policy, — practiced with assiduousness and without ambiguity—which held that subject peoples should never be allowed to
overreach themselves beyond prescribed limits and without official
sanction. From this sprung a tradition, often honored by the subjects themselves, whereby they saw less merit in their own creations
and correspondingly more in those who held them "in fee." To carry
the train of thought further: however commendable, the efforts of
the subject at self-improvement were doomed to failure. Witness the
comments of one of the more enlightened administrators, Governor,
Sir Clifford Irving in 1882: "It is not I think surprising that the attempts to create representative institutions and to establish local
self- government amongst the negro rural population should have
proved a failure."[56] The specific instance, which drew the observation, related to the village councils, which exceeded their authority,
existing as "quasi-municipalities"—much larger than village units.
Villagers had taken the representative principle more seriously
than was intended and moved beyond its parameters to set up large
and more malleable units of government—a practice which was easier for them to do because of the common bonds they shared. Rodney
believed however, that "the key problem with the villages by the
1860s was that local government was no longer acceptable under a
class different from that which controlled the central government."[57]

The precocity of the village council in demanding an increased
share of representation showed a measure of political awareness,
communal sensitivity, and incipient national consciousness. Such
conduct could not be tolerated, for it inevitably challenged the
authority of the central administration. The villagers contributed
their fair share of the tax burden (they largely paid for immigration); and claim for increased representation rested on the sure and
undeniable premises, heard the previous century from the American
colonists. Governor Irving, aware of the contradiction and the threat
posed, suspended village autonomy and replaced it with the rule of
the Central Board of Health. The point needs to be stressed that
civic awareness of the Creoles was not limited to rural areas, but extended to the towns where they sought to bring about social and political change. For example, Creoles ran the popular press, which
consistently attacked Governor Irving, distinguishing between policies of "good intentions" and their implementation. The weekly
Echo, the first newspaper published in a village in Guyana,
Sparendaam, East Coast Demerara, was critical of the incompletion
of village plans during his administration; and when Irving left the
country, the battle for village democracy continued without inter-
ruption.

The closing years of the 19th century was one of conscious activity by local people, who, despite vast economic problems, vi was advancing its own independent political will in democratic form, against a power, which had revealed its vulnerability. Guyanese institutions at the village level were the 'founding fathers' of democracy—and this in spite of substantial obstacles in their path. Indeed, the perceived weaknesses of the resident administrators, the entire governing apparatus, including the Court of policy and the Combined Court, encouraged a grass roots democracy. [58] Village institutions were impatient with the highhandedness of central authority, which discouraged growth and resisted attempts by villagers to regulate their affairs; and the impotence of regulation but stimulated the development of self-help organizations.

The village was helped by the press; and the *Echo* took up the defence of the village of Sparendaam against a proposal by the Central Board of Health to make it a sanitary district: "In the matter of Sparendaam, we question the power of the government to deal in so peremptory a manner with the people who, as a matter of fact, can better manage their own affairs . . . What is wanted is less interference with the people and a wise oversight of what they do in sanitation." [59]

The interference of the central administration in village affairs was keenly felt by those villages that were incorporated i.e. had the stamp of legal approval, which guaranteed repair of roads, dams, maintenance of drainage and irrigation facilities and above all proper health facilities. Incorporated villages were also required to bear a huge burden of the taxes for such relief as they obtained from the government. Relief was not always forthcoming and when it was, often late, so that villagers had to see to the matter themselves. Centralization of authority and function amidst inadequate communications played havoc with the simple requests for relief.

Unincorporated villages, on the other hand, which did not "enjoy" government relief, had to make out on their own. This, they did to their own satisfaction and vociferously withstood attempts at incorporation. Many of the unincorporated villages "maintained during the 1870s and 1880s a political system close to the original agreement of democratic socialism."[60] This explains why independent villages were viewed with such suspicion and even hostility. They had learned the representative principle in the course of activity and that principle seemed the most efficacious way of dealing with affairs. The Central administration was at best a useless and unreliable humbug, ready to incorporate villages in order to tax them, but unwilling to grant them the opportunity to participate in the apportionment of the funds. [61]

The alliance of the press and the villages points to the independence of a free press in the affairs of Guyana; moreover, a press, which was also critical of government affairs. In this respect, not the least of the attributes of the growing democratic movement in Guyana, was the stand taken by the press, which was unafraid. The role of the free press, which exercized an independent function, is unsung in Guyanese history. (At the turn of the century there were some ten newspapers: the *Argosy*, the *Chronicle, Royal Gazette*, the *Creole*, the *Working Man*, the *Villager*, the *Echo*, the *Reflector*, the *Liberal* and *O Portuguese*). The press true to tradition defended every political interest from liberal to conservative, and the more liberal "carried on profuse and abrasive criticism of the governor, senior civil servants, and the judiciary." [62] That this penchant for criticism met with disfavor, could be seen from the conviction of two editors who reported a case in which a Guyanese lawyer, Desouza, was charged with contempt of court. [63]

The press campaign "for non-payment of rates" and "well organized protests", pushed government inexorably towards reform. The villagers, who had taken a decisive stand on issues which affected them, had started a movement with which the Creoles in the towns could identify. Also, the middle class, which had already begun to chafe against the limitations of the Court of Policy and the Combined Court and the power of the planters, joined common cause with the villagers. Business interests run at that time primarily by Portuguese and Chinese, also campaigned for reform "for they considered themselves to have had profound differences with the planter class." [64] Portuguese immigrants who came to Guyana from Madeira in the wake of the emancipation of slavery to work the sugar plantations, never settled down to life on them, but went immediately into business. They had expected that the usual racial inclinations would apply in the colony and they would take their "proper" place among the powers that be; but a vicious system of class prevented this and they were outsiders. They were not British and could expect no relief from the rigorous demands of the social club. Eventually, the Portuguese found their own level and solace in that precarious no man's land between Creoles and planters, mixing rather more freely with the former than the latter; and the editor of O Portuguez once upbraided his countrymen for consorting with black women and speaking Creole English instead of Portuguese. [65]

Class and the worker

Class distinctions were derived from the racial standard set by the dominant rulers. The structures of class were intact and ran relatively smoothly, as far as the upper class could see. If workers were less than happy with the material circumstances of life, they were not ready to do anything about it, as a class. Aware of their despicable state, they sought deliberation, discussion and reasonable argument as a means of bringing about change, as the history of the village councils shows. In fact, the workers understood the social arrangements and material conditions of distress in a more basic and profound way than is realized "by continuing their struggle with the plantation owners under radically transformed legal conditions but under the same material circumstances." [66]

The worker at the bottom of the social hierarchy was the cog who kept the sugar industry going. He differed in other ways from the dominant class: his social expectations were marginal and his labor subject to occasional demand, which varied with the season and the fluctuations of the internal sugar market. To economic poverty was added difference of language and expression, which emphasized where it did not create, psychological barriers, as it is wont to do. "Creole" was the main idiom of discourse among workers. The middle class and the ruling elite, naturally spoke what they considered to be standard forms of English.

Cultural factors constituted a major difference between classes. The nature of slavery and the plantation system institutionalized the system of class in Guyana; and to the inequities of class distinction, add those of wealth, and influence. Among colonials the system of class also operated. Prestige based on class had a firm basis in existence in the colony, for property ownership carried with it the possibility of influential representation at governmental level. This system dominated social relations, but it had other repercussions as well.

Chinese, Indians and Portuguese, who chafed under the management of sugar, even though they were brought for that purpose, left the industry to set up in business. Their departure affected the country, for it created an entrepreneurship conveniently placed to dominate the emerging local business community and also to take advantage of waning prosperity of the sugar industry. The emerging merchant class became in turn identified with business and professional interests viz ownership of land, the legal and other professions. In time these interests became a dominant group, which had the money and the influence to participate more fully in representative institutions, though they did not. They existed on the periphery, content to reap such rewards as accrued through trading and business. They came to an early realization that membership of political institutions did not carry with it commensurate dividends. They could not, for example, break the hegemony of the established elite, even though these latter were cavalier in how they administered and directed the affairs of Guyana. The interests and contributions of this merchant, entrepreneurial class were influenced less by the welfare of the colony than by their own concerns. Membership of the governing administration did in time bring certain tangential rewards e.g. exposure to international business interests beyond their own, as well as a certain kudos, usually as a result of an honor, decoration, or accolade from the reigning monarch. The system of class was therefore rigidly entrenched.

As part of the 19th century machinery of government, the Court of Policy was comprised of people representing the sugar industry, commercial and business interests; professional people, including lawyers and doctors. This resulted in the creation of an institutionalized system of class, which made it possible for legal and medical practitioners to be an integral part of future governing administrations without regard to their suitability or competence. This inevitably enlarged the distance between workers and those who represented them. Also, the tendency for the professional class to look towards the elite for social guidance, accentuated this difference between people. One consequence of the social system—and one which was to have repercussions up to the present day—was the remoteness of the African middle class from the worker. And the reason of upward mobility, disguised as a commitment to representation and reform, was perhaps responsible for Africans becoming absorbed in the "safe" professions e.g. teaching and the civil service. But it must be added that education was viewed as a means of upward mobility by practically all subject peoples, quite apart from its social and other functions.

Upward mobility through education occurred rather late for Indians. There was no encouragement for them to receive schooling. In fact, the opposite was true. Indian children were useful hands in plantation chores. They assisted parents, who were understandably loathed to relinquish them to the doubtful benefits of schooling, especially when this often caused the child to be separated from both parent and land. [67] Officialdom conspired in this recalcitrance by actively discouraging school attendance of Indian children; and in the case of girls, an order, "the Swettenham Circular," restrained prosecution of parents who wished on religious grounds to keep them at home. It was only after this order was withdrawn, as late as 1933, that the way was clear for the compulsory schooling of Indian girls. Indians, who, according to Joseph Ruhoman, editor of The People, were "denied the opportunity of realising the full stature of a decent and upright manhood", thus came to formal education later than other groups in Guyana. It might well be that this spurred such am-

bition and competitiveness as to disturb established routine, leading
to jealousy and antipathy. Rodney believed that this "Creole-Indian
immigrant antithesis at times took the form of an African racial confrontation." [68] But this confrontation was not as acerbic as has been
made out. Religious and cultural observances separated the Indians
from the mainstream of plantation social life. [69] But in the conduct of
everyday, there was less friction between the two groups than might
have been expected, given differences in culture and religion. If one
adds to that planter manipulation of them both and the competitiveness of earning a living, and it is remarkable that so little violence
has taken place, not withstanding that of the sixties. Yet history
shows that the two groups co-operated when they needed to; and after the initial period of uncertainty after arrival in 1838, Indians
and Africans joined ranks to push reform. It was this residue of togetherness that the Peoples Progressive Party, PPP, and later on
Rodney himself was able to capitalize on in forging tenuous national
unity. Much of this was effected at the level of the working people.

In fact, the picture that emerges in the post-emancipation period is that of a gradually awakening working people, comprising
Creoles, peasants, farmers and small tradesmen, immigrants,
Indians, Portuguese and Chinese, working together in assorted
ways, and for equally assorted reasons for social betterment through
reform in a class and race ridden system— "an incipient mass movement organization with discernible class objectives."[70] From these
had come the Reform Club and the Reform Association, which pursued the objective of constitutional reform with singular dedication.
That such varied interests and ethnic affiliations were united in
such an endeavor, indicated a measure of assurance in representative democracy, despite the intrinsic lack of representation under
which they lived. Rodney [71] has suggested that in the operations of
the village councils in the nineteenth century were the beginnings of
"democratic expression."

That the plantocracy, the amalgam of planters, legislators and
expatriates who controlled the affairs of Guyana, was bankrupt of
ideas with which to preserve its rule, was clearly evident from the
1870s, when ex-indentured immigrants began to leave the plantations in sizeable numbers. It was calamitous for planting interests
and although immigration continued until 1905, it never succeeded
in completely fulfilling the demand for labor. In addition, other industries such as gold, diamond and so-called "Minor Industries" like
timber competed for labor. The Indian immigrants went to work on
the plantations, farming rice, which was more immediately important for their needs; also there was the compelling reason that they
controlled the rice industry. The Guyanese working people were in

the process, a continuing one, of harnessing labor in their own interests, as it were, becoming independent of the machinations of the
plantocracy. This is not to suggest that they ceased to depend on the
plantations. But it is to accentuate human development amidst continuing frustations of constitutional reform. vii

Also, the uneven price of sugar, culminating in that disastrous
year, 1885, caused grief to planters. Many sold out and others became bankrupt. The once and glorious predictability of sugar prices
and profits had come to an end. The planters who could fashion no
response to a phenomenon, which they did not understand, and
could not deal with, retaliated in repressive ways. They treated
every impetus to change as a threat to their status and dammed up
the gates to constitutional reform for almost a generation. With
their interests in the Court of Policy and the Combined Court, they
sought effectively to control domestic policy; and the slight opening
of the flood gates to municipal self-government, which had been occurring in the villages, was treated with scant consideration and
discouraged by heavy centralized bureaucracy. Incipient democracy
to which both creoles and peasants subscribed, was effectively
thwarted at the grass roots level. The movement, which was more of
a trend in the villages, encouraged creoles in the towns to focus attention on reform; and together with the more enterprising of the
Indians, Portuguese and Chinese, who had begun to feel left out of
the political process, an electoral crusade began.

The energies of all the disparate groups might even be considered as "populist", as Rodney put it [72]; and it was no small achievement of large scale capital to have succeeded in uniting so many
opposing factions. This indicates that social, economic and cultural
differentiation among the various groups did not stand in the way of
effective co-operation; and the much avowed animosity between
Africans and Indians must be put into proper perspective and as-
sessed with due caution. There is another view of this matter: that
so necessary was it to unite forces against an anachronistic
Constitution "which failed to accommodate the many socio-economic
developments" that mutual hostility was covered up; and when this
was achieved i.e. constitutional change,— as indeed it was this century, coincidentally with another anachronistic Constitution—political independence left the two main ethnic groups to confront one
another. Colonial power may have postponed for a century this confrontation.

The working people performed much of the spade work of the opposition process through grass roots democracy. They showed that it
could work. But it was left to the middle class to exploit the creative
work in the villages at other levels. The reform movement gained

momentum with the formation of the Reform Association, which had
a sympathetic press in support of its demands. The middle class
movement was divided between some adherents who "looked to
their social superiors rather than to the disenfranchised working
people for leadership." [73] The consequence of this was that power
came to be wielded "by merchants who were usually either brown or
white." Thus, the reform movement, which had become a force to be
reckoned with, had compromised itself along color lines. The creoles
from the villages who had been the early vanguard for political and
constitutional change were effectively locked out. Perhaps, one consequence of the division of the reform movement on the basis of
color, was its inability to mount a complete and successful offensive
against the plantocracy until this century, with the resulting post-
ponement of national independence. Middle class perfidy in sacrific-
ing the working people to their own interests is not the least of the
reasons why Rodney's faith rested with the working people, whom
he championed. It is to these we turn.

NOTES

1. Lutchman, Harold. *From Colonialism to Co-operative Republic.*
Institute of Caribbean Studies: University of Puerto Rico, Rio Piedras,
Puerto Rico, 1974, p. 65.
    2. Lutchman, Harold. Op. Cit., 1974, p. 47.
    3. Ibid, Lutchman, p. 47 (Collet to Churchill)
    4. Lutchman, H. Op. Cit., 1974, p. 53
    5. Dwarka Nath. *A History of Indian in British Guiana.* London.
Nelson,
19, p. 167.
    6. Rodney,Walter. Op. Cit., 1981, p. 220.
    7. Clementi. C. *A History of British Guiana.* London. Macmillan, 1937.
    8.Frucht, Richard. "A Caribbean Social Type: Neither 'Peasant' nor
'Proletarian,' In Horowitz, Michael M., (ed.) *Peoples and Cultures of
the Caribbean.* New York: National History Press, 1971.
    9. Rodney, Walter. Op.Cit., 1981, p. 218.
    10. Frucht, Richard. Op. Cit., 1971.
    11. Ibid.,
    12. Nath, Dwarka. Op.Cit., 1950, p. 161.
    13. Chase, Ashton. *The History of Trade Unionism in Guyana.*
Georgetown: Guyana Printers, 1960.
    14. Rodney, Walter. Op. Cit., 1981.
    15. Ibid.,
    16. Ibid.,
    17. Ibid.
    18.Dalton, Henry. G. *History of British Guiana.* Vol. 11, London: Faber,
1955, p. 522.

19. *Report* of the Des Voeux Commission. Georgetown: 1871, p. 63.

20. Rodney, W. Op.Cit., 1981, p. 179.

21. *Report* of the Des Voeux Commission. Op.Cit., 1871, p. 63.

22. Singh, P. *Socialism in a plural society*. London: Fabian Society, 1972, p. 1.

23. Clementi, C. Op.Cit., 1937, vii.

24. Mohr, 1975

25. Smith R.T. *British Guiana*. London: Oxford University Press, 1962, pp. 51-52.

26. Farley, Rawle. "The Rise of the Peasantry in British Guiana," Social and Economic Studies. Jamaica: University of the West Indies, 1954, p. 91.

27. C.O. 111/477, Lees to Ripon, No. 125, 16 April, 1895.

28. Hilhouse William. Agriculture in 1829. Timehri, N.S. vol. 11, 1897, p. 281, quoted in M. Shahabudeen. *From Plantation to Nationalization*. Turkeyen: University of Guyana, 1983, p. 153.

29. Tinker, Hugh A.. *A New Systen of Slavery*, the Export of Indian Labour Overseas, 1830-1920. London: Oxford University Press, 1974.

30. Clementi, C. *Report* on the Condition of the Colony of British Guiana during the Great European War and th Chief Local Problems Awaiting Solution. Combined Court, No. , 21 of 1919, quoted in M. Shahabudeen. *From Plantation to Nationalization*. Turkeyen: University of Guyana. William Hilhouse. Agriculture in 1829. Timehri, N.S. vol. 11, 1897, p. 281, quoted in M. Shahabudeen. *From Plantation to Nationalization*. Turkeyen: University of Guyana, 1983, p. 153.

31. Tinker, Hugh A..Op.Cit., 1974.

32. Clementi. C. Op.Cit. 1983.

33. Ibid, p. 188

34. Hall Douglas. "The Flight from the Estates Reconsidered: the British West Indies 1838-42." *Journal* of Caribbean History, Vol. 10, 1978.

35. W.L Emancipation and Apprenticeship in the British West Indies 1838-42. Lo Indenture had saved the industry, for it brought in needed supplies from London, p. 363, quoted in Alan H. Adamson. *Sugar without Slaves*. New Haven: Yale University Press, 1972.

36. Ibid., p. 33.

37. J.D. Tyson. Report on the Conditions of Indians in Jamaica, British Guiana and Trinidad and Tobago, 1929, cited in M. Shahabudeen. *From Plantation to Nationalization*. Timehri: University of Guyana, 1983.

38. H.J.M. Hubbard. *Race and Guyana: The Anatomy of a Colonial Enterprise*. Georgetown: 1969.

39. Rodney, Walter *A History of the Guyanese Working People,* 1881-1905. Baltimore: Maryland, 1981, p. 31.

40. McLewin, P. Power and Economic Changes: The Response to Emancipation in Jamaica and British Guiana, Unpublished dissertation, Cornell University, 1971.

41. Walter Rodney. Op.Cit., 1981.

42. Rodney Walter. Op.Cit., 1981.

43. Adamson, Alan. *Sugar Without Slaves*. New Haven. Conn: Yale University Press, 1972, p. 71.

44. Ibid., p. 72.

45. Williams, Eric. "The Historical Background of British Guiana's Problem," Journal of Negro History, 30, No. 4, Oct. 1945, pp. 357-381.

46. (C.O. 111/436, Attorney General Haynes Smith to Granville, conf., 2 August, 1886).

47. Williams Eric. *Capitalism and Slavery*. London: Andre Deutsch, 1964.

48. Williams, Eric. "The Historical Background of British Guiana's Problems," Journal of Negro History, 30, No. 4, Oct. 1945.

49. (C.O. 111/72, Barkly to Grey, No. 36, 28 February, 1849).

50. C.O. 111/436, Haynes Smith to Granville, conf., 2 August 1886.

51. For a scholarly analysis of plantation economy, read Lloyd Best, "A model of Pure Plantation Economy," Social and Economic Studies, Vol. 17, No. 3, September 1968.

52. Walter Rodney, Op.Cit., 1981, p. 123.

53. Ibid.

54. Ibid., p. 125.

55. Ibid., p. 126.

56. C.O. 111/538, Swettenham to Chamberlain, no. 436, 13 Oct. 1903, quoted in Alan Adamson. *Sugar Without Slaves*. New Haven: Conn: Yale University Press, 1972, p. 212.

57. Walter Rodney. Op.Cit., 1981, p. 128

58. G.N.A. GD 285, 3 October 1882, C.O. 111/425.

59. Walter Rodney. Op. Cit., 1981, p. 128.

60. Ibid, p. 131.

61. The Echo, 12 April, 1890.

62. Walter Rodney. Op. Cit., 1981, p. 133.

63. The Echo, 22 October, 1880.

64. Walter Rodney. Op. Cit., 1981, p. 140.

65. C.O. 11/450, National Association of Journalists, 2 October 1889.

66. Ibid., p. 143.

67. O Portuguese, No. 420, 14 January, 1888, quoted in Walter Rodney. Op. Cit., 1981, p. 143.

68. Walter Rodney. Op. Cit., 1981, p. 31.

69. Report of the Sanderson Committee, Part II. Minutes of Evidence, p. 323, 1910, quoted in Dwarka Nath, *History of East Indians in British Guiana*. London: Nelson, 1950, p. 167.

70. Rodney, Walter. Op. Cit., 1981, p. 178.

71. Tyson, J.D. Report on the Conditions of Indians in Jamaica, British Guiana and Trinidad and Tobago, 1929, quoted in M. Shahabudeen. *From Plantation to Nationalism*. Turkeyen: Guyana, University of Guyana, 1983.

72. Walter Rodney. Op. Cit., 1981, p. 139.

73. Ibid., p. 43

Chapter Three

Politics in the Diaspora

Race in post-slavery Societies

Rodney was moved to consider, broadly-speaking, the fate of working people in relation to state structure. Concern for the working people led him to examine all aspects of their lives and in doing so implicitly he asked two questions: 'Do they live productive lives?' And: 'What would it take to make their lives productive?' Both questions involve human development and of course, national development. He would work first in criticizing established theory, where it fell short of its objectives; and when it contradicted good sense. When he found finally a structure that was so abhorrent that it seemed beyond hope, he committed himself to radical change, and was destroyed because of it. He had become, to use Horace Campbell's words "an organic intellectual."

His canvas was broad and his agenda was clear: domestic capitalism and international capitalism and how they influenced state structures and the lives of people; race and class and their interrelations with the state; the working people's movement and how it withstood the pressures of domestic and international capitalism by a precarious unity and a threatened solidarity.

Immanuel Wallerstein considers these main themes logically, thus emphasizing mental development and intellectual growth. But the author prefers to look at them chronologically. Rodney was a scholar from the Caribbean and influenced by its culture and environment. Class and race taken separately or collectively would have marked his early upbringing (no one in a British colony could be isolated from an awareness of class and race, both of which in their local as well as international aspects, are a continuing torment to the world's non-white people). Yet, it is often within such a recently independent territory that distinctions of class and race—and their defense—still occupy sections of the society. And Richard Small in his introduction to *The Groundings with my Brothers*, states the

matter succinctly, and in so doing, focuses attention on much that
Rodney would later address; indeed, addressing the issue of the
African identity of a majority of Jamaicans was responsible for the
banning of Rodney from that island. Small noted that the African
presence had been actively discouraged and at best paid lip service
to. And that "these questions could be subversive of 400 years of the
colonial viewpoint and the colonial relationships on which the present society is based." [1]

The tradition of continued worship at the imperial shrine, which
had been part of Caribbean preoccupations was challenged in
Jamaica. But that was incidental. Worship of the various colonial
idols existed at that time in all areas of the Caribbean and no territory could consider itself immune or remain aloof from these rituals.
If Jamaica became the platform for a significant regional challenge
to those that would deny or hinder or ignore black consciousness,
and thus arrest national identity, it was because of the university
there—itself at the time a colonial institution. Thus, we see the
irony of the situation. The challenge to the colonial mentality comes
from an institution of learning set up by the colonialists; but when
that institution seeks to exercize its freedom, its work is threatened
not by the colonialists but by those whom it is trying to liberate.

But the majority of black Jamaicans, "the man in the street" did
not need the university, or for that matter Walter Rodney to understand the reality of the African presence in the new world. This had
long ago taken place; indeed, the Rastafari had established the late
Emperor Haile Selassie as their God and had dared the society to
challenge their beliefs. The Rastafari movement and its mythology
of Africa had been the most conspicuous theology that had existed in
the Caribbean since slavery was abolished and whose modern observance is a national celebration. The word theology is deliberate, for
many first saw the Rastafari as a cultural phenomenon, in which
there were religious tones; and certainly some of the more visual aspects—the embrace of poverty, for example, (existentially, and not
as in the Christian experience, which proclaims its virtue as re-
ward)—contributed to the belief that the Rastafari movement was
uniquely cultural. This may have also had to do with its followers
who are black, and considered social outcasts and were independent
of the accustomed and expected allegiances.

But movements evolve and the Rastafari did. One of the consequences of twentieth century cultural imperialism is the speed with
which internationalism descends on cultures and changes them and
is in turn changed by them. The Rastafari movement became international because of the universality of its message, with which mil-
lions could identify, and its symbols, which could be exploited by the

mass media of communication. The message could claim immediate resonance among most of the world's peoples, certainly among the by-ways of European metropoles at the very least, where many of the exploited congregate. Moreover, they could identify with the message that sought to remedy social injustices, end persecution and transform the consciousness of their oppressors.

The message in its deepest significance is a plea to save the world by a revision of the social and economic arrangements—arguably, what the so-called Third World is after. Pointedly, "the story of the Rasta is the story of the black man, the castaway black man of the New World . . . " [2] The dignity of the black man is at the center of the universe of the Rastafari. It is a dignity which has been trampled upon, affronted and the object of much aggression. But offended dignity is not lost dignity, for the core remains untouched and it is that which indicts the white man and implicitly western civilization for the wrongs done.

The white man becomes 'Babylon', a state of sequestration, from which all must flee, for it is doomed forever from finding the true way. But the 'Babylon' spoken of is not exclusively the prerogative of the white world, it is to be found among those who do not understand the true way: they equally persecute the true believers. The 'Babylon' mentality therefore exists everywhere: in the Caribbean which had been undergoing the trials of growing nationalism and the uncertainties of ethnic identification within the national consensus; in Jamaica, where its most active form came to be manifested; the independent nations of black Africa which were forced to define anew their freedom from foreign incursion that would enslave them; in the Americas, where black assertion and pride came to be seen as violence and therefore to be put down by the forces of law and order, or deflected by enticements from the 'establishment' and co-opted within it.

Thus, the Rastafari starting from basically religious premises had provided a cosmology of the world, which was deceptively simple. On the surface the doctrine was about man and his relationship to the world and the nature of that relationship: a whole system of social, economic and political variables are tributaries to the main theme; and although the Rastafari eschew the more formal arrangements of politics, they are not blind to the political ramifications of their philosophy. But the deeper understandings, "groundings," are about what Fanon referred to as "Les Damnes de la terre", the Wretched of the Earth.

Religion cannot be entirely separated from a political system; indeed, it is the political system that helps feed and nurture belief. And the body of Christian missionaries who practised their calling in the Caribbean during and after slavery was as much influenced by the Church in England as the political system of which the Church was a part. This raises the question of responsibility for the maintenance of the institution slavery: was the Church active participant or passive observer? Did the teachings of the Church support the institution slavery, or did it work to undermine slavery in the long run. If the answer is that the Church helped undermine slavery by exposing slaves to the strength of the liberal conscience, thus reinforcing their own beliefs in liberty denied, then Christianity must be seen as a potent political doctrine. The Rastafari, therefore, and other religious sects, like Shango in Trinidad, Pocomania and Cumina in Jamaica, became implicitly political organizations, combining overt religious practice and covert political education. The Church in the Caribbean with all its rich mixture of African heritage and Christian tradition was a distinct political force; and certainly the teachings of Cumina, the Revivalists, Obeah are evidence of African form in ritual.

Significant about this form was a philosophy which incorporated the religious diversity of things ethereal and earthly experience central to the life force. Form gave it meaning. Indeed, the form of African religions made it easy to assimilate foreign religions rather than the opposite. For example, in Haiti the Roman Catholic church enjoyed a successful missionary and their observances of Bon Dieu embraced the African gods of "Olorun, Amma or Nyamurunga." [3] But it is also true that in the passage of time, African religious forms became susceptible to other influences and Protestantism was as easily accommodated in the English colonies as Catholicism in the French and Spanish possessions,—"an intermingling of mutually congenial elements."[4]

African religions in Jamaica and the rest of the British Caribbean originated in West Africa and their roots are with the Yoruba. i In fact, the Yoruba are the basis of the wholistic view of the world that informs the teachings of many of the revivalist cults of the New World and are their root. Now Yoruba thought and also traditional African philosophy emphasized unity of all the elements. ii Also, religious belief in Jamaica among the Cumina and Bongo cults " rests on the assumption that men and spirits exist within a single unified structure . . . " [5] Belief rests on a unity of matters spiritual and temporal within a coherent system.

African religions which accompanied the slave trade to the Caribbean were kept alive by the constant influx of people from Africa, thus reinforcing continuity and the stability of religious experience. Slaves embraced religion of ancestral worship as a means of spiritual continuity as well as refuge from suffering and distress.

They also looked to religion in joyful moments such as the emancipation. The power of the established church declined after emancipation. Corruption was widespread, inefficiency a by-word and it could not therefore successfully deal with the new social and political arrangements with its moral authority tarnished. In any case it would have been hard put to do this because of the strength and persistence of religious form that sustained belief among freed slaves. African religious practice, reflected in myalism and other cults, was strong enough in the years following emancipation for common cause with native baptist religion. Revivalism of a distinctly Jamaican kind superceded orthodoxy; and even though orthodox religion restored its confidence in later years, it did not succeed in overcoming the hold of Revivalism in the consciousness of the masses. [6] This short excursion in ways of religion is significant, for it explains the particular strength of a revivalist trend in the social history of Jamaica. Its fundaments were zeal and uplift. It is from revivalism with its particular African terms of reference, uniting the elements of spirituality and ancestor worship, from which the Rastafari spring. What makes them different is that they place the black man at the center of the universe. In the Caribbean region, religion, or more precisely, African religious practice, has been and is a source of continuous celebration; also,—and this needs to be said,—it is often a safety valve which soothes more active forms of social disquiet, even as it revolutionizes a sense of self. The Yoruba tradition, which is the basis of African religious influence, embraced with equal devotion philosophy and religion and observed no separation between religious observance and social practice. This makes it easy to understand why the Rastafari could unite religious practice and social justice, even though they did not actively campaign in politics.

Rodney said that the Rastafari, "have completely and inexorably broken with Jamaican society and its values."[7] But this is incomplete. The very separation constitutes a fiercely political act. Yoruba religious beliefs contrast with the theology and practice of Roman Catholicism, which separates the teachings of the Church from more demanding social and political practices. And in our time, the vexed question of liberation theology, wherein some practitioners of the Roman Catholic Church seek to apply its teachings to the social demands of the marketplace—the union of theory and praxis—has caused controversy within Church hierarchy. The physical and spiritual unity between Man and God—or Gods—is the key to understanding the significance of African religious presence and more especially as it is reflected in the Ethiopian Orthodox Church. Yoruba gods are polytheistic. The Rastafari could see no contradic-

tion in the concept and the practice of a living God, such as Haile
Selassie, or his heirs or successors, for the Yoruba religion embraced
all kinds of Gods—the only requirement being that the God could
dispense on a regular basis concern for their life and meaning.

Ethiopian Orthodoxy reflects the coherence of religion and its
unity with people. "It is a church based on the people and their way
of life. Even when converting 'animists' to Christianity, it respected
their previous culture and adopted part of it." 8 Respect for another
culture, another religion, is in keeping with the belief in the unity of
all matter. And the Rastafari with their belief centered in Ethiopian
Orthodoxy weave this respect for the individual into their theology
so that they become one. This makes for a strong sense of individual
awareness and an assertion of self, which is in strong contrast with
the society that has rejected them. The religion of the Rastafari as-
serting self in the midst of 'Babylon', must also be seen as a need to
protect self and culture against forces which threaten to destroy.
The protection of self was a necessary part in preserving the dignity
of the individual, threatened and abused from all sides. The religion
of the slaves during and after slavery had much the same purpose:
to restore psychological strength, to comfort, to renew, and to provide continuity for traditions in danger of being forgotten. Some of
the content of these traditions were naturally disregarded over the
years, or merged with the content from other religions, but the essentials, the form, and the purpose, remain intact.

Thus, the Rastafari congregation followed the usages of the
church in times of slavery, but went beyond it in certain significant
particulars: if the slaves saw religion as awakening a liberal conscience and providing comfort for an assaulted self, the Rastafari assumed a more radical function. They pointed to the weaknesses of a
society incapable of honoring its promises to provide social and economic refuge to its people; moreover, one which actively practiced
discrimination; was indifferent to social injustice, and casual in providing remedies or solutions to social problems. This is all the more
obtuse because of its closeness to organized Christian religion. And
it is precisely there, as Rex Nettleford affirms, that the Rastafari
probe the vulnerability of the church and did so with "weapons out
of its own armoury—the Old Testament, particularly those parts of
the Old Testament which satisfied the needs of a people deprived
and degraded for too long."9 In this way, a fusion of the theory and
the practice of religion was brought about: between biblical scrip-
ture and social and economic needs.

The scriptures were to come to the aid of the Rastafari in other
significant ways: the suffering and torture of black people during
slavery, their continuing wretchedness in Jamaica, the Caribbean

and by implication, the rest of the world and 'Babylon,' is surely akin to the biblical tribulations of the Jews. The Book of Revelations provided both the assurance of after life and the faith which could help and sustain belief in it, when all suffering would come to an end. The sustenance of belief, the righteousness of cause, the sense of the relationship of self to that belief, is a dangerous doctrine when allied to the circumstances of racial ethos. Bluntly speaking, black people can never be allowed cheerfully to have and to hold so fundamental a belief outside of other mediating social and cultural influences. Rex Nettleford believes that the theoretical foundation of the Book of Revelation is unassailable, except within doctrinal debate with other religious bodies; and its practical application is plainly subversive of national and international energies, except where these meet and cohere with shared objectives.

The Rastafari are dangerous precisely because they stand outside of the familiar religious, social and cultural establishment and deliver a message which is so profundly political; and yet,—here is the contradiction,—without seeming to be political. If the Rastafari had founded a political organization and identified themselves conspicuously and overtly as belonging to a group seeking power, they would be forgiven their heresies. But, their symbols, which are their foci, are a union with the Godhead and the universality of love and peace. [10] This explains why the movement has enjoyed such international 'acclaim.' Its 'message' touches a universal human need and this same message, coming from the downtrodden of the human race, the black person, imprisons responses of white people even as it liberates the black person.

Thus, it could then be immediately understood why this liberation of the black person, made it easier to identify with the return to Africa movement. This is not to say that black people have only thought about the Return; over the years individuals and groups of people have actually done so. But the considerable merit of the Rastafari is to have elevated the business of the Return to Africa to the status of myth and thus placed it indelibly on the consciousness of all blacks wherever they are. The Return is therefore part of black mythology. What this does is to place black people outside of the province of 'establishment' thinking, making it possible for them to create their own history. DuBois was aware of the duality; the feeling of being American, and black. One cannot underrate the importance of myths in human history. One lives by them. And it is at least arguable that a people separated from their homelands, buffeted from pillar to post, needs the comforting assurances of myth to sustain efforts at survival. The Return is less about return than the myth of Return. The black power movement in the United States aimed at the empowerment of black people there, but when it departed, as some of the more extravagant of its adherents did, from the fundamentals of what the movement was about, to counsel return to Africa, it destroyed the basis of its own support by trying to convert myth to reality.

This, of course, was quite apart from the vicious racial responses and cumulative depredations to legitimate protest, which also contributed to the demise of the movement. Also,—and this needs to be emphasized—the absence of a coherent theoretical philosophy, which could be converted to practical action to sustain energies of spirit, contributed to its early flowering and premature end. The black power movement in the United States lacked an appropriate base from which to rally its adherents; and 'power,' vague and ill-defined came to be associated with force and aggression, without the balancing influences of thought and reflection. Thus was the movement robbed of its spiritual vitality.

The mythology of the Return is a psychological tool which is to aid in the liberation of all black people from bondage wherever that bondage exists. This accomplishes three things: first, it forces reactionary blacks to deal with their continuing bondage and to admit that continuing bondage exists; second, it sets the stage for a unification of black people everywhere on the basis of the common ritual of suffering and other shared experiences; and finally, it places the struggle beyond place and time.

Some of the faithful who had left Jamaica for London, New York, took the teachings of the movement with them. Most found the religious teachings especially comforting in the unfamiliar worlds of Europe and America. These beliefs became especially meaningful as a bridge connecting the New World with the Old and with the United States of America with another of the Americas. Also, the Rastafari sought refuge in faith from the oppressions of racism and ethnocentrism, intensifying the religious experience through a unity of theory and praxis. The movement now affects all the trappings of a modern international religious practice, and if its symbols are shaky—Emperor Haile Selassie has passed on and with him the Empire, and Ethiopia is at best an uncertain paradise— they have been succeeded by the more permanent symbols of the oppressed in the major metropolitan cities; and an Africa, which is in need of help and identification with her children the world over.

The Rastafari and Rodney

It was this that Rodney recognized. The religious and cultural foundations were intact in Jamaica. A relatively unexplored region of human opportunity was ready, for the ground had already been pre-pared. He had seen it in the early years at the University of the West Indies, when the Jamaican bourgeoisie had consolidated their hold on the growing opportunities for agricultural and industrial de-velopment. For example, as a consequence of increased development capital, which came with U.S. investment, the bauxite industry en-joyed a boon, the effect of which was to further increase the gap be-tween rich and poor, insulating them from one another. Among the poor, who could afford to, many migrated; others remained behind to swell the ranks of the urban poor. Such of the Rastafari who re-mained behind became the conscience of the country, reminding it that it needed to practice what it preached.

The importance of the Rastafari in Rodney's education cannot be minimized; however much one wants to disagree with its theology or underlying theory. Both theory and theology rest on certain in-escapable facts of poverty and material destitution, with which most black people can identify. Indeed, Rodney, writing in *Groundings with my Brothers*, remarked on the oppressive conditions which he found in Jamaica; as Franz Fanon described in The *Wretched of the Earth* when speaking about the Third World. And Marcus Garvey had in five years 1915-1920 so understood the facts of destitution as to see that the only way out was organization of black people on an international scale, to obtain mastery over the environment through economic and political power,—truly, a celebration of the black race through enhanced power and not, as later reactionaries, those who misread or misinterpreted the teachings of Garvey, would claim, a prescription for black racism. That the Garvey movement seemed a threat to the American way is evidence of an endemic racism that would not go away; but more importantly, Garvey threatened to end the system of exploitation under which black people lived. That the revisionist interpretation of Garvey's teachings was limited can be seen in the effect Garvey had internationally. At the height of his popularity, the Garvey movement counted branches in North America, Central America and the Caribbean,—Cuba with 52 was the largest outside of the U.S. Europe, Africa, Asia and Australia had token membership.[11]

While the message was addressed to black people, its contents were such that all people who felt oppressed could identify with it. Thus, in a curious way, black organization and protest, had most un-likely consequences and spawned unpredictable social responses. And the black social unrest, which was a part of the black power movement in the United States in the 1960s, encouraged other op-pressed groups to rally. Instructive, perhaps, is the historical evi-dence that attempts by black people to liberate themselves, be it from the physical bondage of slavery, or other forms of social, economic and political emasculation, have invariably met with strong resistance. But, more encouragingly, perhaps, is that such attempts at liberation and social protest have invariably succeeded in attracting a following among those who perceive themselves in similar circumstance. And in our time the Civil Rights struggle in the U.S. has found immediate empathy with those groups that feel themselves oppressed. This would indicate that race is by no means the only denominator of oppression; and bondage or subjugation of any kind inevitably widely sows seeds of anger, bitterness, leading to discord and social unrest.

What Garvey had to say was also the brunt of much criticism and hostility. In the U.S. he was opposed by Du Bois whose brilliance as journalist and scholar placed him in the unique position to lead the National Association of Colored Peoples and the bourgeoisie and the "talented tenth", who were ready to avail themselves of what the country had to offer. As an educator he taught the important lesson that racism was a negation of the ideals which the nation stood for and a poison eating away at its body fabric. He was among the first to see that Africa had to be brought into the comity of nations, an integral part of the world community and could not remain as an exploited entity. iii It was Du Bois "who gave body and soul to [the] idea of Pan-Africanism and broadened its perspective." [12] But Du Bois had limited appeal. His was not a position with which the common people could identify. "My leadership was a leadership solely of ideas. [13] I never was, nor ever will be, personally popular." His was the moral vision to condemn, to warn, for he was a patriot; and patriotism—arguably, then, the most expensive of luxuries and one which the masses of black people could ill afford—prevented Du Bois from achieving Garvey's following.

Du Bois reasoned—and so did Martin Luther King—that America should honour its commitments to all its citizens regardless of their race, and color. This was no more than the fourteenth and fifteenth amendments of the Constitution stated. But these seemingly routine observances, which guaranteed political equality and social and economic justice, were considered radical in the early years of the century, and even now, while part of official discourse, cannot be taken for granted. Du Bois spent most of his life campaigning for the promise of a better life for blacks through the legal rituals. His duty "stern and delicate" for equality contrasted with that of a Booker T. Washington, who counselled black appeasement to the will of whites in the South, in the fond hope that eventually better counsels would prevail. "By every civilized and peaceful method, we must strive for the rights which the world accords to men . . . "[14] These rights were denied not only in America, but everywhere black people lived and Du Bois with commendable foresight saw the Pan-African movement as championing the rights of Africans to rule their own societies. ("The rights which the world accords men.") It was not a popular position among blacks, nor for that matter, among Americans generally, which perhaps accounted for his lack of financial support from even his liberal white friends. "They had no schemes for internationalizing in race problems and to many of them it seemed quixotic to undertake anything of this sort." [15]

The internationalizing of the movement for the civil rights of black people became Du Bois' major preoccupation over the first half of the twentieth century. What had started as a campaign to end racial oppression in America, had incorporated similar grievances elsewhere. Five international congresses were held by the Pan-African movement. What had begun as deliberations against racial injustice, became involved in the nationalist struggle for independence in Africa and the political and economic freedom of Africa. With commendable prescience the last Pan-African Congress, meeting in Manchester 1945, warned of the possibilities of racial conflict in Kenya and Africa if the inalienable rights of Africans continued to be abused. The Congress made sweeping recommendations on social, economic and political matters, which are still on the agenda of international institutions: economic stangulation of the developing world, the cancer of apartheid in South Africa. Moreover, the Congress took a stand on all matters affecting the freedom and dignity of African peoples. And just as Du Bois had challenged America to live up to its own Constitution, so the final Pan-African Congress challenged the Atlantic powers to live up to the Atlantic Charter they had created. But the declaration of the Congress was not an olive branch appeal. It said that if the Western powers were not prepared to respect the principles of their own charter, then African nations might well use force in order to achieve their aims. But the appeal to force as trenchant as it sounded in 1945 was not then a realizable possibility and never overshadowed one of the real aims of the movement which was economic democracy " as the only real democracy." Du Bois advocated "national self-determination, individual liberty and democratic socialism" [16] for Africa. These were the essentials of his Pan-Africanist policies. Du Bois still hoped that an indifferent and sometimes unfriendly West would see its promise before it was too late. But the organization went on.

Pan–Africanism, which was Du Bois' great contribution to the history of African peoples, stimulated nationalist movements in Africa and brought life to their objectives. International pressures mounted as a result of which internal self-government then political independence of many African countries was achieved in the 1960s. African unity, an unforeseen possibility, at the turn of the century, is now more than rhetoric. The welfare of African peoples, which so singularly exercized Du Bois, has reflected his tact and diplomacy amid a great deal of hostility. His contribution to the movement might have been in internationalizing the struggle. He made Africans aware that their concerns were shared by American blacks and American blacks realize that they had a role to play in the development of Africa.

But Garvey harbored no such illusions. He had long since despaired of black people ever obtaining justice in America. It is from this conviction that his Back to Africa movement stemmed. The movement was more a rallying call to action, which lacked the essentials of a coherent philosophy. Though it must not be inferred that black power is not susceptible to this coherence; but it is to say that Garvey's strengths were also his limitations and he did not succeed in translating black power from the domain of slogan to that of realizable alternative. Black power as a viable philosophy is a great deal more subtle than Garvey realized. For him, black power involved separatism from the persecution of white people in America, an end to European exploitation in Africa. What was to be done when American blacks reached Africa and set themselves up was not fully explored though plans were made. But there is sufficient evidence to show that Garvey envisioned institutions under his domination and control. He lashed out against capitalist exploitation but understood what was to be gained through capitalism.[17] But the separation that was a fundamental part of the Garvey movement was not racist and it would be inaccurate to refer to it as racism in reverse. A mass movement with objectives independent of the American state, implicitly seemed to threaten the existence of the state. Black power, then as now, in the words of Martin Luther King Jr., "is a call for black people to amass the political and economic strength to achieve their legitimate goals . . . " [18] There is nothing inherently disturbing or frightening about such a point of view, for it must be on the agenda of all who would aspire to the leadership of black people. But it must not be exclusive. Garvey made it so. Du Bois did not. And Rodney must be considered—in the early stage of his career—as assuming the mantel of Du Bois rather than Garvey.

" . . . Black people there have a stake in that land, which they have watered with their sweat, tears and blood, and black leadership is aware of the necessity of fighting white power simultaneously at home and abroad." [19]

Compare this with Du Bois' An Address to the Country, 1905:

"We claim for ourselves every single right that belongs to a free-born America, political, civil and social; and until we get these rights we will never cease to protest and assail, the ears of America." [20]

Every leader of black people this century has sprung from the wellsprings of Marcus Garvey or William Du Bois; and the black movement needs both: the passions that Garvey could arouse among the masses and the intellectualism of Du Bois, the man of ideas, who could help chart its course. Rodney was heir to the universalism of Du Bois rather than the focused vision of Garvey. The tragedy is that both Garvey and Du Bois came at the same time and provoked such untoward responses among themselves and followers.

Marcus Garvey could understand a popular movement precisely because he did not fear its consequences. His experience among the Jamaican middle class had already exposed him to the exploitation and class warfare from which racism was an inevitable growth. iv Instinctively Garvey went to the heart of the matter. Black consciousness of Africa was the antidote to white imperialism.

Du Bois was a patrician-like figure who could appeal in a limited way to a social class that identified with the objective of liberation as it understood it. His was a formal reading of the liberation script, which prescribed an agenda which, while it appealed to many blacks of goodwill, was not offensive to the white liberal establishment. Garvey's purposes were more ambitious and encompassing. They were also radical: nothing less than the economic liberation of black people from the domination of white people. That America took more kindly to Du Bois than to Garvey is a commentary on its fear of the consequences of Garvey's message: economic liberation led to political freedom, whose dimensions could not be forecast. Political freedom in its true meaning was as dangerous then as it is now.

One of the obstacles to political freedom was the non- empowerment of black people. Both Garvey and Rodney shared this belief and the latter has been called a disciple of Garvey. But this is incomplete. Garvey gave meaning to the life of tired blacks, with his vision for Africa and liberation. They who had been searching in diverse ways for a ubiquitous messiah both in Jamaica and the Americas, found his message comforting. He wanted an independent Africa for black people, where they could build up economic power, organization and political power. The return to Africa fulfilled all their aspirations.

Rodney too spoke of Africa but not in the same way. In Jamaica and elsewhere he spoke of an Africa which people did not know and about which they had received all the wrong instruction. They knew nothing of the its former economic power, nor of its greatness and glory, its leaders and its institutions, which had changed the world and contributed to the greatness of Europe. Thus, the Return fulfills certain psychological objectives: it situates in the mind the vision of a civilization complete and functioning and active long before the arrival of foreign influences; and these same foreign influences, barbaric at their worst, and exploitative at their best, never succeeded in destroying it, though they did inevitably wound it.

Rodney's discourses on Africa became therefore information as well as propaganda—not in its modern affiliation to lies and distortion—but as a sower of seeds bearing fruit. Thus he posed the question in the first line of *How Europe Underdeveloped Africa*: 'What is Development?' Which is a prelude for the analysis of the etymology of the word and a discussion of how its meaning has changed to reflect an exploitative, capitalist nomenclature. That change was accompanied by denigratory associatons and value-judgments, and it is these, he pointed out, which define underdevelopment.

Jamaica provided the crucible of experience where the ideas of history, an emerging nationalism,—which it shared with his own Guyana—with all the inherent contradictions of social class and attendant sensitivies, came together. Class as a measure of social, political or other determinants is susceptible to categorization. But the lines separating one category from another are not clear; there is often overlap. Also, there is rigidity, when class barriers define social, economic and political movement. Rigid class barriers create an awareness of class, which frequently leads to the exercise of political remediation e.g. at the polls, or other avenues of change.

The class phenomenon in Jamaica can be looked at in four ways: class as ideology; in economic terms; as symbols of status; and as an affair of power and powerlessness. [21] But that is an objective perception, and not necessarily how people in Jamaica look at it. The late Carl Stone, an eminent Jamaican political scientist, found that more people understood social class as an economic condition i.e.between rich and poor, than any other category, including the ideological.

Rodney's assessment of the Jamaican situation was that class was an economic condition that reflected ideological conditions based on exploitation of the poor by the rich. In fact, he observed "the dilemma faced by alien class elements", [22] who are so out of step with their own society that they were embarrassed when Haile Selassie visited the island.

Responsibility for the oppression of the poor masses of Jamaica, Rodney placed squarely at the door of the rich, who act as representatives of metropolitan-imperialist interests. And the "local ruling elite", the rich "was primarily brown, augmented by significant elements of white and other groups, such as Syrians, Jews and

Chinese." [23] Thus, he broadened the class category to include varia-
tions of colour, which closely parallels perceptions of status. [24] This
latter position seems to accord with that of another observer of the
Jamaican scene: "colour is the social determinant of status and suf-
fuses most relationships." [25] But race is declining in significance in
Jamaica's class structure. [26]

The correlation of class and color in Jamaica created some confusion among those blacks who could not identify with the main
ideas and beliefs of black power. Identification with the ruling elite
through habit and custom caused them to be isolated. They took
refuge in the comforts of a social class to which their education and
upward mobility gave them relative access. In the U.S. education,
motivation and drive to move up the economic ladder and the frustration and anxiety caused by its denial, was one factor responsible
for the radical ambitions of the civil rights movement of the sixties;
other factors included, the persistent and wanton neglect of the
black minority in a host of areas like housing, health and employment, to name the essentials; and the Vietnam war. [27] But the example had already been set by Marcus Garvey.

Social class division in Jamaica affected the attainment and performance of national goals and was divisive of national unity. But it
also promoted inequality and uneven development and further exacerbated those factors responsible for social impoverishment. The
Jamaican working classes—like the working classes anywhere in
the Caribbean—were vulnerable to economic as well as social inequality. Many believed—and Rodney among them —that capitalist
development was responsible for the uneven, and in most instances,
untoward development of both economic and educational systems in
Jamaica. But this did not prevent attempts at a national agenda and
the unity of the middle class and the worker-peasant.[28] Common aggravations—discrimination on the basis of color, intellectual and
job-related—served to keep the alliance together until independence
was achieved. Upward mobility assured, though perhaps not guaranteed through independence, the middle class continued to develop
through education, legitimizing upward mobility with the aid of
Christian morality. And further, it was education and especially
higher education, confirming status and setting its seal of impreg-
nability, that drove a wedge between the middle class and the working class. C.L.R. James puts it nicely: " . . . for centuries they have
had it as an unshakeable principle . . . that they are separate and
distinct from the masses of the people." [29] It was a distinction which
paid certain dividends: jobs, patronage, position, status and even
wealth. But the sacrifice was immense, and not only in Jamaica.
The impossibility of the middle class in the Caribbean to articulate a

position outside of strict material possessions, was only matched by its inability to understand the depth of the plight of the masses of the people. It stood for nothing outside its own narrow class interests and would not be moved from them. The Jamaican working class did not succeed in achieving gains proportionate to its contribution to the independence movement.

The betrayal of their interests frustrated national development, led to anger and unrelieved bitterness and made them prey to unholy influences. And since the working class is predominantly black people, it is clear that any fundamental change should have as the main focus of its energies the mobilizing of black people. Institutionalized poverty, exacerbated by the lack of political power, are the main ingredients of its destitution. The Jamaican working class became for Rodney a symbol of the condition of black people everywhere in the face of the representatives of capitalism.

Yet it was not a helpless position, as such illustrious Jamaican forebears as Paul Bogle, Marcus Garvey had found: stasis provided its own conditions for movement and revolutionary activity. Rodney observed: "What matters above all else . . . is the action of the black masses in their various capacities."[30] And this activity was not limited to Jamaica or the Caribbean. "Black Power can be seen as a movement and an ideology springing from the reality of oppression of black peoples by whites within the imperialist world as a whole." Moreover, "it [the movement] . . . is confident of the potential of black power on this globe."[31]

The oppression of which he speaks was as much cultural as it was materialistic and cultural freedom was an important point of departure for black power. Indeed, Rodney was aware of the influence of cultural and political ascendancy of the white establishment over the psychology of black people, on self-esteem, self-hatred.[32] The adoption of a standard, a cultural standard, distinct from one's own, is treated in the literature of alienation of our time.[33]

Black people have been treated as fodder, tools, and reduced to the status of objects in the history of western civilization, in exploitative productive relations from which struggle has been inevitable. This experience falls into the Marxist category of the class struggle, but the literature of alienation does not seek philosophical justification on these premises. The literature studies the images of blacks and their status in the world. [34] But the significance of race and doctrines based on race dwarfed considerations based on purely class and would explain why class could never replace race in the primacy of black struggle. The modern tendency to substitute class for race, while invigorating the debate of political liberals, is without foundation. Hence, alienation is alienation on the basis of race and this is reflected in the work of such Caribbean writers as George Lamming[35] and Aime Cezaire.[36] The theme of racial alienation is intense in Caribbean writers: discrimination on the basis of race, added to an enforced rootlessness and or exile, and identification with a western value system that dehumanized even as it partly fulfilled certain yearnings. The intellectual of sensitivity cannot for long accept the system as it exists and learns to reject it or come to terms with it.

The history of the intellectual in the Caribbean this century has been one of ambiguity. Each territory has known people who have advanced the revolutionary tradition in their own ways. Each has been stung by the victimization of race and, to the extent that protest has been active and vociferous against racial injustice, and powerlessness, it has taken the movement of black struggle further along the road to economic and social justice for all. Walter Rodney, the intellectual, was committed to that revolutionary tradition.

But it was not a tradition that was uniform, in the sense that all those who felt abused, protested against the main causes of that abuse. Some suffered abuse indifferently, indeed tolerated it. The Caribbean intelligentsia in general found themselves privileged in so far as the material conditions of life were concerned—"measured in terms of the front lawn and the huge American car"—and this dulled any tendency towards radicalism and consciousness, "depriving the black masses of articulate leadership." Still, it would be a mistake to relegate the intelligentsia, however misguided, to a passive role. Violence, both manifest and latent, is never far from the surface. And certainly violence for the Caribbean man of intellect is a separation from the more oppressive features of a western value system, the colonial system, the system of capitalist relations, indeed any system, that dominates and dehumanizes, including the system of governance within his own territory to which he can be more exposed and therefore vulnerable. Violence also means the destruction of "white symbols" and a defiance of all cultural elements that would subvert the continuing influence of white people on the psyche of black people.

The conscious destruction of colonial symbols, a re- discovery of an African cultural integrity, of reinforcing the myths of black cultural existence dissipated over centuries, constitute the main thematic elements of Negritude—that body of work which sought to re-affirm the humanism of blacks. In literature it is seen in romantic attachments to Africa; and Leopold Senghor has sought to capture the essence of this relationship in the poem Black Woman, who is the metaphor for Africa, endowed with qualities of beauty, grace and an eternal mother.

NOTES

1. Richard Small. *"Introduction." Groundings with my Brothers.* London: Bogle L'Ouverture, 1969, p. 7
2. Owens, Joseph. Dread: *the Rastafarians of Jamaica*, with an Introduction by Rex Nettleford. Kingston. Jamaica, Sangsters, 1976.
3. Jahn, Janheinz *Muntu.* London: Faber, 1961.
4. Lewis, Gordon. *Main Currents in Caribbean Thought.* Baltimore: Maryland, The Johns Hopkins University Press, 1983, p. 20-21.
5. Patterson, Orlando. *The Sociology of Slavery.* Mass. Harvard University Press, (1977)
6. Ibid.
7. Walter Rodney. Op. Cit., 1969, p. 13.
8. Ibid., p. 45.
9. Nettleford, Rex. "Introduction." Joseph Owens. Op. Cit., 1976, p. xiii.
10. Owens, Joseph. Op. Cit., 1976.
11. Martin,Tony . *Marcus Garvey, Hero.* Dover. Massachusetts: The Majority Press, 1983.
12. Padmore, George. *Pan-Africanism and Africa.* London: Dennis Dobson, 1972, p. 96.
13. W.E. DuBois. 1966 p. 42-43.
14. Ibid.
15. DuBois, W.E. *Dusk of Dawn*, p. 275.
16. Padmore, George. Op. Cit., 1972, p. 84.
17. Fox. C. Elton C. Fox. *Garvey: The Story of a Pioneer Black Nationalist.* New York: Dodd Meads Co., p. 149.
18. King, Martin Luther King. 1967, p. 36
19. Rodney, Walter Rodney. Op. Cit., 1969, p. 21.
20. Quoted in George Padmore. *Pan Africanism or Communism.* 1972, p. 91.
21. Stone, Carl. *Democracy and Clientelism in Jmmaica.* New Brunswick. N.J.: Transaction Books, 1985.
22. Rodney, Walter. Op. Cit., 1969, p. 13.
23. Ibid.
24. Foner,Nancy. *Status and Power in Rural Jamaica: A Study of Educational and Political Change.* New York: Teachers College Press, 1973.
25. David Lowenthal. *West Indian Societies.* London: Oxford University Press, 1972, p. 93
26. Stone, Carl. Op.Cit., 1985, p. 22-23.. New Brunswick. N.J.: Transaction Books, 1985, p. 22- 23.
27. Gitlin.T. *The Sixties: Years of Hope, Days of Rage.* New York: Bantam Books, 1987.
28. Munroe, Trevor. *The Politics of Constitutional Decolonization* 1944-62. Jamaica: Institute of Social and Economic, University of the West Indies, Social and Economic Research 1972.

29. James, C.L.R.. *Spheres. Of Existence.* Westport: Conn.: Lawrence Hill publishers, 1980, p. 137).

30. Walter Rodney. *The Groundings with my Brothers.* London: Bogle L'Ouverture, 1969, p. 14.

31. Ibid, p. 20.

32. Ibid.,.

33. Lamming, George. *The Pleasures of Exile.* London: Michael Joseph, 1956; and Vidia Naipaul. The Mimic Men. London: Penguin, 1962.

34. Abiola Irele. The *Journal* of Modern African Studies, 3, 4, 1965, pp. 499-526.

35. George Lamming. Op. Cit., 1956.

36. Aime Cezaire. *Cahiers d'un retour au pays natale.* Paris. Gallimard,1961.

i. A comprehensive analysis of Yoruba religions in the New World appears in R. Bastide. *The African Religions of Brazil.* Baltimore. Maryland: The Johns Hopkins University Press, 1978, pp. 59-62.

ii. Janheinz Jahn discusses in Muntu, several studies about people from different regions, which are far a[art. where languages are dissimilar, but where neverhteless, despite differences of detail, the core of belief is the same.

iii. Henry Sylvester-Williams, a barrister-at-law from Trinidad, first conceived of the idea of Pan-Africanism as an affair of fellowship among people of African descent. The problem of race prejudice in London, where Sylvester-Williams practised law, as well as the common afflictions, which accompanied students of African descent, moved the infant organization in a more active direction.

European expansionism in Africa had not as yet ended and fresh onslaughts on African institutions continued to be made and Sylvester Williams became legal adviser to some African chiefs who came to England on political business. For example, the Bantu nations in South Africa were the object of increasing aggression by the South African government. Cecil Rhodes and his British South Africa Company started to establish hegemony in Central Africa and European plunder could scarcely be contained in the rest of the continent. Thus, political events dictated the policy of the Pan-African conference in 1900. Sylvester-Williams did not live to see his idea take root, for he died soon after his return to Trinidad.

iv. Franz Fanon also deplored the tendency of the middle class of the Third World to subvert national liberation movements. Read. Franz Fanon. *The Wretched of the earth.* New York: Grove Press, 1965; also for critical analysis on Fanon's political theory, Renate Zahar. Franz Fanon: *Colonialism and Alienation.* New York. Monthly Review Press, 1974.

Chapter Four

Slavery and Black Power

Jamaica is the microcosm that reflected Rodney's view of that assured and inexorable movement of oppressed black people,— ["there is nothing with which poverty coincides so absolutely as with the color black."] [1]—who in their several ways are moving to rid themselves of the burden of history. Some of the manifestations of the movement within the Caribbean, with its intricate composition of peoples, merits attention. Slavery cast a shadow over the whole of the Caribbean and affected the social and ethnic make-up of its peoples. Now how did the institution of slavery influence societal relations. To neglect to do so is as fundamental an error as to underestimate its importance. Much work has been done elsewhere on one or other of these elements and their details need not concern us here. [2] But it is important in so far as black power is concerned to trace the more important antecedents of the modern phenomenon and the tendency to sensationalize in popular journalism and to see black power as a response and reaction to white imperialism is facile. This excludes the history of black power, its emergence at different points in time, how its responses differs with the society in which it emerges.

For example, black power in the Caribbean is quite different to the form that emerged in the United States. In the US, historical conditions dictated a complete separation of the races, and a corresponding denial of the opportunity for meaningful and continuous social exchanges; and this was institutionalized in law and custom. Black power in the U.S. is a demand by black people for equal rights in law and for full participation and exercise in social, economic and political institutions. In the Caribbean, black power is not about legal rights denied; it is more about the delicate shades of custom and habit that have prevented their emergence of those rights. Black power is a protest against the ambiguities of class and color. For custom and habit foster socio-psychological attributes of mind, derived from slavery, that distract even as they encourage defiance of the status quo.

More to the point, these attributes are a consequence of the persistent demand for economic power and the pursuit of economic justice that is inherently a more "subtle undertaking requiring negotiation by individuals so as not to antagonize the other races." [3] It is a balancing act of no mean proportions, requiring skill and judgment. Also, and herein lies the complexity, it requires, as Lloyd Best suggests, "the abandonment of the monoliths of race, class and culture that provide deceptive rationalization for exploitation of one sort or another." [4] But it is not the abandonment of race, class and culture that will alleviate pressures on communities or temper anxieties. To abandon race, class and culture would be in any case ahistorical and run the danger of perpetuating myths that are not accurate. Rather, a more prudent course, in our view, is to accept these monoliths—race, class and culture—and to deal with their contradictions—and be free of their burden.

Opposition to black power in the U.S. consists of elements within the white establishment and some reactionary blacks, who find themselves in positions of responsibility within the "establishment." The situation is altogether quite unique; the strength of the opposition to black power varies with the nature of the challenge; and in times of assertion, the opposition is more pronounced than in times of relative quietude. Opposition to black power follows a certain mathematical formula: economic or other gains achieved under conditions of challenge and protest are apt to be reversed when those conditions no longer exist. This is disturbing for social harmony, and wearying of effort, and it ensures that each generation begins anew the battle for civil rights. In the Caribbean, the opposition is more subtle and consists mainly of the ethnic mix of people, who differ in number in each community, but who nevertheless are afraid for the positions they occupy, the wealth they possess, and is content to follow examples from abroad unthinkingly and without reservation.

Rodney understood the relation of black power to the world of capitalism. "Black Power can be seen as a movement and an ideology springing from the reality of oppression of black peoples by whites within the imperialist world as a whole." [5] The Caribbean has been victim of foreign exploitation and indeed its "most oppressed section because we were a slave society and the legacy of slavery still rests heavily."[6] To which Gordon Lewis adds: "The conquest and colonization of the Caribbean . . . can only be properly understood if it is seen as a chapter in the expansion of early capitalist society." [7] That conquest inevitably posed problems for the colonizer,—the European man in the metropolis and his acolyte in the Caribbean—and the transported African. It was to lead to revolts, disturbances, and a great deal of suffering on both sides, and shining through it all was the desire for liberty, what C.L.R. James calls "the ridding oneself of the particular burden which is the special inheritance of the black skin."[8]

The domestic burden of capitalism was exercised through, and by means of economic relations, specifically through sugar and the products of sugar i.e. rum, molasses etc. It is these that defined relations initially through the planter class and the white labor in the fields, then later on between the planters, overseers, field managers and an entire coterie of subsidiary and subsidized classes among whom were petty bureaucrats, surveyors, technicians, field workers and slaves; and among the slaves too, there were relations based on class—the household slaves having absolute control over the field slaves and later on the children who resulted from liaisons between slaves and the white managers. These social relations stemmed from the nature of the productive relations that occupied the capitalist exploitation in the Caribbean. It is the one and enduring legacy of the Caribbean. And the withdrawal of white labor from the fields changed an essentially economic relationship to a social one—if it is possible to consider slavery as a social relationship.

Black people who replaced white people in the sugar cane fields became identified as slave labor; and white labor became associated with "property and domination." This occurrence is important to understand the social relations, which were defined by the productive relations of sugar and its by-products: a hierarchy of social patterning in the Caribbean derived from them, not to mention the confused mosaic of psychological ambiguities, which at one time or other infected its communities. But this worked not only in the Caribbean. It is impossible to exploit without reciprocity and there grew up between exploiter and exploited a productive relationship, whereby the exploited not only produced material goods and things, but was also responsible for a great deal of what was produced on the periphery—shipbuilding, and its by-products, the commerce and industry of whole towns and cities and the development of nations at a particular period when capital from slavery financed the genius and talents, which sparked the industrial revolution.

The study of this exploitative relationship—and how its truth was masked, hidden and discolored for centuries through brazenness and ingenuity—is the central theme of Rodney's How Europe Underdeveloped Africa. It is the same productive relations and their residue of social and political conflict and ill-will that created them, kept alive the myth of black inferiority.[9] The perversity of the myth of black inferiority was only equaled by its devastating effect on black people, some of whom believed in it and still do. The capacity for self-hate is one of the least studied of the psychological consequences of slavery.

Yet, this crippling psychological malaise has affected the ability of newly independent countries with a prominent black presence to overcome such limitations to nation-building and unity. "Even the blacks became convinced of their own inferiority." [10] And it must be added that attitudes of passivity and compliance bred by self-negation, were hastily aroused when they perceived they had been made fools of. "Though fortunately we are capable of the most intense expressions when we recognize that we have been duped by white men."[11] Despite the apparent tranquillity of the Caribbean, its history has recorded a consistently revolutionary people active in the defense of its liberty and resistance to outside authority. Understandably, the bulk of that resistance has come from slaves and their descendants, who are in a majority in the Caribbean. And such gains that have taken place have not always been commensurate with the efforts put in. "Black power recognizes both the reality of black oppression and self-negation as well as the potential for revolt."[12] The potential for revolt is always there, for the conditions that would discourage such occurrences have not gone away. [13]

Slavery and its abolition did not end imperial designs; on the contrary they brought into play new and more subtle means of dependency. The immediate post-slavery era was significant in revealing imperial policy and how that was to be the fulcrum of relations between the Caribbean and the metropolis. While Britain emancipated the slaves, relations on which slavery were based did not end. New policies every bit as moribund as the old came into effect. Rodney attacked the business of compensation for planters, who were paid 20 million pounds to compensate them for the loss of their property " . . . we black people should have got the 20 million pounds compensation money. We were the ones who had been abused and wronged . . . " [14]—an argument made by the Rastafari. The wrongs, he insisted, persist.

The injustice of the economic exploitation of the Caribbean in the aftermath of slavery deeply affected Rodney's humanity and with that his later political vision. He immediately drew a parallel with the serfs in Europe who "usually inherited the land as compensation and by right." The Caribbean man on whom so much of the industry rested was left without any provision at all. "White property was of greater value than black humanity." Indeed, when the now freedmen left the estates to set themselves up as peasants, thereby robbing the plantations of labor and threatening them in the process, indentured Indians were imported to work the plantations. The indentured traffic that began with the Indians and later took in Chinese and Portuguese, illustrated the power and control of British capitalism which "could move non-white peoples around as they wished." The power to dispose of humanity—non-white humanity—in the interests of perpetuation of a system of exploitation was not limited to indenture. Even after the Caribbean ceased to be a paying proposition, this "power to dispose" continued unabated.

In Jamaica in 1865, for instance, Britain rescinded the Constitution and ruled the island through the Colonial Office, using as excuse the hostility of the natives to white power. That very year 1865, Britain had suppressed the revolt of Paul Bogle, the Jamaican black. Trinidad had previously in the century suffered the same reversal of its political freedom, which had prompted Trinidad politician Andrew Cipriani, to remark that "the West Indian barefoot man was able to hold his own with any sort of people anywhere"—an assertion that reflected his performance during the 1914-1918 war and which also held true for unrealized political experiences i.e. independence.15 Rodney submitted that these constitutional movements were directly racially motivated.16 And the Caribbean shared with Africa and Asia the butt of political disadvantage. But Australia and Canada, the white colonies, were encouraged to move towards self-rule and independence. Racialism for Rodney was essentially an economic condition resulting from capitalist exploitation. Remove the capitalism and men would be bound to see the self-destruction implicit in racialism. This view was to seriously affect his later analysis of the relations between Africans and Indians in Guyana.

But capitalism could not be easily removed. In fact, as the value of the sugar industry declined as a consequence of the abolition of slavery, competition from beet sugar and cheaper sugar production elsewhere, institutional supports became quite marked. And with these came overt racialist policies. The system of indentured labor under which Indians came from India to work the sugar plantations was "a form of slavery" and the traffic became so abominable that it was terminated in 1920, eighty-six years after it started. 17 The horrors of the indenture system were shared with other colonies; and the Indian government, reflecting a new nationalism, sent a Committee of Enquiry to Surinam, Mauritius and Fiji to study the workings of the system. It was ironic that by the time the Committee published its report, conditions between the indentured and employers in Guyana had begun to improve, though this was not so in the other territories. Indenture propped up, temporarily at least, the decline of the capitalist system in the Caribbean and elsewhere. But property belonging to white people was and still is safe-guarded and one way of ensuring this was to keep power in their hands or those of their stooges, who had passed the test of accommodation. And since the system was overtly racial, then the color standard became the litmus test of accountability. The social and class system in the Caribbean display a quite marvelous sense of color gradation existing in descending order from the ultimate standard, white.

But it was not sufficient to maintain a color standard. An institutional standard of politics also served to preserve controls. In fact, the constitutional development of the Caribbean region and elsewhere reflected a design to keep the colonies benignly though firmly in place. The emancipation of slavery the previous century therefore did not mean that freedom existed, though it might be inferred that the conditions for freedom existed. Rodney called this "hypocritical freedom", which 100 years after emancipation was so humiliating to the blacks in the Caribbean that they revolted (1934-38). Herein lies that contradiction in British colonial policy between theory and practice. It has always been the declared objective to bring colonial peoples to independence when their own level of consciousness seemed ready to its demands. Yet in practice this objective was not always met and many a British government has been known to delay independence—and the national exercise of freedom—deliberately, until it suited them: the case of Guyana is well known. There, the popularly elected government of Dr. Jagan in 1953 so upset predictions that the Constitution was overturned with cavalier attention to legality. Often this delay occasioned, as in Kenya and Zimbabwe, to take two examples, much bloodshed.

Colonial policy in the Caribbean was less dictated by a concern for humanitarian orthodoxy, or even by periodic outbursts of violence, which in any case could be contained. In fact, as Rodney declared when disturbances against British rule erupted, they were very surprised. [18] The crucial factor as far as the Caribbean was concerned was its proximity to the United States, whose tenuous legitimacy over the region rested on the Monroe Doctrine. British policy therefore had to take into consideration the demands of an imperialist power, which had emerged triumphant after World War II. A power, moreover that would not stand idly by, while an unruly Caribbean run by black people, embarrass its own domestic, social arrangements. Thus, the assumption of power by black people, which had been the logic of a century of gradualism was thwarted by British ambivalence and American interests.

But there were other reasons why the Caribbean was neglected by Britain, according to Rodney.[19] A lack of economic importance did not end Britain's commitments. Poor colonies were colonies nonetheless and could some day be useful as they waited for political independence. The state of casual indifference was rudely shattered by World War II. Colonies provided useful manpower in the military as both Britain and France found out "to fight the white man's battles." This eventuality stemmed for the moment the distressing news of the Report of the Royal Commission of 1938 about the wretched state of the Caribbean. Economically the region was destitute, politically it was backward and Crown Colony government was not the most advanced of representative institutions. While in theory such institutions allowed local representatives a chance to participate in government, the practice of it was quite different. Crown Colony government was of a limited franchise, meaning that property qualifications discriminated against the majority; and only those who met these qualifications were allowed to vote. In addition, there were positions in government that were held for special interests, usually those which supported the maintenance of imperial interests or were themselves part of those interests. " . . . local government was given to a white, brown and black petty-bourgeoisie [who] were culturally the creations of white capitalist society . . . " [20]

Thus, from the start, the political dismantling of the imperial state was compromised from within and what emerged was a motley collection, owing allegiance to outside interests rather than to individual territories. Seldom could democratic intentions have had such undemocratic and oppressive consequences. The growing representative institutions formalized inequality, while purporting to achieve social and economic justice; and by dividing the population between those that supported imperial interests and those that did not - quite apart from the various derivative racial and color components—these institutions maintained the inequalities. The consequence of which was to further oppress black people and to promote the black consciousness movement and eventually black power. Rodney put it decisively: "I maintain that it is the white world which has defined who are Blacks—if you are not white then you are black." [21]

Racial definitions are facile, unreliable and inadequate, and, most would argue, unnecessary. They are also incomplete, for they often do not deal with matters that go beyond race but which nevertheless refer to race and are a part of the limits of the definition. The definition of who are black by white people does not address the culture and the psyche of those who are black and who choose to identify with the culture of white people. Franz Fanon carefully studied the mergence of culture and psyche in Black Skins, White Masks and other works and Rodney dealt with the significance of culture as a liberation and revolutionary tool in Africa, particularly in Guinea and Cape Verde and the work of Amilcar Cabral, whom he admired.

In the Caribbean, Rodney scorned those blacks "who were the cultural creations of white capitalist society",[22] and who are manipulated by the "media of education and communication . . . to perpetuate white values." It is these same white values that infiltrate the psyche of Africans and Indians and thus make it difficult for racial understanding: "both groups held captive by the European way of seeing things." [23]

Culture is a dynamic of the liberation process and an important form of political activity. Culture is the embodiment of the life, will and struggle of the masses. It is the masses who lead the struggle for liberation and independence and they in fact who had to bear the burdens. Culture is important too, for it is through this agency that the subjugation of peoples was and is facilitated. A particularly telling modern example is the effect of Disney comics and the fantasy world of American mass media on the rest of the world. [i] During the colonization period, information on colonial territories was amassed, the easier to prescribe, to exploit and to dominate. With the start of the liberation struggle information became a crucial asset for undermining resistance and analyzing the characteristics of the societies where the struggle took place. Culture is essential armor in the liberation struggle, for it mobilizes opinion behind the ideology of freedom. Since culture was a means by which oppressed peoples were subjugated and conquered, "physically and mentally", it must be at the center of the liberation process. In fact, the African diaspora and its extended following in the new world made such a cultural process necessary for black liberation.

The African presence in the new world has been marked by a great deal of schism and division. The more obvious division naturally reflected the fears of the slave owners, who split up families and tribes, in order to insulate themselves from the possibility of rebellion. But the divisions did not end there. There was separation of function: field slaves, house slaves, etc., and these work routines created different kinds of social expectations and awareness. For example, slaves who were of the household could be expected to be more acculturated to the domestic plantation system than those who worked in the field. Also, understandably, individuals could be expected to have different levels of awareness, which would make them more or less receptive to the dominant value system. But the end result was the same, the creation and evolution of classes within the subject group, giving rise to different perceptions and levels of perception. Therefore, the cultural process had to allow for these disparate levels of consciousness and awareness. To put the matter

in a nutshell: ." . . . the West Indian situation is complicated by factors such as the variety of racial types and racial mixtures and by
the process of class formation."[24] Given this admixture of people,
only a cultural movement dominated by the black masses could succeed in throwing off the shackles of cultural imperialism: "the cultural reconstruction of the society in the image of the blacks."[25]
Those who had been victims of the system should lead in the reconstruction of their destiny.

Rodney was clear on this point: the black masses are the people
who are uniquely capable of leading the societies out of their
malaise to a more just state. This is not idle sentiment. The deprived
black masses have a residue of energy and purpose, which have been
untapped; and it is they who must take charge of their revolution.
His view is also influenced by the history of empires, which rested
on wilful force camouflaged, and further disguised as the consent of
the governed. And this history showed that such control was exercised by means of a combination of factors: the economic, social, cultural and political. To dominate people it is necessary to concentrate
all available energies on all aspects of their lives. The Caribbean itself provides convincing examples of this.

Education and culture have been the twin pillars on which were
built all the idealism of the post-emancipation period. Through education a new world was to be obtained and all had visions of personal
progress if not prosperity. It was what the slave imagined for his
children, and education was the acknowledged way out of physical
and mental destitution. But this way led to integration within an
imperialist system that seduced through the prospect of personal
gain. Education distanced those who were fortunate to obtain it
from the masses, who were thereby deprived of "articulate leadership." Also, the educational opportunity came at a heavy psychological price. Some who were exposed, were scarred and became
apologists for pro-imperialist stances, which led to self-denigration
and lack of trust or confidence in any institution that was not white
. . . "white hearted black men."

Black people in the Caribbean, in Rodney's opinion, have had
the wrong kind of education: "the brainwashing process has been so
stupendous that it has convinced so many black men of their inferiority."[26] National efforts at reconstruction therefore must address
the proper role that the universities should have in the various territories. Curricula changes were peripheral to larger questions such
as the nature of the relationship of the educated to the uneducated
masses. More particularly, what was the role of education in a developing country?

Rodney answered it decisively: " Black Power . . . must aim at transforming the Black intelligentsia into the servants of the black masses."[27] And more importantly: "Black Power, within the university and without must aim at overcoming white cultural imperialism."[28] And Guyana, to say nothing of the Caribbean, has suffered from the ghosts of imperialism which continue to haunt. Indeed, the racial unrest that has bedeviled Rodney's own Guyana has come about because "both groups are held captive by the European way of seeing things."[29] The assumption here is that the removal of the imperialist presence could bring about some basic understanding and an end to confrontation. And the imperialist presence is especially dangerous, given the strength of its symbols. Rodney was under no illusion about this. And this dominion over the Caribbean has been through the agency of cultural symbols, an all-important one being Christianity. "Why should Christianity come to us all wrapped up in white?"—is his plaintive cry. His response: "When Africans adopt the European concept that purity and goodness must be painted white and all that is evil and dammed is to be painted black then we are flagrantly self-insulting."[30]

Rodney and black power

Rodney was no crude Black Power advocate. In an argument that came close to defining his version of a pluralist society, he supported the celebration of religious symbols by different racial groups. "There is absolutely no reason why different racial groups should not provide themselves with their own religious symbols."[31] He trod very carefully there, for he did not wish to champion symbols that could deflect from nation-building; and would not support the adoption of any foreign symbols contrary to indigenous development. Still less did he wish to perpetuate the myth of "a multi-racial society living in harmony" .He saw the danger immediately. A harmonious multi-racial society justified the continued exploitation of one group by another: "the blackest of our population, at the hands of the lighter-skinned groups."[32] He meant Jamaica, but the same was equally true of Guyana, where the myth persisted of five peoples living in a state of bliss, until this was rudely shattered after independence.

Myths define and perpetuate beliefs, often false ones; they can create a reality that does not exist and thus delude. For Rodney, it is necessary to debunk these myths that shelter deception, harbor untruths and facilitate exploitation. Blacks must never be exploited again and all myths which circulate these illusions must be done away with. This is very important for developing a position of solidarity with working class peoples. It is even more important for worker solidarity to do away with the myths that had been circulating about black power.

"Black power is not racially intolerant." He assured us that black power is not aimed at the Indian and is not at the expense of the Indian. "That would be a denial of the historical experience."33 Indeed, the Indian is as much a part of that historical burden as the African; and both of them were exploited and victimized by the crushing demands of capitalism and imperialism. Together both of these racial types have shared the "same racial contempt" of the white power structure and both together and in separate ways have responded to its brutality. The uprisings in Guyana in 1938 "were actually led by Indian sugar workers";34 and in the previous century there were pockets of isolated resistance at all levels and noteworthy was that of Peter Ruhoman, the Indian editor of the first working people's newspaper. And even though "some Indians (like some Africans) have joined the white power structure in terms of economic activity and culture", 35 poverty pervades their existence and as a consequence "power is denied them." The unity of African and Indian in Guyana and by implication in the Caribbean, stands above and beyond the transient and divisive significance of race. The unity is also of meaning for the furtherance of a dialectic of independence, for throwing off the definition of what constitutes blackness, and reasserting a sense of self.

This phase is inconceivable without the destruction of a certain well-established myth: that of "a harmonious multi- racial society." To persist with that erroneous belief is to be guilty of the historical error of underestimating the cruelty of slavery in the Caribbean and to ignore its consequences. The excessive cruelty of slavery in the Caribbean has been well documented elsewhere and need not detain us. But the consequences of slavery in that region outside of the academic world and social scholarship, remains an unknown mystery to most of the people. That this ignorance continues to exist lies heavily at the door of the intellectual in the Caribbean, who involves himself in the particular constituencies such as teaching and writing to the exclusion of broader social commitment—an altogether limited commitment, as Rodney would say. Also, it could be argued that this area of public knowledge has been played down because of the need for the more wholesome, though erroneous myth, of social compatibility among many differing shades and groups of people. Rodney suggested that the reason for the persistence of the myth is that at a theoretical level, it has a certain appeal and supports goals "which nobody . . . would oppose."36 Thus, the wider populace is deluded into embracing a myth that has little relevance to its daily functions at any level—spiritual or material. Indeed, its perpetuation is entirely in the interests of a social class, "an elite", that would continue to dominate them. This explains, no doubt, the relations between the intellectual, as a class, and the dominant class. The intellectual is beguiled through favors, goods and services, to abandon roots and to support the dominant class. This also explains why higher education assumes such importance in the region.

An instrumentalist belief persisted that higher education was the key to open doors of privilege. This legitimized the elite and was its seal of membership. Agriculture, agricultural industries, and farming are less valued as areas of study because they were not deemed occupations of the elite. George Lamming, the noted Caribbean writer, laments this stratification and an "educational system . . . designed to reinforce such a stratification." [37] Lamming also is distressed about the failure of the intellectuals as a class to support the worthy aims of the working people, "to root this knowledge—that labor in all its stages of organization has been the most powerful democratizing force in Caribbean history—within the ranks of the working people."[38]

For Rodney, the absence of this knowledge has not been among some working people, a major obstacle to spiritual fulfillment. "In our epoch the Rastafari have represented the leading force of this expression of black consciousness." [39] They turned from the philistinism of "white West Indian society" that would not admit to its continuing racial torment, and sought in Africa "their cultural and spiritual roots."

Rodney was specific about white people as the social roots of the oppression of black people. He did not, of course, discount the shade identities of those who are the lackeys of imperialism and those "who are often outdoing the whites in their hatred and oppression of blacks",[40] even as he admitted some of the same "who are in the forefront of the movement towards black consciousness." [41]

The pluralism debate

Black consciousness and the raising of it presents the Caribbean scholar with many difficulties. Certain questions must be raised and responses given. The racial and ethnic canvas presents difficulties that are susceptible to diverse interpretation. Race, color, class are significant factors that inhabit the Caribbean marketplace of ideas. Lines of social responsibility and power are not always clear and politics confuses judgement. Hence the debate about pluralism is less about its meaning in the dictionary of the common man, than about the political ramifications about who or what groups define, and or, control the living arrangements. Fundamentally, it is about how power is distributed, to whom and for what purpose.

Pluralism as a concept of social relations was first used by the sociologist, J.S. Furnivall, with regard to Burma and Java,—colonial societies in which Europeans, Chinese, Indians and the native element lived side by side. Each spoke its own language, followed its own cultural practices, traded in a common marketplace under the same governmental rule. "They mix but do not combine." The Caribbean immediately lends itself to such comparisons. But pluralism is replete with interpretations and schools of opinion divide over its meaning and application. This is no academic exercise but crucial matters affecting the terms upon which a society addresses issues of governance, of domestic policy and shape the national debate.[42]

Furnivall saw pluralism essentially in economic terms because that was an area in which all the people shared and which brought them together. In the Caribbean more than an economic variable is involved. Pluralism has other associations. The area is rich in diversity and its social structure provides a tempting array of models from which to assess such differences in social structure. Plantation society, occupational roles and Marxist analyses define social structures; and in order to understand the conviction of Rodney's black power ideology, it is necessary to look at the alternative voices that have contributed to the debate.

Not the least of the models of the social structure of the Caribbean is that which represents the frame of reference of a prominent British scholar, R.T.Smith, whose anthropological work in Guyana has been the subject of much critical attention. R. T. Smith sees the Caribbean as a unit, a victim or recipient of European influence and ethnocentricity. The way of seeing the Caribbean defines the research problem and affects its outcome. Such research biases the outcome by erecting false signposts in history, which can lead to directions taken that do not reflect the letter though they might reflect the spirit of the problem.

Thus, for example, the nineteenth century was not only about the emancipation of slavery and the beginning of a new era. It was also about the evolution of the institutions that freedmen constructed. Nomenclature is important, for it is a psychological signpost that is part of the problem studied. Black slavery, a convenient heading for most historians, could just as well be white slavery, based on the presumption that he who enslaves another is himself a slave. In fact, slavery must be seen as a despicable interlude—but an interlude nevertheless—in the continuous development of African peoples and their experiences in the Americas and elsewhere. So distinguished a historian as the late Elsa Goveia avoided this trap in her "Historiography of the British West Indies," by studying the literature using the century as a signpost, and avoiding the temptation to assign value judgements through nomenclature: thus, the seventeenth century, the eighteenth century, etc. Scholars from the "mother country" must be protected from the consequences of their own value judgements and frequently also from their benevolence.

R.T.Smith, sees the Caribbean as a plantation society, evolving into a Creole society and finally a modern society. Clearly unhappy with the notion of a pluralist society - one in which two or more races are present who share the same landscape, have distinct cultural observances, but display some feeling of solidarity to one another - he sees the social structure as emerging from colonial institutional arrangements represented by slavery, post-slavery and institutions of the future. The idealism of his social stratification sees only the cementing characteristics, those which bring the society together, particularly with regard to Guyana and Trinidad and R.T.Smith's sharing of the common weal diminishes racial considerations, the role of colonial power and other defining characteristics. His model maps out the future development of the territories and sets them firmly on the path towards integrative institutions. Would that it were so simple!

In Guyana, Africans and Indians have never shared a common culture, but each has lived locked together inside the bosom of its own, emerging at times to participate in a common polity, as each does now. This is not to imply that these moments or periods of co-operation have not been marked by much mutuality and good feeling. But it is to suggest that each group has shown loyalty to itself as a cultural entity and a certain loyalty to the shared interests of the territory. Indeed, it might be said that the strength of group loyalty enables one group to give generously to the demands placed on it by the need to participate in territorial affairs alongside the other group. Also, the strength of group loyalty enables some togetherness and cooperation at crucial times in the country's history. This is clearly evident in Guyanese politics of the nineteenth century, where both Africans and Indians joined forces to press their constitutional demands and to combine their slender resources to strike against injustices.

R.T.Smith's plantation model is static and does not go anywhere. It is a rudimentary typology that serves a certain historical purpose: it delimits the colonial experience in Guyana and charts its future development. R. T. Smith must be protected from the consequences of so naked an optimism. In fact, a cursory reading of Dwarka Nath's History of Indians in British Guiana should restrain enthusiasm. Published in 1950 to commemorate the arrival of Indians in Guyana a century earlier, it represents the most partisan examination of the country there is; and Dwarka Nath admits he was driven by the scant attention paid Indians in the literature of the period.43 Still, his book is admirable evidence of the strength of a society, divided culturally, though possessed of a resilience, enabling it to combine and to cooperate when it needed to. In fact, the history of Guyana is one of resilience, perhaps characteristic of Caribbean territories, which have managed, despite considerable obstacles, to survive the hazards of uncertain fortune.

Leo Despres, whose quantitative analysis of Guyana's ethnic situation supports the pluralist argument, and reaches similar conclusions to Dwarka Nath's historical critical analysis. What Despres did was to provide the quantitative basis that refined the tentative opinions of Dwarka Nath and others, who wished to arrive at conclusions by close but questionable observation. Despres looked at both African and Indian communities to determine in what way they differed and also where they interfaced culturally; his study was completed prior to independence, when it might be supposed that both communities would temporarily bury differences in common interest, which they did. The areas in which they differed dealt with the family and kinship organization, religion and economics of daily living and the organization and disposition of their villages and communities. But the two communities shared public organizations such as local government and education and later on a tenuous national consensus following the Second World War. Even though many African and Indian organizations cemented relations in order to present a common front against the colonial power, each still was intensely loyal to its ethnic group. And the author well recalls the once prestigious League of Colored Peoples, which had a strong affiliation with the now defunct National Democratic Party, led by Sir John Carter, a prominent barrister, who later represented Guyana at the Court of St. James. The League was a worshipful congregation for Africans, in much the same way that the Muslim League and the Hindu Association were points of foci for their respective brethren. Separate cultural identities, however, did not hinder political awakening. The granting of universal suffrage occasioned strong urban and rural unity among both the African and the Indian working class, resulting in victory for the Peoples Political Party, PPP, at the 1953 elections. That both their leaders, Cheddi Jagan and Forbes Burnham, came from the two main ethnic groups contributed in no small measure to political solidarity. Yet, it was precisely this that led to the suspension of the Constitution, the imprisonment of some of the leaders and the restriction of others.

The working class consensus collapsed and ethnic unity, precarious at the best of times, foundered in the face of the assertions of the Colonial Office. The re-emergence of ethnic sovereignty in the government of Chief Minister, Cheddi Jagan in 1957-64 and the corresponding build-up of African frustrations under the opposition leader, Forbes Burnham, finally destroyed possibilities for national cohesion. The strikes, racial disturbances and civic strife that attended this period, frustrated any attempt at governing and made impossible the routine exercises of civilian administration. Chief Minister Jagan's lip service to radicalism offended many and scared a few, including the United States, which wanted him removed. A constitutional device was found which duly removed him. Jagan was induced to agree to proportional representation, a construct, that the whole country as one constituency, and electoral seats were won on the basis of voting percentages of the parties contesting the elections. As a consequence Burnham's party, PNC, was voted into power with the help of the United Force, UF, and Jagan's PPP became the opposition party. It was Burnham's party that led Guyana into independence.

The period of these stormy happenings was marked by a great deal of civic and racial strife. That this could take place strongly suggested that national consensus of Africans and Indians was superficial at best and temporary. Indeed, how both groups quickly resorted to ethnic and divisive political loyalties indicated the inherent fragility of both earlier and continuing relations not firmly rooted in mutual attentiveness. Also, that working peoples' solidarity was quite feeble in the face of ethnic challenge and could not muster any countervailing force. That the working people failed to deflect ethnic hostility indicated the tenuousness of its unity, a situation that remained substantially unchanged though not unchallenged since the previous century; but it is tempting to see periodic flexing behaviors as proof to the contrary.

Rodney was himself aware of this, and his book, The History of the Guyanese Working People, 1881-1905, is a tribute to a people who were still emerging and had not reached the dimensions of a working class. And the Burnham government, which had been then the only administration in an independent Guyana, exploited these ethnic divisions as a means of cementing power. It manipulated the opposing (majority) faction into chronic belief that national unity was of the essence, in the face of multiple dangers: the border disputes with Venezuela and Suriname provided ready support for national anxieties; and economic and other disabilities contributed their fair measure.

It can also be argued that Burnham's machinations were not

original at all and that he merely capitalized on the well-known ethnic divisions that had always been there, but which had remained
dormant during the colonial period. These divisions were in fact
there, had always existed, reinforced by language, culture, religious
observances, and also space. Indians had until the mid-fifties
worked on plantations in the country and this amounted to a functional but incomplete separation. [44] And once the threadbare lines of
national unity were severed by the suspension of the Constitution,
each group began to see to its own interests. The speed with which
social organization was marshalled to fan mutual dislike, enmity
and racial conflict demonstrated the strength of latent systems of
animosity that continued virtually unabated for a decade (1957- 68)
and during national elections of the same period. [45] Racial polarization aptly described the state of affairs that gave rise to considerable
disquiet and apprehension about the future of Guyana. [46]

The plural argument is sustained largely because of the continued existence of the two racial communities—Africans and
Indians,—which had been living side by side since the previous century, and had developed institutions of their own, which nominally
excluded the one from the other, though they continued to live in
harmony. Certain objective conditions also existed, the main one being the existence of a single form of government which was, for the
largest part of Guyana's history, a colonial government. But pluralism is much criticized and one of the most eloquent critiques, has
come from H. Hoetink, [47] who places importance on the racial factor,
seemingly ignored by M. G. Smith.

The view of race as understatement, "social myth", omitted the
ultimate question: upon what structure did political power and its
distribution rest? Walter Rodney emphasized that it was crucial to
explore and discuss that question, for "revaluation of ourselves as
blacks and with a redefinition of the world from our own stand-
point." [48] Hoetink complained that M.G. Smith saw plural societies
in too rigid a manner "based too much on political and territorial notions", and excluded the historical evolution of societies; in brief, societies change and are in the process of changing and it is wise to
take this into account.

But the main changes in Guyana occurred, leaving racial divisions virtually intact because the institutions of the two communities remained largely untouched. Religious institutions of Hindus
and Moslems still controlled the allegiances of their respective followers and often there was considerable rivalry between the two
faiths. The strength of these institutions and their cultural hold on
their followers could be seen from pilgrimages of non-Muslim and
non-Hindu politicians in courtship of the Indian vote. [ii] The courage,

and expediency, (which inevitably brought rewards of one kind or another) of individuals willing to cross racial and party lines, remains, perhaps, the only hope for a vital political system, without the troublesome factor of racial involvement. Constitutional advances, which increased representation and responsibility at the national level, made a degree of political sophistication absolutely necessary; and the slim increases in economic growth since the country became independent, did not bridge the gap between the two communities. The relative poverty from which the country as a whole suffered caused both Africans and Indians to seek comfort and shelter behind their respective institutions. [49] Indeed, the maintenance of such separateness was encouraged by the colonial power, not merely because of the need to divide and rule, attributes associated with colonial rule everywhere, but because separateness enhanced the perpetuation of myths; and myths were important to preserve the status quo.

Thus, differences in religion, culture and language became part of symbols which justified the separation of the two groups and the continued subservience of them both to the colonial power. [50] These symbols—religion, culture and language—for the most part also became part of the machinery actively working to promote class distinctions. And the functional and occupational division of Guyana after slavery,—with the Africans populating the villages and the towns, the Indians working on the sugar plantations and in small businesses, the Chinese and the Portuguese involved in trade and commerce and the European exploiter class in government—the stage was set for the complete structural division of Guyana by class, and occupation. Occupational division encouraged and cemented class divisions, which were already created by the myths of racial distinction. Social class stratification, supported by the colonial power, did not induce mixing between the two predominant communities, but actually reinforced their separateness. Race definitively divided the social structure of Guyana, despite the presence of other variables such as class, color and status. It is tempting to consider class, color, status and race as units in the Guyana social stratification matrix, as one scholar actually did in assessing the Caribbean.[51] But to apply this model to the social structure of Guyana is to add complexity to an already complex situation, without the saving grace of clarification or understanding. Nor does an occupational model of Jamaica applies to Guyana. [52] The concept of a plural society is in the final analysis, a comprehensive position that explains a part of the complexity of the social structure in Guyana. [53] Pluralism accounts for culture and other complex diversities; and it is important that this be said, for it explains the growth and development of both the African as well as the Indian communities and their subsequent relations after independence. The readiness to acknowledge the strength of pluralism is important for the future development, as Guyana charters its nationalist course and seeks to end racial disharmony, now subsumed under a barrage of constitutional niceties, uncertainty, apprehension and apathy. But pluralism alone is incomplete.

Rodney's unit of analysis was the plantation—how it evolved, the forces at work both within it and outside it, its inner dynamic. Both the pluralism and the plantation models as tools of social analysis were limiting. Pluralism concentrated on "non-material culture" and did not examine "common conditions of work . . . That is a fundamental aspect of culture."[54] Moreover, by placing non-material culture at the forefront of analysis, pluralism did not explore other ways in which "the various segments of society related to one another."[55] Conditions of work were important for analysis of the influence of plantation life on the development of both African and Indian communities; for it was these same conditions of work and the stereotypes they embodied, which were responsible for the manner in which each community saw the other.

The plantation model went further than the pluralist model, which was "inadequate." In the plantation model all else was subservient to the production of wealth; and social relations were important only in so far as they subscribed to this design. It also placed Guyana and the Caribbean within the context of the "international scene", allowing the region to see itself" as an integral part of a larger system."[56] But this model too was limiting. Having told us about the constituents of wealth and its relationship to the international scene, the plantation model could do no more. The direction of the society could only be explained by an analysis of the class struggle between workers and planters. Indeed, it was as a consequence of this contradiction that the shape of the society could be determined. Rodney made the point that both the macro view of social analysis—the colonial system—and the micro view—analyses of the details of a society—were treacherous. In the first case, the analyses could see the whole picture but miss the details. In the second case the details might obscure the total view. He believed that analysis should be made at the points where both interrelated. [57]

History and its aftermath

The continued presence of the colonial power in Guyana assured that both occupational and class divisions—both in a Marxist and non-Marxist sense—would be maintained. On their departure, however, differences, that had over the century grown into accepted wisdom, started to reassert themselves. In this respect one must not underestimate the importance of education as a psychological tool in the creation and formation of opinion and belief. As a result, both Africans and Indians inherited as part of their belief systems, unexamined and therefore potentially dangerous ideas and notions about one another, that later were regrettably tested in conflict. This is not to deny the importance of differences in religion, culture and language—and later occupational functions—but it is to emphasize the role of the colonial power in cementing these differences into a concretized system of class.

The concreteness of the class system governed social mobility, general as well as particular relations, except in the city where social interaction mitigated class differences. This accounted for the question whether race or class is the more crucial variable in the social structure of Guyana. Indeed, it is one which divided Rodney's attention, and others as well, and he travelled both directions, though not, of course, at the same time. With Rodney, there was always the need to clarify the fundamentals and sort out the ambiguities.

Rodney was alive to the significance of the black power movement, its broad canvas sweeping the Americas, its clarion call for black unity, its short-lived dynamism, objectives and limited accomplishments. Life in Jamaica as an undergraduate and later on as an instructor of history would have exposed him to the uncertainties of a society, where people of African descent constituted a majority, but had not fully realized economic power. His writings, and in particular *The Groundings with my Brothers* indicated strong commitment to more specific objectives than the movement had up to them been able to direct. Race was uppermost in his mind.[iii] Echoing Garvey, a race without power was a race impoverished. Consequently, black power must assert itself by proclaiming sovereignty in those regions in the Caribbean in which it was in the majority. Blacks must seek power. But the emergence of black power was not to be at the expense of other groups in Caribbean society, as we have already noted. Race is fundamental because race was significant in Caribbean history and it is the duty of the historian to assess its influence, to redress the past in the interests of those who have suffered at its hands.

When Rodney talked about the Caribbean and the American South as "being the breeding ground for world racialism" [58], he had in mind duties that necessarily impinge on those most affected by racialism. "There must be no false distinction between reflection and action."[59] Thus, the man of letters, "the intellectual", is commissioned to work for the liberation of his people from continuing servitude of one kind or another.

Fanon had no such compunctions: he would free blacks and

whites from the prison of history by forgetting history. For Fanon, the discovery of the past was not a source of celebration at all. The past could only impede the liberation of the present by placing people in watertight compartments, creating victims rather than free people.

> The discovery of the existence of a Negro civilization in the fifteenth century confers no patent of humanity on me. Like it or not, the past can in no way guide me in the present moment . . . I will not make myself the man of any past. I do not want to exalt the past at the expense of my present and of my future.[60]

Fanon's preconceptions were dictated by his profession: as a psychiatrist, he had seen the sufferings of those who had been victimized by the past—in itself a refusal to accept the present—and whose mental health depended precisely on this acceptance, for only by so doing could they be free. "Disalienation will come into being through their refusal to accept the present as definitive"; [61] and "in no way should I derive my basic purpose from the past of the peoples of color." [62]

Racism and its implications—injustice, inequality, powerlessness—assumed great importance as universal discourse, which most assuredly were informed by his reading of history of the cumulative depredations and persecutions suffered by black people. But Rodney could not allow race to triumph over his Marxist preoccupations. He could not defend the contribution of the working people of Guyana by resorting to the racial imperative. Time is important here. The Rodney of 1969 saw race as both affirmation and negation. Black power is an affirmation of race in the face of the power that white people exercise. Black power in its Caribbean manifestations must be clear about its objectives and benevolent and not disinclined to share. It is about pride in past achievements and the future and it is humane but does not shrink from revolutionary possibilities. But there is the negation: racial considerations alone negate the spirit of a movement that is humane, wishes to reverse the tide of history; these are antithetical to the development of working class unity everywhere. Race is a contradiction pure and simple.

For Fanon, the world of science, "scientific objectivity," frees the black man and the white man from becoming victims of their past and prisoners of it. His position is that of universal brotherhood. "There is no Negro mission; there is no white burden . . . I have one right alone: That of demanding human behavior from the other." [63] Fanon did not dismiss black power; he was wary of it, of slogans in a world which demanded "annihilation or triumph" and where "words wrap themselves into silence," and where "moral law is not certain of itself." Black power was a retrograde step because it limits the vision of people who should wish "to recapture the whole past of the world" and "not responsible solely for the revolt in Santo Domingo." [64]

Rodney's vision was also a universal one. It is a necessary step that oppressed people must take in their own interests, "for the recovery of human dignity."[65] For Rex Nettleford, there is parallel concern "to give substance to the form of freedom which was won in 1838 . . . but which has never attained full reality."[66]

Both Rodney and Nettleford see Africa as a point of reference "for the spiritual transformation of Jamaica society" and the Caribbean in general. For them, both the black power movement represents both the coming of age and a continuing of the humanism of Africa in the New World. It is a spiritual process that can liberate the energies of the Caribbean people as a whole. And for Rodney especially and for Nettleford also, black power is the motive force behind social justice and freedom in the region. Also, Rodney took black power seriously as a political means to achieve social and economic justice. Black power is as much a political manifesto, a prescription for socialist action as it is part of the humanist tradition. Rodney united them both.

The humanist tradition

That humanist tradition sought to both understand the meaning of Africa in the contemporary world, and Africa in relation to itself. History was guide. It would serve to recover the past and to locate the myths that were so deeply embedded in the consciousness of black peoples everywhere and which stifle their growth. "To expunge the myths about the Africa past that linger in the minds of black people everywhere." [67] Myths were destructive of freedom, and independence. They were also dangerous. Because of that, their elimination was "the main revolutionary function of African history in our sphere."[68] These myths were imposed through white colonization and they were kept up and maintained in the new world and indeed they are part of the legacy of European peoples everywhere and their destruction a necessary process. This view assumed particular cogency because of their impact on black people, their belief in them. That the myths were white people's egocentricity made their eradication of great importance. [69]

Two qualities were embedded in the myths: the first had to do with the persuasive ethos of capitalism; and the second, which derived from the first, the superiority of white peoples and their institutions. Both qualities stemmed from economic determinism.[70] Placing the economic factors before any other amounted to the "moral terminology of capitalist accumulation", which neglected, where it did not deny the previous existence of African development and the specific accomplishments that arose. [iv]

How Europe Underdeveloped Africa is an indictment of the process by which history was falsified and the resulting prescriptions that resulted in consequence of this, not the least of which, were theories inappropriate for development. The second of these myths: the superiority of white peoples stemmed from the nature of capitalist development, as Franz Fanon has observed. "Race prejudice in fact obeys a flawless logic. A country that lives, draws its substance from the exploitation of other peoples, makes those peoples inferior."[71] Rodney, reflecting on the Guinean experience at the hands of France, when it left the French colonial empire: "The only culture of colonialism is the culture of command: a form of brutality of human beings, both colonised and colonisers."[72] The humanist tradition, which predated the coming of the Europeans to Africa, should be part of the education of contemporary blacks wherever they might be. That tradition rested on the firm ground of social and cultural relations. It was a wholesome view of the universe as a system interrelated and dynamic; and social and cultural relations were integral parts of the harmony of the cosmos. Social and cultural relations upon which African civilization rested "had meaning and value." It was a system of social behavior that defined both domestic and external relations.[73] Standards of hospitality governed social conduct, a benign system of laws carried out social justice, and the same benignity regulated welfare among the people regardless of age.

For example, travelers in Africa from the 15th century spoke flatteringly about the hospitality received from African peoples. A total system of relations, suggests Jan Heinz Jahn, was universal and existed among different groups and also different regions; and but for differences in detail, they are basically the same - the Baluba, Ruandese, Dogon, Bambara and Haitians - who show the resilience and perpetuation of African culture in the new world. The African "system" is really one that encompasses the world, metaphysics and religion. Such a system represented "the African contribution to the solution of problems posed by man's existence in society." [74] And in assessing that cosmology, Rodney insisted as so many anthropologists do—even though their warnings are not taken seriously—that such an assessment be on their (African) terms. It needed an especial distance, training and commitment to do this; and there was a suggestion that it could only be done in ideological terms. A failure to understand the terms upon which knowledge was built up, could lead to serious mistakes in appraisal and analysis, misinformation, patronage and value judgments. For example, a remarkable feature of European scholarship was the bandying about of words such as "pre-logical" to explain systems of thought that Europeans could not understand, or again "mystical" to explain the relationship between divinity and the occult. Edward Said discussed how far these narrow views spanned centuries of ordinary people's knowledge of the Orient; also how dangerous they are, how they persist and their influence on political and other realities. [75]

Epistemology, which is a methodology of knowledge, stresses the relationship of all knowledge and mutual dependency. It is a unity of all things—be it philosophy, theology, birth, death—and as Adesanya shows, the removal of a part disturbs the functioning of the system. "This is not simply a coherence of fact and faith . . . but a coherence or compatibility among all the disciplines." And what drives the total system is Nommo, the word, which is a unity of " water, seed and blood in one."[76] Nommo is important to Rodney's understanding of African humanism. It is a philosophical tradition that governs all relations and does not compartmentalize knowledge. It is Nommo, the 'word' that addresses Muntu, the problem of man in all his guises,—and which is central to Rastafari belief that so preoccupied him. "But you learn humility after you get into contact with these brothers."[77] The humility radiated through the community of people and energizes them. It is a shared humility, a poet's humility. The African poet speaks to and on behalf of the community in contrast to the poet from other lands, e.g. the European poet, who is an individual and speaks of feelings and motivations. The African poet belongs to his community for whom he is at once its seer, its chronicler and its prophet. "For in the last analysis every artistic manifestation is collective, created for all and shared by all."[78] This included the novelist or writer of stories as well. For example, the work of Amos Tutola must be seen "as the power of Nommo, 'the word', the mechanism of sorcery, the laws and the order of forces."[79] Rodney was an admirer of the work of Amos Tutola, precisely because he embraced the sense of community and the continuity of the word - a discipline shared with the Rastafari.

The artist then had a social function to perform on behalf of the people of the community. Devotion to the cause of the community reflected the humanist environment that had always been a part of Africa and African humanism informed Rodney's later Marxist sympathies and reinforced them. African humanism could be taken to excess, frequently by those apologists in the European tradition, who sought philosophical justification for social custom. Negritude was in that tradition.

Negritude

Negritude in literature attempted to re-discover a traditional past, temporarily distracted or transformed by alien influences,—specifically, colonialism—and to re-interpret this in ideological terms. Negritude was a re-invention of the past that assumed certain mystical overtones. Central to this view was that colonialism didn't last very long, had a cursory influence on Africans in general; and with colonialism out of the way, Africa could go back to being its traditional self. This view was escapist and "tries to run away from the problem altogether"; namely, that the colonial system did have certain very strong consequences economically, politically and socially. Negritude denied this. The attitude was that there was a fundamental difference between the African and the European that colonialism did not reach. Africa had a residue of feeling and sensitivity that European thought and intellect did not touch. That feeling and sensitivity still existed in traditional form and it was the strength of these values that resisted the imposition of European cultural values in Africa.

Rodney did not take kindly to negritude. The traditional Africa of the villages "are totally involved in a series of production and social relations in an international division of labor that makes it impossible to describe them as traditional." [80] But he assigned a dominant role to Islam, which sustained resistance against Christianity. [81]

The debate about negritude assumed ideological tones because it was ideology that was instrumental in causing denial and neglect of the past.[82] The policy of discouraging knowledge served certain appropriate ends. First, it supported the view that there was no history in Africa before the coming of the white man and a people without history could have but a limited future and that identified only with the oppressor. The historian of Africa and the New World had to contest the foundations of this myth and many did. Rodney's monumental work, How Europe Underdeveloped Africa, is of the same order as Cheikh-Anta Diop's, *The African Origins of Civilization, and Ivan Van Sertima's, They Came Before Columbus,*—works that *contested* accepted myths. Diop's major contribution was his writings on the African origins of civilization, which he firmly established in Egypt, the initiator of "western" civilization. Van Sertima dealt with the legacy of Africans in the Americas before the coming of Columbus. These are only a few of the more scholarly works that have helped to destroy myths: W. E. B. Du Bois, Aime Cezaire, C.L.R. James, Franz Fanon, Janheinz Jahn and others have accomplished the same task in distinct ways and over a wide spectra of disciplines. But each generation must exert itself anew in its own defense, given the nature and multiplicity of the challenges. Second, ignorance of Africa's past imprisoned the mind, making it hostage to cultural oppression.

Cultural oppression is the lynchpin in the battle for the minds of men. The literature of negritude recognized this and asserted the cultural independence of Africa and its history before the coming of Europe. The refusal of black people to be dominated culturally and spiritually was the key to understanding the roots of black power. "This is the ultimate end of negritude, and much of the literature is dedicated to a rehabilitation of Africa, a way of refurbishing the image of the black man." [83]

But negritude didn't start that way. The Caribbean origins of the movement are well documented. David Caute in his excellent book on Fanon declared that negritude sprung from diverse themes in Caribbean literature in the 19th and 20th centuries[84]. Haitian independence brought to life a forgotten history to the other territories in the throes of slave rebellions of one sort or another, and dispiriting attempts to fashion representative institutions; and the later American occupation this century so offended sensibilities as to provoke a revival of African culture, or perhaps an identification of it among certain classes, for it had never ceased to be at the center of life of the working people. This resulted in a spiritual union between the creative person and the worker, who symbolized the flourishing of mother earth and a return to nature. The myth of the return to Africa was also a protest against the evils of European civilization, which had desecrated the earth, destroying that synthesis between nature and man, which was such an intimate fact of African cosmology.

The more recent manifestations of the movement are historical, for Aime Cezaire, negritude is inseparable from an awareness of color and a consciousness, which carried certain profound responsibilities. Cezaire's poem, *Cahier d'un retour au pays natale*, which popularized the movement, was the symbol of the Caribbean intellectual, who had just begun to take up the spirit of resistance and who became active in a liberation shared with the worker. The poem celebrated the strength and vitality of the toiler in the fields "who does not produce anything", but whose existence, close to nature, rendered him sublime. The salute to the worker as aesthete, was a cultural response to a history, that had betrayed, neglected, and finally abandoned him. Thus, negritude was an aesthetic celebration of a process, that had its social roots in history, fomented by the continuing ambiguities of European rule, but which sensitized the creative to forms of protest. Indeed, negritude is a form of cultural liberation from the acknowledgements of European hegemony.

What was significant, as Caute reminds us, was that the prophets of negritude were part of the metropolitan French cultural establishment and well known in European literary circles. For example, consider *Damas* of French Guiana, *Cezaire* of Martinique, *Tirolien* of Guadeloupe, *Roumain* of Haiti,—all men of literary ambition, who had achieved merit. Negritude was also their protest. Intellectual recognition was as far as they could go before the vexed question of race confronted them in the wider society.

Negritude in and of itself i.e. literary style, form, racial harmony and spirit was not sufficient as a tool of liberation. These men were part of the very thing from which they wanted to flee. Culture without an ideology for change had its limitations and *Amilcar Cabral,* who fought the Portuguese in Guinea, added that culture must be part of an ideology for change. "Our struggle is based on our culture, because culture is the fruit of history and it is a strength." [85]

Fanon discussed this in *Black Skins and White Masks* in the chapter on 'The Negro and Psychopathology'. The struggle, or confrontation if you will, affected the psyche of the black man and his social behavior. For Cabral, there was the residual culture of Guinea on which to depend and for the inhabitant of Guinea, who had not lived in Europe, the battle was easier, for he had not been exposed to foreign influences; but to the black person in the Caribbean, the confusion is more apparent. Fanon acknowledged that this conflict could be seen when Martinicans went to France, who became more aware of their color than of the cultural similarities with the French. This could lead to neurosis and then inevitably the colonialist turned to the white person for replacement of a shattered self-esteem.[86] Such dependency created confused relationships and was responsible for the fact that the "Negro is in every sense of the word a victim of white civilization."[87]

The confrontation of psyches—the case of Martinique was studied, but it is not unique—enslaved everybody and white people also were victims. Cultural imposition had its other side: and he that will enslave another is himself enslaved. Sexual neuroses with their attendant fears disturbed relationships and created racial animosity. Racism was fundamentally based on sexual fears. The white feared the sexuality of the black and oppressed him for it. For the white, the problem defined in whatever terms, is the black. For the black, however, the matter is economic.

Both Fanon and Rodney eschewed the racial imperative: the

problem was economic. For Fanon, it is " . . . Negroes exploited, enslaved, despised by a colonialist capitalist society that is only accidentally white."[88] This explained the social roots of negritude. It was also why Rodney found negritude unsatisfactory as a way of dealing with then contemporary problems of independence. Negritude as protest Fanon could identify with. Negritude as a return to a mythical past was vague and in any case we have seen that the past did not enslave him. "Like it or not the past can in no way guide me in the present moment." [89]

Negritude as romantic idealism that glorifies elitism, Rodney had no patience with. His words were unmistakably clear: "We must create a national policy . . . for the masses. We ought never to lose contact with the people . . . " [90] He could find no difficulty coming to grips with his ambiguity in European society and like Cezaire, destroyed the European in himself. And what does it mean "to destroy the European in himself?" It is to refuse to accept the notions of color and race as significant considerations for defining existence. Fanon was "interested in the future of France, in French values, in the French nation." [91] But he did not blind himself to the reality of violence as an act of liberation, which raises the consciousness of the masses in the independence struggle. "Violence is a cleansing force."[92] But for the worker, the task was monumental, for his human worth was defined by race, class and the nature of his work, all of which could hinder understanding of self and the objective situation. Fanon suggested that the slaying of the white dragon imposed certain responsibilities on the intellectual. [93]Rodney shared this view, as we have already noted, but the point is worth emphasizing: that the man of intellect must participate fully in the life of the community and partake in the fruits of his experience with the worker to safeguard life, the life of them both. For Senghor, though, "negritude is the cultural heritage, the values and particularly, the spirit of Negro-American civilization."[94]And for Sartre, who wrote the Preface to Fanon's The Wretched of the Earth, negritude was a step, a negation, on the road to a synthesis of a complete person—without regard to race.

Fanon and Rodney were both Marxists. Fanon's position was at times existential. "There is no Negro mission; there is no white burden . . . I have one right alone: That of demanding human behavior from the other."[95] He wanted respect for human values "that constitute a human world";[96] and the environment was the key to the mental health of the individual and mental illness resulted from the inability of people to control, and to take care of the demands of the environment and its pressures. Edward Braithwaite, on the other hand, believed that the revolution placed demands on the en-

vironment within which people live, forcing them to break out of
limited structures, and to impose meaning and interpretation on reality. [97]

Rodney saw the cultural renaissance as a means of achieving
unity between all African people, regardless of the hemisphere in
which they lived. " . . . To make a contribution to the development of
African culture, helping to free it from European imperialism." [98]
The unity of a wider understanding of common culture shared is inseparable from independence and cultural nationalism.

Both Fanon and Rodney looked beyond race and racial considerations. Fanon, however, wished to ignore race because it arrested
present and future development.[99] It was the universe of man that
absorbed him.[100] Fanon would act "so that never again would a people on earth be subjugated", but "my black skin is not the wrapping
of specific values."[101] Race and the implications of race cried out for
"a restructuring of the world."[102] Rodney understood this, accepted
it and went further. He would involve the intellectual in direct political action, as it were, chartering a course for Fanon's thesis. He
would not cry out for "a restructuring of the world", but would re-
structure it through direct political action.

Culture and the State.

For Rodney, culture was an ideological frame of reference that
served to mobilize the masses for definitive political goals. Black
power and all that entails was less about race and about racialism—although both are necessary stages requiring protest and
refutation—than about political power. It was indeed through political power and a synthesis of common interests that historical revision takes place and a people can have understanding of its destiny.
"The road to Black Power . . . must begin with a revaluation of ourselves . . . and with a redefinition of the world . . . " [103] Needed
though was confidence to take that leap from servitude of mind to
independence of spirit; knowledge of Africa and its achievements in
science and the arts—a cultural endowment—was central to the
task.

Indeed, this knowledge is firmly rooted in the literature of the
Caribbean and the works of its poets have reflected the sensitivity
and longing for the African past. Edward Braithwaite explored the
question of exile and what it contributed to psychic experience. The
exile was, of course, that of the nations of Africa, which had been
transported across the seas to the Americas. The theme is rich, re-
warding and present. It assumes permanence in the ethos of the
Caribbean; and a restlessness of spirit prevails over the mundane

affairs of everyday and the demands of exile itself. George Lamming's *The Pleasures of Exile*, traces the evolution of the colonial and his rise to an understanding of himself through study and exposure to an alien environment, the substance of which is already known in the colonies. The psychological dimension is the uprooting of the spirit, which is in need of re-fertilization from a bankruptcy caused by rootlessness. For Braithwaite it is a "re-education of a Black mind towards self-fulfillment." [104]

Cezaire extols the traditional ways in *Le Tour au Pay Natale*, in its way a re-education too, but an affirmation of life, threatened by the rootlessness of exile, uncertain feeling, and the cultural impositions of capitalism. For Rodney, " . . . the struggle (to free and mobilize black minds) will not wait until the re-education of the mass of the black people reaches an advanced stage." [105] Braithwaite speaks about the need " . . . to connect my history with theirs, the bridge of my mind now linking Atlantic and ancestral homeland and heartland." [106] Exile, renewal and regeneration of spirit is shared by Caribbean thinkers as a response to the hazards and depredations of alien cultures. Rodney warned about this, as he analyzed Fanon: "Fanon exposed the limits of Western culture and its counter-productive aspects as far as a Black revolutionary was concerned."[107]

Rodney's rejection of negritude was less a failure to acknowledge the romantic side of the movement, or indeed its redeeming characteristics, than the irrelevance of its contentions. In the total scheme of things, negritude was a bourgeois preoccupation that did not go far enough to explain the more important and substantive realities, which people must face up to for their liberation. Cezaire is the apostle of negritude, a man of ideas, an aesthete, whose particular contribution was to herald the movement and place the problem in its historical context. Cezaire, who helped raise the consciousness of black people, lit up the Caribbean stage for a moment, but was too much a part of the European system to finally separate himself from it. An important footnote to history, he remains a man of understanding, but not of vision. Senghor, the other apostle, is a distinguished poet and leader who injected the Republic of Senegal with paternalistic vigor. Both Cezaire and Senghor have the same responses to the presumptions of the European world. Theirs is as radical an aesthete possible for the bourgeoisie, one which breaks down barriers to self-knowledge, even as it fosters, nurtures pride and humanity among Africans.

Rodney would have approved of the responses as a worthwhile contribution of the bourgeoisie to their own salvation and valuable as a methodology for self-examination. But he despaired of the cap-

italist system ever reforming itself, or effecting major, or fundamental changes. For Rodney, culture without politics was without
foundation, literature without social commitment was shallow and
image without defining ideology useless.

Culture then is a dynamic of the liberation process. It is a necessary step for African peoples who have been exploited by white
people; and though racial consciousness is an understood part of the
cultural autonomy, there are other significant currents that grew
out of racial consciousness. One was power over one's own destiny
[108] and the opportunity if not the will to remake the world in one's
own image. But this went hand in hand with tolerance for other
people and their institutions. Implicit was the argument that black
power should not be intolerant. Rodney rejected any racialist ideology. Indeed, he saw black power as a catalyst for promoting equality between groups; and a multi-racial society in which "each
individual counts equally" [109]; and where power is equitably distributed, there would be no need to fear black power. First, he advocated the reassessment of the role of blacks in a multiracial society;
second, an understanding of it as it related to social, cultural, economic and political relations, finally the definition of a plan of action based on such relations.

Societies must recognize the need to practice equality and
share power on the basis of equality and to eschew fake harmony as
practised in Jamaica, where there "is the current image of a
multi-racial society living in harmony."[110] The need to re-evaluate
the terms and conditions of living arrangements was central to
the movement of Africans everywhere and understandably so.
Re-evaluation defined the ideological framework on which freedom
and equality was based and is a constant theme in the writings of
black scholars.

For example, Harold Cruse, suggests that the methodology of
attempts by black people at integration in the United States is open
to question and this could destroy legitimate and wholesome ends.
[111] In the rush to integrate—seen as a necessary and sufficient prelude for legitimate social goals—blacks, in Cruse's opinion, have
sold themselves short. No organizational goals based on cultural,
economic and political realities slowed their progress; blindly, they
believed in and pursued integration as national rite and salvation.
The consequence was that cultural form and substance that had
been so distinctly a part of the black experience were abandoned in
favor of forms more easily acceptable to the white majority. Cruse
carefully points out the folly of separating culture from social, economic and political goals. He reminds blacks that the civil rights
era is over and they can expect no especial consideration or redress

for the disabilities of race.[112] Needed is a new beginning based on reality and promise and belief in themselves. A political party based on African aspirations and an economic and cultural identity is the surest guarantee against "a paternalistically racist, economically predatory and culturally irresponsible society." "Cultural survival" is of the essence. But it must be predicated on "cooperative economic efforts." Cruse's latest work represents a radical departure. He has seen through the sham of pluralism, which is unequal and hallucinatory and has disposed of that American condition. His might be the prescription for the salvation of African people in the Americas.

Molefi Asante also stresses survival.[113] He argues that racism has so warped the minds of white Americans that they can no longer, if they ever could, develop a critical perspective that is shorn of racist presumptions in dealing with Africans. He reminds us of the tradition of Africa to which Africans in the New World are heirs and "a society of harmonies, in as much as the coherence or compatibility of persons . . . is at the root of traditional African philosophy." [114]

Roger D. Abraham arrived at the same conclusion in his study of African speech and cultural behavior in the Caribbean: that an African cultural heritage exists and triumphs over obstacles.[115] Rodney himself had earlier addressed the matter of survival. "A fantastic amount of physical and social energy went into the defensive task of sheer survival."[116] These directions in modern African thought in the Diaspora, stress continuity in survival and the strength and resilience to overcome obstacles. Cruse, though, is impatient and wishes to establish firm foundations based on economic and cultural identity.

Rodney took up the theme of destiny for the masses of the Caribbean. If the destiny of its people was to be free from the chattels of continuing subservience through the persistent ghosts of foreign imperial power, then people must transform themselves by transforming their social relations, totally. The intelligentsia and those who had been exposed to higher learning must become "the servants of the black masses;" and united they could overcome alien cultural impositions.

NOTES

1. Rodney, Walter. Op. Cit., 1969, p. 19.

2. Patterson, Orlando. *The Sociology of Slavery.* Cambridge, Mass: Harvard University Press, 1968, and Freyre, Gilberto. *The Masters and the Slaves.* New York: Alfred A. Knopf, 1956.

3. Best Lloyd. "Black Power." *New World.* Special Issue, 1971, p. 15.

4. Ibid.

5. Rodney. Op. Cit., 1969, p. 24.

6. Ibid., p. 25.

7. Lewis, Gordon. *Main Currents in Caribbean Thought: The Historical Evolution of Caribbean Society in Its Ideological Aspects, 1492—1900.*Baltimore. Maryland: The Johns Hopkins University Press, 1983, p. 13.

8. James, C.L.R. *Spheres of Existence.* Westport. Conn.: Lawrence Hill publishers, 1980, p. 177.

9. Rodney, Walter. Op. Cit., 1969, p. 25.

10. Ibid., p. 25.

11. Ibid., p. 25.

12. Ibid., p. 25.

13. Rodney, Walter. "Problems of Third World Development." *Paper* delivered at the African Studies Center, UCLA, May 30, 1972, p. 23. "Imperialism has used racism in its own interest but it turns out to be a double-edged blade, and the very unity that is engendered among black people—the unity of common conditions and common exploitation and oppression is being turned around as a weapon to be used against imperialism."

14. Op. Cit., 1969, p. 26.

15. James, C.L.R. *Selected Speeches.* Westport. Conn.: Lawrence Hill, publishers, 1980, p. 188.

16. Rodney, Walter. Op.Cit., 1969, p. 27.

17. Nath, Dwarka. *A History of Indians in British Guiana.* London: Nelson, 1950.

18. Rodney, Walter. Op. Cit., 1969, p. 27.

19. Ibid., p. 27.

20. Ibid., p. 28.

21. Ibid.

22. Ibid., p. 28.

23. Ibid., p. 33.

24. Rodney, Walter. Op. Cit., 1969, p. 28.

25. Ibid.

26. Ibid., p. 25.

27. Ibid., p. 32

28. Ibid.

29. Ibid., p. 33.

30. Ibid., p. 33

31. Ibid., p. 33

32. Ibid., p. 29.

33. Ibid., p. 28.

114   CHAPTER FOUR

34. Ibid., p. 28.
35. Ibid., p. 28.
36. Ibid., p. 61.
37. Lamming, George. *Cimarron.* Vol. 1 1985, p. 16.
38. Ibid.,
39. Rodney, Walter. Op. Cit., 1969, p. 61.
40. Ibid., p. 29.
41. Ibid.
42. Smith, M.G. Culture, *Race and Class in the Commonwealth Caribbean.* Jamaica: Department of Extra-Mural Studies, University of the West Indies, 1984.
43. Nath, Dwarka. *A History of Indians in British Guiana.* London. Nelson: 1950, p. xv.
44. Despres. Leo. A. *Cultural Pluralism and Nationalist Politics in British Guiana.* Chicago: Rand McNally, 1967.
45. Premdas, Ralph. "Elections and Political Campaigns in a Racially Bifurcated State: The Case of Guiana." *The Journal of Inter-American Studies and World Affairs,* Vol. 14, 1972, pp. 271-296.
46. Lutchman, Harold. *From Colonialism to Co-operative Republic: Aspects of Political Development in Guyana.* Rio Piedras, Puerto Rico: Institute of Caribbean Studies, 1974.
47. Hoetink, H. *Two Variants in Caribbean Race Relations: A Contribution to the Sociology of Segmented Societies.* London: Oxford University Press, 1967, pp. 93-96.
48. Rodney, Walter. Op. Cit., 1969, p. 34.
49. Bonnet, Aubrey Op. Cit., 1981.
50. Thomas, Clive Y. *Plantations, Peasants and State.* Jamaica: Institute for Social and Economic Research: University of the West Indies, 1984, p. 83.
51. Hall, Stuart. " Pluralism, Race and Class in Carib bean Society." In UNESCO, *Race and Class in Post-Colonial Society: A Study of Ethnic Group Relations in the English-speaking Caribbean, Bolivia, Chile and Mexico."* Paris: UNESCO, 1967, p. 150-182.
52. Stone, Carl. *Stratification and Political Change in Trinidad and Jamaica.* Beverly Hills, California: Sage Publications, 1972.
53. Smith, M.G. Op. Cit., 1984.
54. Rodney, Walter. Op. Cit., 1989, p. 20.
55. Ibid.
56. Ibid., p. 21.
57. Ibid., p. 24.
58. Walter Rodney. Op. Cit., 1969, p. 25.
59. Ibid., p. 51.
60. Fanon, Franz. *Black Skins, White Masks.* New York: Grove Press, 1967, p. 225-226.
61. Ibid., p. 226.
62. Ibid., p. 226.
63. Ibid., p. 228-229.
64. Ibid., p. 226.
65. Walter Rodney. Op. Cit., 1969, p. 22.
66. Rex Nettleford. *Mirror, Mirror: Identify, Race and Protest in Jamaica.* Jamaica. Kingston: Collins and Sangster, 1970, p. 121.
67. Walter Rodney. Op. Cit., 1969, p. 58.
68, Ibid, p. 58.
69. Ibid., p. 51.
70. Ibid., p. 57.

71. Fanon, Franz . *Towards an African Revolution*. New York: Grove Press, 1967, p. 27—37.
72. Rodney, Walter. *A Tribute to Walter Rodney*. Hamburg: University of Hamburg, 1984, p. 95.
73. Rodney, Walter. Op. Cit., 1969, p. 53.
74. Ibid., p. 56.
75. Said, Edward. *Orientalism*. New York: Vintage Books, 1979.
76. Jahn, Janheinz. *Muntu*. New York: Grove Press, 1977, p. 101.
77. Rodney. Walter. Op. Cit., 1969, p. 67.
78. Senghor, L. "L'esprit de la civilisation ou les lois de la culture negro-Africaine." In *Presence Africaine*. viii-x, Paris, 1956.
79. Jahn, Janheinz Op. Cit., 1958, p. 150.
80. Rodney, Walter. *A Tribute to Walter Rodney*. Hamburg: University of Hamburg, 1978, p. 56.
81. Ibid., p. 50.
82. Rodney, Walter. Op. Cit., 1969, p. 35.
83. Abiola Irele. *"Negritude—Literature and Ideology."* The *Journal of Modern African Studies*. 3, 4, 1965, pp. 499—526.
84. Caute, David. *Fanon*. London: Fontana, 1970
85.Cabral, Amilcar. *United and Struggle: Speeches and Writings*. New York: Monthly Review Press, 1979, p. 58.
86. Fanon, Franz. *Black Skins White Masks*. New York: Grove Press, 1967, p. 154.
87. Ibid, p. 192.
88. Ibid., p. 202.
89. Fanon Franz. Op. Cit., 1967, p. 205.
90. Fanon, Franz *The Wretched of the Earth*. New York: Penguin Books, 1957, pp. 150—151.
91. Fanon, Franz. Op. Cit., 1967, p. 203.
92. Ibid., p. 74.
93. Ibid., p. 187.
94 Kesteloot, L. *Les Ecrivains noirs de langue francaise: Naissance d'une Litterature*. Brussels. Editions de l'Institut de sociologie de l'Universite libre de Bruxelles, 1971.
95. Fanon, Franz Op. Cit., 1967, pp. 228-229.
96. Ibid., p. 222.
97. Braithwaite, Edward.. *Race and Class*. Vol. xxii, Spring 81, No. 4.
98. Rodney, Walter. Op. Cit., 1969, p. 37.
99. Franz Fanon. Op. Cit., 1967, p. 225.
100. Ibid, p. 227.
101. Ibid., p. 227.
102. Ibid, p. 82.
103. Walter Rodney. Op. Cit., 1969, p. 34.
104. Rohlehr, Gordon, *Pathfinder: Black Awakening in the Arrivants of Edward Kamau Braithwaite*. Trinidad: The College Press, 1981.
105. Rodney, Walter. Op. Cit., 1969, p. 52.
106. Braithwaite, Edward, Kamau . Timehri, Savacou, No. 2, Sept. 70, p. 38.
107.Rodney, Walter. "C.L.R. James and the African Revolution." *Paper*. University of Michigan, March 3, 1972.
108. Rodney, Walter. Op.Cit., 1969, p. 29.
109. Ibid., p. 19.
110. Ibid., p. 17.
111. Cruse, Harold. *The Crisis of the Negro Intellectual*. New York: William Morrow, 1967, p. 85.

112. Cruse Harold, *Plural but Equal..* New York: William Morrow, 1967.
113. Asante, Molefi. *The Afro-Centric Idea.* Philadelphia. Pa.: Temple University Press, 1987.
114. Ibid., p. 65.
115. Abraham, Roger, D. *The Man of Words in the West Indies.* Baltimore: Maryland, Johns Hopkins University Press, 1983.
116. Rodney, Walter. Op. Cit., 1969, p. 58.

i. Ariel Dorfman and Armand Mattelhart. *How to Read Donald Duck Imperialist Ideology in the Disney Comic. Bagnolet: IMMRC,*

ii. J. E. Greene. *Race vs Politics in Guyana: Political Cleavages and Political Mobilisation in the 1968 General Election.* Jamaica, Institute of Social and Economic Research, University of the West Indies, 1974, p. 139-140. Greene suggests that the movement of individuals to vote across racial and party lines and a " system of political patronage," are reasons why the political system has not "disintegrated."

iii. Rodney's preoccupation with race at this time must be seen within an international context: the unjustified domination of white people over black people. If the Caribbean was a European crucible, Guyana was its testing ground. But there were two directions to this matter of race and what it portended. His earlier beliefs were more narrowly focussed, because he was concerned with rights denied Africans, a neglect of history. In his later work—and especially his political work—he demonstrated that the active concerns of race must be subsumed by a broader understanding of the place of race within Guyana.

iv. It is easier to subjugate peoples by denying custom and culture, so that they appear to have no history; and a people without history must invent one, thus initiating dependency and other compulsions.

Chapter Five

Intellectualism and its Demands

The role of the intellectual in the Caribbean is inseparable from the wider social obligations of maintaining unity with the masses. The unity is not gratuitous or designed to serve some distant or non prescribed purpose. Unity was essential for the struggle against capitalism and for the emergence of a socialist society.

Socialism, in his view, "has gone much further than capitalism in the liberation of man."[1] For while capitalism has freed the bourgeoisie, who are in a minority, socialism "in even the immature form in Eastern Europe, and China", has emancipated the workers and peasants, who are in a majority.[2] Freedom is associated with socialism and slavery of a certain kind and certainly economic disadvantage is associated with capitalism. Economic disadvantage was the clue here to understanding the role of the intellectual and also that of the university in a developing Africa. Economic disadvantage imposed certain demands inseparable from development. Indeed, socialist development was the only means of successfully assaulting economic disadvantage wrought by rapacious capitalists. The intellectual was expected to be in the vanguard of the struggle for liberation; and "with the help of the universities . . . those who stand in the way will ultimately be swept aside as irrelevant." [3]

The demands on the intellectual were not limited to such skills as he might have, or such pretensions to leadership as he might claim. [Rodney believed that all claims to leadership must be derived from the masses and any other was pretentious.] This explained his suspicion and rejection of middle class leadership as irrelevant to the tasks of development because it represented the imposition of class domination over equality of condition, one objective of socialism. The intellectual was expected to be a part of the struggle for national liberation and development. If history was a chronicle of the social development of human beings and the satisfaction of needs, triumph over nature and search for free institutions, then it was the purpose of the intellectual to analyse this development for the benefit of and in the interests of the masses.

In Africa and much of the developing world, such freedom was in jeopardy, and forms, slogans and empty rhetoric prevailed over meaning and substance. The masses were deceived. The economic and social chains that bound Africa to the imperialist system still existed and the imperialists had reinforced their domination within a world capitalist system that is not easily broken. The exploitation of labor and natural resources continued unabated, resulting in lack of development and exploitation, the more destructive because it was insidious and seemingly out of control. Nor were there possibilities for respite through technology and technological invention. These facilitated further dependency, even as they encouraged the growth of capitalism. Growth was at the expense of development, which could be seen in the decreasing terms of world trade; and annual figures indicated the loss of both skills and other opportunities for technological growth. The so-called "brain drain" was a clear example of the drain in resources and the flow of skilled personnel to the developed countries. Rodney declared succinctly: "This is a logical consequence of the imperialist system which is parasitic in essence."[4] The drain on resources of the poor countries negated development and was responsible for inequalities and threatened freedom. In fact, inequalities perpetuated oppression locally by encouraging wide disparities in income, and social services. Those few who could afford to lived at extravagant rates of consumption and the majority lived in destitution. Poverty, destitution and want created conditions of frustration, bitterness and anger, resulting in spurious attempts at remedies. Retribution on the part of the government was a direct consequence of the attempts by peasants and workers to initiate changes in their lives, resulting in the growth of state apparatus in the form of military, and para-military apparatus.[5] Oppression, unfortunately, bred oppression, which can have dire consequences for the state and of course, the masses, who continued to suffer from injustice. But Rodney was hopeful, for he believed that injustice could not continue indefinitely and he had "full confidence in the creative capacity of our own people."[6]

The creative capacity, Rodney referred to, was the marshalling of intellectual opinion within the university, to promote, build and strengthen opposition to such inequality, dependency and lack of freedom where it existed. The university was the revolutionary seat of the universe of mind in a developing country. Because of its seminal position at the heart of the nation's affairs—the sifting and analysis of information and its transference into useful and available knowledge, enculturation of national affairs, harbinger and transmitter of cultural values, a guardian, and sponsor of its international relations and a common leveller in social relations—the university must be at the center of the intellectual, social and political life of the nation. It was the institution that should transcend the transitory basis of politics because it was beyond politics in its narrow sense. The university must be subject to the control of the people of the country, must owe no allegiances and submit to no authority other than that of the people. This last point is especially crucial.

Rodney was nervous about the university losing its mission and worried that its purposes could be diluted by foreign and other ideologies. Because the university occupied so central and important a place in his scheme of things, the likely penetration of it by influences, which did not reflect the philosophy of the nation, disturbed him. This was primarily because of his awareness and sensitivity to the strength, and resilience of political systems that could threaten and eventually destroy the chances for development. Specifically, investment in one of its several guises could "penetrate our intelligentsia and perpetuate a system of values conducive to capitalist exploitation."[7]

Investment in information and mass media are branches of the ruling estate of developed countries which support their economic hegemony.[8] The contributions and forms of assistance given by foundations such as Ford and Rockefeller, were staging posts for assaults on the values of developing countries. Such assistance as given by these foundations were confined to the social sciences and law and "conspicuously absent" in other areas. He attributed this to the need for ideological penetration, which was dangerous. This was so because of the presence within the university of faculty and staff who because of training, disposition, or inclination were particularly vulnerable to absorption. Many of these were reactionary and readily adhered and responded to foreign bounty; others, either because of a mistaken belief that they are apolitical, or through lassitude, leave undone things which they ought to have done, postponed political development and deprived the masses of the people of leadership. All, and these included the progressives, were members of the elite and occupied positions of much kudos.

The university was as much a seat of learning, education and refinement as it was a shrine that epitomized the philosophy and spirit of the nation. Students from the former colonies who had studied in the metropolitan countries were often too well aware of this; and their return home after such exposure could be traumatic. Exposure to "the values of capitalist education" could lead to "confusion." Rodney here placed an educational system, which historically had been concerned with the perpetuation of a system of class relationships against his vision of what the function of higher education should be.

A university in a metropolitan country was established because of certain distinct and particular relations peculiar to that country at a certain point in history. In capitalist countries, universities represented institutions where knowledge could be acquired for purposes, which had to do with productive relations. Thus, the popularization of universities in Europe from the 16th century, as Elizabeth Eisenstein has noted, was not unrelated to the invention of the printing press by Gutenberg in 1485.[9] Universities sprung up in response to the need for learning and for channeling printed material to the emerging bourgeosie, who had begun to grow fat on trade. The printing press encouraged book production, but it also pushed the eventual development of magazines which came before newspapers. More than that, the printing press stimulated communication between the bourgeoisie in other lands, thus promoting productive relations internationally.

Bourgeois system of thought, which Rodney identified with capitalism, was responsible for a great deal of suffering in the world: slavery, and the "all pervasive racism which underlines modern bourgeois scholarship."[10] Thus, aided and abetted by the universities and the skills derived therefrom, the bourgeoisie could confidently reach out to non-European peoples, who became fodder for exploitation. Universities and their development are inseparable from the rise of capitalism in Europe and helped to promote the onward march of capitalism. New literacy skills advanced learning and technological development, which became central to the establishment of European outposts overseas.

What Rodney found particularly discouraging was the lack of "enquiry into the dynamics of social change and to the inter-relationship of things on a global scale."[11] Bourgeois education system did not, in his view, deal with its historical evolution. It was as though it did not wish to confront its history because of what it might find there, and be forced into admitting its contradictions: it was destructive of the very premise upon which it is built. More to the point, Rodney believed that it was an unwillingness to admit that a scientific view of society could exist; moreover, one which was free from "irrationality, exploitation and barbarism." Thus, the university which was a seat for reflection on the larger issues of our time, had become instead a place devoted to the exercize of the commonplace. The university did not study itself. And the vigor of the assault on socialist studies in some places was only matched by the caricatures of meaning derived therefrom.[i] But the bias against the scientific application of principles to society was not universally applicable; and the university, despite its unwillingness to commit it-self to self-criticism and examination, was made up of warring and competing factions, representative of the very interests, which it de-nied. And there "exists, at least in embryo form, the struggle be-tween capitalism and socialism."[12] The struggle manifested itself at all levels and not least at that of the state, which could be more rad-ical than some of its institutions of higher learning. Whether the balance tipped in favour of the state or that of the institution, it represented in the final analysis, the direction and the character of the university in the development of Africa.

That character, in Rodney's assessment, was not necessarily permanent. The idea of the university should persist, but its form and corresponding content must also be subjected to further study. The university everywhere inherited the tradition of scholarship, that was itself elitist and class oriented. It could be a harbinger of prejudice, oppression—when it serves the interests of a minority—or it could be exclusive and traditional. The university was not meant to occupy such a position of privilege; and Africa and the de-veloping world, might have to examine its role as an agent for de-velopment.

What he had in mind, was the concept of the university emerg-ing from common objectives, defined by the people themselves, and based on their understanding of the facts and experience of develop-ment. Such a concept, rooted in the community, avoided elitism, es-caped the absolutism of class warfare and the indignity which accompanied it. Workers and peasants alike would share in its mu-nificence and the social and other exchanges would mutually rein-force the growth of the community. Inevitably, the university would merge with the community from which it received sustenance and derived its raison d'etre. The concept of the university as the exclu-sive prerorgative of people who had pretensions to scholarship of one form or other, who desired to enhance or complete skills in a certain direction, was obsolete. Given the equally enormous preten-sions of socialism as a scientific study of society, it was clear that the university in its present form could not continue to exist un-challenged and unchanged.

Rodney's vision of the functions of a university at the very cen-ter of national development, explained no doubt the alarm with which his application for a position at the University of Guyana was viewed. The familiar, conventional idea of a university—certainly that of the universities in the Caribbean—could not have long re-mained uninfluenced by his presence. His campaign for change would have been immediately loud and clear and the familiar bas-tions of middle class respectability, which is life on the campuses in the Caribbean, would have resounded to calls for change, as indeed occurred at the University of the West Indies in the short time Rodney was there. Nor would these calls have been unanswered. There is a continuing restlessness about academic life, reflecting perhaps the instability in the region, which has had to come to grips with, for example, the aggravations against Cuba, the invasion of Grenada, the lopsidedness of continued development efforts, vast gaps between the rich and the poor and persistent economic and social pressures, to say nothing of political upheavals of a kind to disquiet the sober and comfortable middle class. And beneath all of the more obvious examples of uncertainty, would have been the less obvious understanding of the anxiety that can be a part of the life of many Caribbean countries.

Rodney shared Lamming's vision of a university where the more important functions united communities of people. Lamming agonized over the exclusion of the working people from the intellectual life of the community and the schism between them and the intellectuals: "an artificial status which separates the educated from the uneducated."[13] This schism was one which developing countries could ill-afford in the interests of development. Knowledge was the common frontier of the intellectual and the worker sharing a cross-fertilization of ideas for mutual growth. Indeed, it was in this area of knowledge that the challenge rested, for knowledge was that "commodity", whose possession is crucial in the business of power and relations based on power. It was knowledge that presently insulated the intellectual from the working people, and left them both wanting. That this state of affairs existed, reflected the perfidy of unbending and inflexible class relations, and the continuing strength of the middle classes as arbiters of these relations. It was this chasm that Rodney tried to bridge in his History of the Guyanese Working People, 1881-1905. To recognize the contribution of the worker to the intellectual life of the nation, to extend a dialogue rooted in diverse experience, forge a common destiny and participate, in Lamming's words, in the "humanization of the Guyanese coastal landscape."[14] Rodney's method was through socialism and Lamming's is a "humanization" which, though not precisely defined, leaves room for any system whose curriculum fuses "organic links with all mass organizations."[15] Such links are inseparable from the development of the nation and the focus of all development.

Ambiguity, contradiction and development

Development studies are a creation of the 20th century and reflect the influences, where they do not derive, from power relations,

profit motives, and human needs. They also have to do with two objective situations: first, the emergence of the United States at the
end of World War II as the supreme industrial power, and, second,
the relative decline of Europe, and the impoverishment of the rest
of the world.

U.S. industrial supremacy translated into great material
wealth and prosperity, high standards of living for its citizens, a
substantial military superiority over the rest of the world,—"the
military- industrial complex" dates from that time—and economic
productivity, which showed little evidence of slackening.[16] In fact,
because it was geared to a war footing, productivity was artificially
stimulated. Also, as part of the industrial complex was a sophisticated information structure, which interpreted the world for the
'power elite.'[17] The elite was not confined to government but included private enterprise and common interests ensured that the
industrial complex operated to maximum efficiency. Advertising
messages were the creative arm of the military-industrial-commer-
cial complex. All shared—unequally perhaps—but shared nonetheless in an understood philosophical relationship.

The word philosophical is deliberate. Capitalism is a working
system generally associated with the production of goods and services by private individuals for profit. That system has been part of
the economic usages of the West since the fifteenth century and it
could hardly have been better formulated in its modern aspect than
in the late President Truman's speech to Baylor University in 1947.
There, the limits of capitalism were spelled out graphically: . . .
"Goods move from country to country in response to economic opportunities. Governments may impose tariffs, but they do not dictate the quantity of trade, the sources of imports, or the destination
of exports. Individual transactions are a matter of private choice.
This is the essence of free enterprise."[18] That system of free enterprise has been responsible for defining the parameters of development for much of the Western world and a substantial part of the
newly independent countries in the post-World War II period. It
was development based on the permissive application of free enterprise without restraint. Free enterprise rests heavily on the unhin-
dered passage of information in the international spectrum. Thus,
both economic freedom and informational freedom go hand in hand;
both are essential props of the system of free enterprise.

As the United States emerged from World War II as the dominant super power, it was able not only to expand its production of
goods and services, but also its markets in other countries. As the
country prospered, its industrial strength mushroomed and with

that a rising hegemony over the rest of the world; and what is more, acknowledgment internationally of the wider limits of its hegemony. This is often attended by exploitation of poor countries and not infrequent attempts to subvert fragile nationalism to maintain power.[19] The details of the plunder we pass over for the moment, and it is enough to say that it is reflected between the developed nations and the developing ones at the level of international division of labor, trade and the movement of capital. At the same time, it is necessary to note the modern developments that place greater emphasis on international monopolies and less on national capitalist systems.

Thus, plunder assumes an ill-defined and amorphous character, but it nevertheless strives to define the world according to its dictates. For example, economic development in the developing countries has witnessed changing nomenclatures: and underdevelopment, emerging, development, the Third World, represent new vocabularies for states of mind which camouflage social, economic and political arrangements even as they define them. [20]

Those definitions Rodney found limiting, incomplete, inaccurate and capricious and false to the experience of history. "Development in human society is a many-sided process . . . universal because the conditions leading to economic expansion were universal."[21] Indeed, survival demanded that the individual explore different and varying avenues. Where survival was the main purpose, the individual and the community within which he lived had to adapt to nature and the environment. History records that man's capacity for adaptation and flexibility is only equaled by his will to survive.

Social relations both within his orbit and beyond manifested a gathering concern for mastery of the environment in assuming responsibility for such matters as personal safety for oneself and the group to which one is affiliated. Thus, systems of governance started as an extension of survival behaviors and adaptability. But equally important was the tendency for all societies and the systems that governed them, to increase productivity, which naturally influenced the quality of life and "the character of the society." China is cited as an example of a society in which adaptation to nature, led to increases in productivity, specialization and division of labor, and the emergence of a political state complete with religious orders. The process by which China emerged from self-governing communities to the nation state indicated the levels to which quantitative changes in production affected the quality of life. Inevitably, such changes as there were took their human toll in the form of inequalities that arose from land ownership. As fewer people owned land, this created a division within the society, between landlords and peasants with attendant class divisions.

But China never became capitalist despite its social divisions. That it did not is attributed to a complex of factors including religion, education, intrinsic beliefs, attitudes; above all, because China remained for the most part an agricultural land, in which state bureaucracy negated any tendency for the growth of local capitalists. This is why development is not entirely an economic affair, but one in which complex social relations derive from the very nature of the development considered. Rodney suggested that in Europe, as distinct from China, the emergence of a bureaucratic class allied to landowners, superimposing itself on the mass of people, led eventually to social domination—as they needed to protect their wealth and property—and conflict, which has been an inevitable accompaniment of wealth and privilege.[22] As a consequence revolution cannot be separated from the growth of class consciousness; and both capitalist on the one hand and the exploited worker on the other felt the need at various times to resort to violence as a means of either defending interests, or on the other hand overthrowing the status quo in their interests. Thus, the growth of capitalism is accompanied by crystallization of social class, leading inevitably to violence as power is seen to be in the control of one or other group.

In Africa for the most part, social classes in Rodney's view were "incompletely crystallized", meaning that the various sectors were not rigidly demarcated, indicating perhaps the absence of exploitative relations. What concerned him more was the unevenness of the development process. It is an important point, for so much of development policy this century has centered on aid and its distribution. For example, the readiness of some donors to fund some projects and a reluctance to fund others is often based on unfair, quantitative comparisons of similar projects elsewhere, where other standards might apply. The larger question is why have people and nations developed thus unevenly.

Rodney's response is grounded in the material facts of existence. The responses people and nations make to their environment is largely responsible for uneven development. Such responses create "forms of social relations, forms of government, patterns of behavior, and systems of belief."[23] These different forms in turn interact with human beings and nations and they reinforce one another. Each society is qualitatively different from the other because the nature of the response to the environment is different and their reaction to science and changes brought about by science especially so. Thus, man's technical ingenuity which enabled him to conquer the environment, causing people to reach a new stage of development, is influenced by the peculiar conditions of the society within which he finds himself. Development is affected by conditions which are peculiar to a given society.

But more than that: human life is informed by the daily challenges to material and other needs; and these needs were similar in some instances and dissimilar in others. It was indeed the material needs which informed Man's other concerns. And these same material needs varied with the continent, the climate, the hazards of nature and so on. This is why people and nations develop unevenly and any theory of development that seeks to define objectives of one kind or another, must understand this. Moreover, Rodney suggested that uneven development, which varies with the society, has always made sure "that societies have come into contact when they were at different levels."[24] This explained the crucial role of development in social and economic growth.

As a general rule when two societies of unequal development come in contact with one another, new relationships take place which can more seriously affect the weaker: it is "adversely affected" and can only get back on track if it ultimately sustains a level of productivity which is higher than the dominant society. This also explains the vulnerability of countries of the developing world when faced with the more productivity economies of highly industrialized countries. The advantages which the latter countries have gained over the centuries in terms of capital accumulation, political, military and cultural hegemony have encouraged further exploitation, domination and dependency. Those countries which have been thus victimized by such conditions have found in socialism a doctrine, or a way of ordering the world, is in harmony with human needs; moreover, a doctrine, that can establish economic equality, the foundation of political equality and "equality before the law." To this effect the planned economy must be seen as a corrective to laisser faire capitalism which only "fitfully and partially" intervened in the economy to regulate it in the interests of economic egalitarianism.

Rodney's complaint was that development was an extremely complex business and inadequately treated in the literature where treated at all: that development seen through the eyes of bourgeois scholars was a restricted process, narrowed, limited and skewed to economic variables, omitting what was real about development: and that was the human process. These considerations also omitted those influences that hampered development, chief among them was human exploitation in the interests of capital formation and power.

Development was not simply a collage of economic variables; this would be limiting in the extreme; besides which it would not be true. Development must be looked upon as a process that includes the rise of capitalism, the evolution of social and class relations and political systems. Indeed, capitalist development, which increased profits with the assistance of technology, promoted Western democratic institutions. The linking of capitalism to Western democracy suggests that the latter could not have succeeded without the compulsions of many who did not benefit from it; yet no mention is made of their contribution. Rodney's prescription is firm: capitalist development was at the expense of the lack of development and cannot be studied apart from the underdevelopment which it created.

It was the task of the historian to do this: to revise this historical neglect and then to move on to other considerations. [In his case it was to intervene in history to set up the conditions for the overthrow of capitalism]. Capitalism had to be overthrown for other reasons, one of which was that it retarded the ongoing and continuous development of people and nations who worked diligently to support it. Besides, "capitalism stands in the way of further human social development." [25] But he was careful to insist that capitalism in its march towards its aggrandisement, did contribute marginally and peripherally to the well being of significant numbers of people, but that time had long past where its continued existence could be justified. People the world over had decided to take their destiny in their own hands and that was significant. Indeed, "such a determination is an integral part of the process of development." [26]

Such development has not been understood by scholars in the field of development. For example, the work of Walt Rostow,—selected because he represents so much of the thinking of the post World War II era—defends the view that each country has a stage of development that is appropriate to it. [27] Thus, at a certain stage, industrial capacity is appropriate to a certain level of technological skills and human resources. But surprisingly Rostow does not mention the contradictions of capitalism, which exploits human beings for its own welfare and which influences the developmental stages of these countries. Moreover, development defined or considered in this way, severely limits that overall march of humanity which we know as social development. And this is the crux. Economic development such as is generally considered by capitalist countries restricts the process of human development. It is a theme that Rodney returns to time and again, suggesting, for instance, that the relatively advanced methods of rice cultivation among communal tribes in the sixteenth century in the Upper Guinea Coast, were responsible for the "'humanization' of the landscape."[28] This is not to be taken as an attack on industrial society so much as a challenge to it, not to ignore the human perspective. Inevitably such concerns center on factors of production and their consequence for the development process.

The development process is also about underdevelopment; indeed, development cannot be conceived without underdevelopment, which stands in contrast with it. Underdevelopment is a stage in the development process and without it development cannot be conceived. Looked at this way, development is a feature of all societies, for all have had to deal with the problems of facing nature and conquering the environment. This is, of course, routine understanding that disguises complexity. But it is necessary to delve deeper into the precise nature of underdevelopment in order to unmask its true causes. This is a vital step before tackling development.

Structural dependency initiated first through the colonial system, then reinforced through capitalist and imperialist systems, created conditions of on-going dependency. These conditions were further reinforced through trade agreements, foreign aid, educational and cultural institutions, including universities. Continued pillage was the consequence of this dependency, the net result of which was the perpetuation of conditions of gross inequality and poverty. The contrast with development then becomes clear and questions come unbidden. Rodney derived the theorem: those countries that are rich have become so at the expense of others exploited, that have greater natural wealth and resources. The entire system of relations is kept in place by ruthless economic efficiency, "experts," military apparatus and not least, the administrative ranks within the exploited countries "who dance in Abidjan, Accra, and Kinshasa when music is played in Paris, London and New York."[29] Rodney again faced the consequences of this exploitative relationship, when he attributed political instability to underdevelopment, "a symptom of underdevelopment." Since "real" power is concentrated outside of the exploited countries, then political decision-making, or a national politic was also outside of their control. Thus the fibers of nationalism were weakened within and led to a weakening of all national ties. The history of Latin America and the involvements in Vietnam were ample illustration; and the Chilean experience provides the most recent copy.

Underdevelopment was thus a challenge to peasants and workers to "mobilize to offer an alternative to the system of sham political independence."[30] Moreover, this alternative was within the grasp of the exploited and the downtrodden, for it could not have escaped them that their wealth upkeeps oppressors. This is a weakness in the capitalist system. Still, capitalism was resilient and capitalists with former colonies could bring their dependency to an end by encouraging and stimulating manufacture elsewhere, or through the manufacture of synthetic products.

For example, beet sugar replaced sugar in the last century and brought about the decline of the Caribbean sugar plantations, from which the region has scarce recovered. Also, monopoly of the market institutionalized control over the disposition of products from countries under capitalist yoke e.g. the world's coffee and cocoa markets, to mention but two. In addition, technological advances increased the production of synthetic goods, making it even more certain for capitalist countries,— usually the more technologically advanced,—to assume a giant share of the world market.

This litany of concerns was, of course, expressed in the literature of the time. The sixties and seventies were marked by critical examination by third world scholars and others of the wider limits of capitalist expansion after the euphoria of post capitalist investment; and the increased industrial capacity among Western nations, national independence and the movement to end formal colonial structures, provided the opportunity for a great deal of international energies.

Industrialization and modernization became catch-phrases, with the former largely implying the latter among true believers; and newly independent countries became part of these aspirations. [ii] Much ethnocentricity adorned the literature and even a relatively enlightened view of modernization that interpreted the process as total transformation, fell down when it used the yardstick of "the stable nations of the Western world."[31]

These stable standards were pressed into three cubicles, though their implications go well beyond. They did indicate the prescriptive nature of development theory—[do this, do that and you'll succeed]—and the limitations. One researcher analyzed the three approaches which characterized development theory among Western nations—"the index approach, theories of differentiation and theories of exogenously induced change."[32] The first is an economist's tool and development becomes a measurable index, where GNP per capita correlates with population growth, education, literacy, health and so on. It is an ingenuous system in which quantity is superimposed over quality to the evident demise of the latter.

The second example, "theories of differentiation," looked at role and institutional separation and prescribed the kind of differentiation required if development is to succeed: institutions of one sort or another were to perform certain functions; sectors representing particular interests were pressed into service; and each function had its accompanying "set of structural conditions under which it optimally served." [33] Central to these theories was the belief that changes in attitudes create the conditions for modernism. Attitudes, role models, behaviors are all constituents of a process whose ends justify the means. Modernism is supported by rational behaviors, which can be subject to discipline, order, management and a frame of mind that was conducive to work. But is this really so? These new performance criteria are by no means universal. They do not relate to specificity of class and other constitutents such as education, social mobility. They do not therefore relate in their entirety to the Third World countries, some of which have long established and distinct institutional hierarchies and have no need for artificial and ad hoc institutional separateness.

The third approach to development, "exogenous theories," assumed that the prescriptions of Western Europe and the United States for development and modernization were more important than they actually were. Much of this was of course, psychological. Achievement, motivation, empathy, each had its accompanying sympathisers and supporters. Each had its cornucopia for progress— identified with modernization: one might be literacy, another might be exposure to the mass media, hurried industrialization, the Protestant work ethic, consumer demand, behavior appropriate to the changing times; a middle class seeking opportunities to utilize its entrepreneurial skills,—and all the ingredients of capitalism were in place. Together all of these elements constituted a system that militated against the peasant, the worker, and installed an oppressive class domestically; and internationally, it allied itself to a system that was responsible for the rape and subversion of both national independence and sovereignty. Further, that this very system continued to be responsible for much of the suffering of the developing world.

Rodney cited as examples works on Brazil and Latin America, which examined relations with the metropolis and arrived at conclusions similar to his.[34] Also, Samir Amin's The Class Struggle in Africa—another cited work—must be seen as a significant contribution to the study of development in Africa and the furtherance of the debate as to why socialism is a viable system for the Third World.

For Rodney, an undiluted or unqualified socialism was not the final answer—some socialist governments have been as rapacious as capitalist ones, though "not involved in the robbery of Africa." Human social development was the measuring rod and capitalism had failed to improve social relations between people in most lands, where it had existed. Socialism stood as an alternative to a system that is exploitative; and "every African has the responsibility to understand the system and work for its overthrow."[35]

Technological expansion

European domination of the world had begun with naval vessels, seafaring ships under sail, which had designed the rape of Abyssinia must be seen in this context. More specifically, the need to defend colonial interests led to increased naval research and also the development of armaments; and . . . "By the end of the Second World War, military research had become the most highly organized branch of scientific research . . . "[36] And that started in the 19th century with the great impetus, which came from colonial expansion.

Military research and other forms of scientific activity were part of that inexorable movement of machines and men that came down to us as the Industrial Revolution. It involved the harnessing of energy and its application for productive purposes. The colonies were ideal in this respect, for from them came wealth and resources to fatten the coffers of the metropoles. Together all the resources of technology, be they in the military, or the factory, succeeded in dappening, where not depleting any social energy for conflict on the part of the colonized. Indeed, it would have been most hazardous to do so: uranium for atomic energy was first mined in the Belgian Congo, copper came from Zambia, iron ore from Sierre Leone, chrome from Zimbabwe, and bauxite from Jamaica, Guinea, Guyana, and Suriname. All the elements were in place for the later amalgamation of the military-industrial complex of the present day. This indicated that the transnational corporate structure came out of the early beginnings of European industrialization. The greater dynamism of the United States ensured that what started as a household relationship—between metropolis and periphery— would grow into a worldwide concern in which the "international division of labor" would consign each worker his rightful place in the scheme of things. Quite apart from the centralized control of men and their productive output, which this involved, was the maintenance of a system heavily geared to the metropolitan workers who had the skills. The maintenance of this corporate structure placed in the hands of transatlantic capitalists, literally the wherewithal to control the world through the movement of capital, the productive processes, the skills, marketing and above all the distribution of good and services. Rodney underlined distribution. [37]This was crucial. For it was the crux of his contention: that capitalists unfairly distributed the products of their wealth. They gave it to a minority class, the bourgeoisie, "the white race and resident in Europe and North America."[38]

Much of this wholesale exploitation took place as a result of government policy, directing, influencing and cajoling colonial and later capitalist development. But government was not the only one to profit from investment. Individual firms did so as well. For government investment helped to regulate economies often distressed domestically by encouraging overseas investments and interests. Thus merchant banks, shipping interests and manufacturing companies, such as Unilever, represented some of the wider limits of capitalism shared by European powers. Rodney reasoned that all capitalist nations profited—perhaps unequally—but profited nonetheless in colonial expansion, even those, which had no colonies. "The exploitation of Africa gave European monopoly capital full opportunities to indulge in its tendencies for expansion and domination." [39]

But Africa alone was not exploited. The European worker, the cog in the machinery of Unilever, or one of the larger enterprises, also suffered exploitation. Inevitably, the ensuing dissatisfaction between exploiters and exploited led to a clash; governments resorted to methods of repression in order to prevent cohesion and unity among the working classes. Where they did not do so, they prevented such a possibility through concession, which like repression, served the same purpose; they were, in short, part of the same method of damming up the spread of working class unity and preventing its social, cultural and political development. Both led to the growth in state power, the results of which have been clearly spelled out elsewhere. [40]The struggle of the workers against government attempts to control them first through social manipulation structures like the church, the school and other social services, and finally by corruption of union leaders, was but another example of the lengths to which the state imposed itself on legitimate aspirations of workers.[41] Inevitably, state repression—and concession also is a part of the machinery of statecraft—led to a growth in the total state apparatus and the decline of standards of representation.

This had two consequences: class lines became rigid and social conflict became increasingly part of the national agenda. It was finally state repression of the working class that drove them to socialism as the only remaining alternative. Internationally, the continued desire for expansion of markets and redivision of territories led to "wars of redivision." It was only then, according to Paul Sweezy, that the national working class could exert its proper claims to socialism.[42] When imperialist countries are weakened economically and socially as a result of warfare, the time is propitious for socialist revolution. The second consequence is the growth of nationalist opposition in colonial countries. This comes about because of the stagnation of the economy in colonial territories because of the continuing influence of imperialist countries—an influence that is exercised at the level of the local bourgeoisie and continuing legislation designed to facilitate exploitation of the national resources. The nationalist movement is thus compromised and split between the working class and the bourgeoisie, who themselves are divided between some who pursue their own interests and others who identify with the national interest. Leadership "wavers between accepting the support . . . of socialism . . . and temporizing with imperialism in order to keep in check the socialist menace." [43] In default, the working class thus became the repository of national aspirations towards socialism, a position which it shared with the peasantry. [44]

This state of affairs, which Lenin anticipated, is precisely that which Rodney faced on his return to Guyana: a national leadership which in order to remain in power, had compromised itself by flirtations with the capitalist world, amid socialist rhetoric; [45] moreover, a leadership of ill-conceived if not grandiose development plans;[46] a country in which the bourgeoisie were divided racially;[47] and the working people restless and uncertain. It was these social, economic and political conditions, so distracting to scholarship and challenging to a Marxist that propelled Rodney to enter the troubled waters of Guyanese politics.

The problem of development

For Guyana, as for Africa, the problem of development had to be re-stated as a question. Rodney asked: 'Who was/is responsible for underdevelopment in the Third World?' The answer to that is clear: the imperialist countries, their representatives and agents have had a major role in this underdevelopment through the creation of structural impediments to development. "Restrictions were placed on African capacity to make . . . use of its economic potential—which is what development is all about."[48] Rodney explained that underdevelopment was not a phenomenon that must be considered apart from development. Underdevelopment does not exist apart from itself, but is always relative to development. They are two sides of the same coin. The only way to end it is by exorcizing dependence and that is a political problem.

Indeed, it is a political problem, which confronts the Third World whose 2 billion people continue in poverty by almost any standards and the gap separating the poor countries from those exploiting them continued to grow; and whatever increases in income came their way hardly touched the level of the population where it was most needed. Rodney was not alone in describing and assessing the nature of the development/underdevelopment equation. Marxist economists Gunner Frank, Samir Amin and Clive Thomas did so too.

Gunder Frank, whose work concentrated on Chile and Brazil, attributed "the development of underdevelopment" in Chile to three contradictions, and the first of these was "the expropriation/appropriation of economic surplus."[49] Frank saw the concept of development or underdevelopment of any part of the capitalist system within the context of the world capitalist system. Chile has historically had strong external as well as internal monopolies and it was these monopolies that siphoned the economic surplus, appropriating it for other parts of the world capitalist system, or for their own use. And since these monopolists were small in number they had a disproportionate share of the national wealth and whatever was not distributed they kept for themselves. Thus, external capitalism fed the growth of internal capitalists who in turn fed them. Development ensured the continuation of underdevelopment.

The second contradiction lay in the firm relations between metropolitan centers and the countries on the periphery and the contradiction applied also to regions within the same country. Briefly, the contradiction must be considered in the following way: because of structures of centralization within the metropolitan centers, control is exercised over the countries on the periphery which are unable to get access to their economic surplus. As a result the economic surplus accrued to the metropolis and impoverished the periphery. "One and the same historical process . . . continues to generate—both economic development and structural underdevelopment."[50]

The third contradiction which detained Frank was "the continuity and ubiquity of the structural essentials of economic development and underdevelopment . . . "[51] This "continuity" in Chile and Latin America began in the 16th century when the foundations of mercantile capitalism were laid. These foundations affected the future development of all the institutions of the region; and these institutions, pointed out Frank, were still in place, as any study of the role of the church, the armed forces, the trade links would indicate. These capitalist structures existed both externally and internally and affected the development, or rather its lack, over a whole range of areas: they were responsible for the perpetuation of internal exploitation of the native Indians who are the agricultural slaves and later industrial workers of the local aristocracy tied to foreign interests; these structures were responsible for the growth of the city as the center of business and the corresponding lack of growth in the countryside.

Samir Amin argued that these structures were in place in Latin America from the beginning of the mercantilist period and persist to this day.[52] The "structural essentials" of which Gunder Frank speaks are those which created an agrarian economy, complete with latifundia and peasants who were maintained in an inferior slave like status, and a rapacious bourgeoisie with permanent links to Europe. Later on, they replaced these allegiances with North American connections. The plight of the Indian in Latin America illustrated just how capitalist relations produced underdevelopment among people, in much the same way that slavery supported earlier forms of capitalism. The subjection of the Indian to the demands of capitalist economy is illustrated in the often contradictory relations between the city and the countryside; the city with the advantages of its channels of communication, used these as a convenience for its pillages of the countryside and for carrying the gospel of European capitalism.[53]

Amin had studied the concept of development in "tribute paying formations" and found that these developed according to their own inner dynamic, and certainly without recourse to capitalism. This explained the evolution of China, Egypt and India, countries which had achieved their own rhythm in the development process before the advent of capitalism. "Tribute-paying formations" were centralized, controlled by a state-class bureaucracy, which regulated economic and political affairs. The kind of development, which these espoused, was quite different to the feudal societies of Europe. In fact, the break-up of feudalism let loose energies of people who were not tied to a nation-state and could therefore utilize the opportunities for pushing the idea of capitalism without the restraint of citizenship. Thus, suggested Amin, the so-called pre-capitalist societies came into existence on the periphery of the tribute-paying countries and derived much of their dynamism from them. Perhaps, in this way, the idea was reinforced, which linked pre-capitalism, or capitalism in embryo form, to the exploitation of "tribute-paying formations," which had already established a developmental pattern of their own.

Rodney's position has always been that European capitalism interrupted the progressive development of Africa and impoverished Africa while enriching Europe. Amin arrived at a similar viewpoint: he analyzed the roots of development in pre-capitalist Africa, and indicated how these were uprooted and replaced by a system that was so different as to be totally disastrous for its present and also for its future.

Amin, himself an economist and head of the African Institute for Economic Development, also explained how the countries of Africa and Asia came to be peripheral to the capitalist system. The movement from a subsistence economy to a money economy carried certain profound dislocations, affecting agriculture and the fledgling industrial crafts; and by emphasizing the need to export products above all other considerations, it ruined the possibility of growth of a sizeable domestic market and sucked the country into the international capitalist system. Nor was there any attendant relief for so doing. The countries on the periphery were forced to manufacture specialized products and they did not derive the benefits for so doing, for their earnings went to support the international capitalist system. The structural dislocation of these countries on the fringe of the international capitalism was not confined to economics alone. Inevitably, this invaded other areas as well and it had profound effects on the emergence of social classes, which indicated the domination of metropolitan countries on those of the periphery.[54]

Frank reinforced Amin with regard to the emergence of social classes in Latin America. The bourgeoisie became the class that were the main supporters of the metropolitan countries locally. They most benefited from the economic system and could therefore be expected to ensure its continuing success. This was at the expense of the Indian. "The development of capitalism, then, generates even more underdevelopment in the Indian community just as it does in most others."[55]

Walter Rodney, Gunder Frank and Samir Amin were kindred souls who charted the course of capitalism, explaining on the way, the theory of capital accumulation, tracing its history from earliest times and showing how its application to the Third World is disadvantageous to its short as well as long term interests. Such a system must be done away with. It remained an imperative if the crisis that afflicts the Third World is to be ended. Fundamentally, therefore, the problem is a political one, and one of political will, in which a maximization of the human resources and their application to the problem at hand, together with other more stringent measures, are needed. Development, for Rodney, was inseparable from the more demanding areas of ideology and will.

Clive Thomas, a friend and contemporary of Rodney, who shared his political vision, framed this in an eight point agenda, which represents the most coherent plan of development. for the Caribbean region and deserves to be seriously considered. [56] The Thomas agenda acknowledges the need to consider development within the context of historical experience and like Amin and Frank to learn from the lessons of history.

From the outset it must be clear that in the Caribbean, the masses have not been placed at the center of any development plan; they have always been on the fringes and this has made for uneven development, quite apart from sustaining a chronic inequality. Indeed, Thomas suggests that any development must be seen within the context of a world movement of the poor and the powerless to rid themselves of a historical burden. This is why development must be in the interests of "The Wretched of the Earth," to use Fanon's poignant phrase. These include the satisfaction of basic needs; self-reliance; democracy and democratic procedures of decision-making; protection of the environment and the enhancement of life; worker participation in the life of the state; recognition of the common dangers which the Caribbean region is exposed to; and finally, a "regional alternative" in the face of the mounting pressures from outside the region. Development is a total program of social, economic and political uplift in the work of Gunder Frank, Samir Amin and Clive Thomas. The state is called upon to enact measures for the benefit of the masses and to be concerned about the emergence of social and class differences which often attend the development process.

Center and periphery relations

Theoretical constructs provide a useful framework for examining the historical origins of the transition to peripheral capitalism. The transition process involved all institutions and all were affected by the process. As a consequence countries on the periphery suffered economic, social and political dislocation. This took the form of agrarian crises brought on by concentration on the export market to the exclusion of the local market and the lack of growth of the latter. The same conditions applied to industry, where an overemphasis on the export of exotic products catered for a fluctuating market and left the country vulnerable to changing conditions.

The pattern of the relationship between the center and the periphery was defined and controlled by transnational corporations, as Samir Amin, Gunder Frank, and Clive Thomas agreed. The continued cycle of dislocations led to the persistence of inequality and the inability of the countries on the periphery to break from what has euphemistically become known as "the cycle of poverty." Above all, these dislocations created such conditions as to need "development policies . . . that are different from those on which the development of the West was based." This suggests the existence of certain "structural features" that perpetuate inequality and underdevelopment in perpetuity, i.e. regardless of the production levels obtained.

The countries on the periphery can never hope to overcome their afflictions.

Amin like Rodney emphasized that while these febrile structures were influenced by their historical circumstances, they had common ingredients that compose them: "agrarian capital" and private communal investment, usually from countries of the center. These interests are preserved by certain compulsions e.g. force of arms and political relations. The circumstances of endemic dependence really created two cultures: those on the periphery and those at the center, each with its own particular system of operation, and its own bureaucracy and management to sustain it.

Consequences of underdevelopment

Underdevelopment was brought into focus with colonial relations. Prior to this time, one could speak, according to Rodney, of "comparative development", meaning by that the conditions within which productive relations existed. Did they, for example, exist in harmony with the expectations of the people of the country? Were these relations such as to sustain the routine fellowship in which the growth of the individual would not be incompatible with that of the state? Each society had to establish its own rhythm in nature and this was where Africa was before the continent became the object of colonial conquest. This historical analysis was central to the case for understanding the enormity of the responsibility that Europe bears for the underdevelopment of Africa. It was not a barren historical exercise. It was an important stage for launching and devising development strategies. Rodney himself addressed the closeness between theory and strategy in the development process. "The aim is to identify the salient aspects of socio-economic and socio-political development in so far as development is consciously pursued . . . "

Colonial conquest distorted traditional development and the normal routines of a society moving along at its own accustomed pace. For example, the disruption of village economy, the replacing of a subsistence economy with a commodity exchange economy and the introduction of competitive measures to promote growth. In Africa, competitive measures to spread capitalist development were political and they were also brutal. Political, because they employed the resources of the foreign state to bring about desired changes; and brutal, because these measures stopped at nothing to bring about these changes. For example, the introduction of a manufacturing economy to encourage exports and the consequent provision of channels for the importation of goods and services; the ruthless use of force to change traditional land policy in Kenya; and the continued brutality against workers in the mining industries of South Africa. Thus, appropriation of land, living, and other imprecations converted traditional structures into capitalist, economic, money-producing accumulations, disturbing to all sections of the country, in that changes in one area inevitably brought changes in another; and the assault on traditional agriculture could not fail to involve the occupational status of the rest of the village e.g. in handicrafts and other crafts.

Colonial conquest also had its subtler modes of operation: illusions of development under the guise of foreign aid. Given the destruction of the local agricultural economy, its dependence on the economy of the center, it was entirely expected that foreign business would be attracted to investment; and the prospect of low wages, cheap labor and more than adequate returns for investment ensured that such business would enter into competition.

Investment was usually in hard industry to the prejudice of agriculture. Because they paid low wages and made high profits, return on their investment was high. The bauxite mines of Guyana and Jamaica provide good copy in this respect. Also, there was reflected in this pattern that continued principle of profit maximization at the center and at the periphery. The operation of that principle could be seen in import substitution. Here, the importation of consumer goods gave place to that of capital goods, encouraging the formation of an industry that had little relevance to the excluded masses. They could not obtain employment in it.

Production relations between center and periphery underwent change in the form of the multinational corporation, which ever since World War II dominated international trade relations. The multinational corporation is a new and more incisive form of dependency. The previous form of dependency, colonial relations, was based on the supply of primary products by the colonies and the manufactures derived from them which were sold for profit e.g. sugar was refined and exported and the same process involved raw bauxite which was converted to aluminum. The dependent relations comprised the familiar structures of social and economic history and are not a part of our study.

The new economic arrangements, which came into operation with the transnational corporation, created greater dependency. They were more inclusive because the vertical hierarchy of the structure of the transnational corporation, bound countries of the center more closely with those of the periphery. This interfered with development. Control was exercized from the center over all aspects of the social and cultural development. This explains how values from the center become easily absorbed in the periphery. These eventually help perpetuate in the main stream the same system of governance and dependence. For Rodney, the transnational corporation was a dangerous development of capitalism. It was a system, which had the potentiality to dominate economic relations around the world and did.

Rodney was moved to consider the effects of this system on the economies of Africa. The question he asked was simple: What factors were responsible for the plunder of Africa over a period of 400 years? The answer was complex: it was not sufficient to say that the capitalist countries were responsible. It is necessary to consider such domestic changes within these countries as might have affected certain strategies and refinements to the very system of exploitation. Also, it is important to assess the details and the methodology of oppression in order not only to understand it but to develop antidotes. But there is a larger reason and that is to bear witness to a history that is a continuum of human development and can be seen in the social, economic, and political affairs of the Caribbean, Africa and Europe. Prospero can not be separated from Caliban.

Such benefits, which accrued from the tenuous association with international capitalism—subject to price fluctuation shifting economic alliances and changing trading patterns—went mainly to the local bourgeoisie and to the countries of the center. This explains the unevenness of growth in third world countries, where poverty amidst plenty is so much in evidence; and the growth in the power of the local bourgeoisie who control and maintain control by duplicating the system at the center: both in the bureaucratic machinery as well as in other ways, the similarities between the two can be seen. Thus they were able to continue exploitation in the absence of imperial structures; and thus contributed both to the hegemony of the center as well as to their own financial well being.

A similarity of ideas, ideals and outlook was shared by the bureaucracies at the center and those on the periphery. Inevitably, since their common purpose was exploitation and management of resources, it would be surprising if this were not so. Mutual confidence was fostered by interchanges at various levels and certainly at universities and institutions of higher education; uniformity of training if not of disposition, would in some instances explain the smoothness with which local administrations accommodated the social and political changes which came with independence. This was evident in post-independence development strategies in Africa.

Post independence development strategies in Africa

Rodney was of the opinion that development strategies in post-independence Africa were not strategies at all, for "there was no clear picture of the role and objectives of government in relation to development." Many countries did not have a coherent plan at all, except what was given them, or what they borrowed, or what was devised for them, usually at much cost, by outside experts. Whatever plans that were formulated did not have the benefit of long experience. In fact, development plans, Rodney acknowledged, had not been part of the economic history of western nations and were a comparatively new development "fashionable only after the socialist and anti-colonial revolutions." Custom was to relegate such matters to the private concerns of laisser-faire entrepreneurs operating in the 19th century mould.

Rodney analysed the Sierre Leone development plan 1962—1972 and immediately took David Carney, an economist, to task. Wrote Carney: "The theory and technique of development planning have in the last several years evolved into a fine art with rather complicated refinements." Rodney suggested that technical skills, which he presumed Carney had in mind, were not the be and end all of development. Ellul shared the same view and criticized the more obsessive inclinations of the twentieth century in the direction of quantitative measurement. "The technical phenomenon . . . is really a question of finding the best means in the absolute sense, on the basis of numerical calculation." Twentieth century man has surrendered himself to the superficial in preference to the real and in following technique, allows means to dictate ends. To put the matter succinctly: "la technique" brings about specific changes through manipulation of variables, without considering the overall effects of those changes on the body politic. It is the endless search for means. The economist might be the metaphysician of the twentieth century.

Opponents of the view which saw development defined in relation to the philosophical premises of statehood and people, did not ask themselves the ultimate question: 'what sort of society is contemplated by such and such a development plan?' Or again: 'what might the future of such a society be?' For Rodney, this question was fundamental to a development plan and its answer the key to defining the universe, the participation of people in it and their relationship to nature. Essentially, therefore, development became the center of a philosophical debate in which both the individual and the State can have common dialogue. Economic development, in Rodney's words, "necessarily implies historical transformation." And we might add, of the social relations between the individual and the State.

Rodney's ethical position—and to concern oneself with human conduct is to assume an ethical position—did not rule out quantitative economic analyses. In fact, he understood the use and function of statistics and factor analysis as important tools for achieving certain objectives in economic development. He reminded us that "techniques of measurement . . . used in standard neo-classical economic theory, were developed in Soviet Marxist theory since the 1920s."

The economic development plan for Sierre Leone was the microcosm of a systematic attitude to economic development in Africa and so much of the Third World: technical expertise, "la technique" became synonymous with theory and "the distinction between the two was not maintained." This lack of critical perspective in the development process in the face of marginal theories of development was glaring: there had been no previous body of work that had been successfully applied to the pecular condition that confronted two-thirds of the world's peoples, existing under conditions of emergence, independence and challenge. Rodney emphasized that an entirely new condition of being had come about, which demanded different responses and scale of values; and these were not being met.

National plans for development should be concerned with "how to take one type of economy and to transform it qualitatively into another type of economy." About this" . . . available theories said nothing whatsoever about that problem." Rodney went further: "There was no theory to turn to, in or out of Africa, not in Western countries or even within the Socialist bloc." Equally damaging to the process of economic development was the fallacy of believing that there were people competent to plan development in Africa in the absence of a substantial body of theory from which to work. The violence of these presuppositions—that there was theory and people who could meaningfully apply it—explained the rash of "experts" in the field in the immediate post-independence years. Rodney believed that these were unqualified for the positions they claimed for themselves; and in some cases aspired to; first, because their qualifications did not "fit" the nature of their tasks; and second, because the ideology—and this cannot be separated from their occupation or their expertise—rendered them unfit for the enormous work of development. Because of these reasons, the subjugation of Africa— and by implication the Third World—to the judgment of experts, could not be but a monstrous and "quite amazing fraud."

Rodney's assessment was neither new nor original. The questioning of experts and their applicable knowledge, had always been a part of the established routine of governments, foundations, universities. But such assessment had invariably been concerned with and devoted to the methodology of the process. Rodney questioned the system which was itself inherently bankrupt.

Fundamental to the process of development and its critical perspective was the kind of society experts and the people who hired them envisaged. Either through lack of vision, or ignorance, errors of the past were compounded. In the case of Sierre Leone—similar errors obtained elsewhere and that country simply illustrated the common practice—development plans were a mosaic of unfinished projects from colonial times. The colonial development plan had certain characteristics, one of which was its dependence on loans, which mortgaged the country's future for a long period; and any development plan comprised a rigid schedule for repayment of interest on loans. This basic consideration harnessed the country's future to the past and ensured the perpetuation of an economic system that would stifle development completely.

That a development plan such as Sierre Leone's was routinely drawn up as part of official development policy, mocked the use of the word. Yet, in another way, cynically, development plans were not designed to assist those in whose interests they were drawn up. And even though "every development plan is premised on a philosophy explicitly stated or implied," plans for the colonies had certain built-in contradictions against which Rodney prevailed. The Sierre Leone plan under consideration addressed the need "to channel the energies of all the constituent elements—the state, private capital . . . and a mixed section . . . " Rodney attacked these "constituent elements" as based on false premises. They stemmed from the belief that former colonial territories existed outside of the clutches of capitalism and also socialism; also, that worthwhile development could be harnessed to this or that aspect of capitalism, socialism or whatever was the preferred brew. Rodney pointed out the "theoretical falsity" of the premise. "At independence Africa was an integral part of the capitalist system." Still, it did have some choice in the matter "whether to continue to be capitalist or the extent to which it could depart from capitalism."

These premises led to illusions. One obvious one was that a country "could stand outside history" and not be a participant in historical forces. Such a limitation made it difficult to decide what "social forces will be represented in the new economy." Foreign capital could not therefore be prevented from coming into the country;

and it was a mistake to believe "that a government could prescribe conditions for its entry." or when it did enter inevitably to direct or influence its flow. To do so is to fail to understand the enormous capacity of capitalist enterprise to absorb "certain sectors of the economy." More than that, so pervasive did foreign capital become in the economy that it was only at the interstices that indigenous capitalists could make any inroads. For example, the main foreign currency earner in which foreign capital had invested were diamonds and iron ore. Local capital interests were left with transportation and other social services.

The Sierre Leone plan did not contribute to the growth of local capitalism at all and actually prevented it from developing. In fact, this was compounded by the plan's failure even to safeguard national interests; for example, it did not make any provisions to curb the outflow of capital. For this country, read Guyana, Jamaica or any independent country of the period, where not even rudimentary concern for the flight of local capital was considered.

For example, national independence brought but minimal change in Guyana and Jamaica, even with the nationalization of bauxite, a main foreign currency earner; and to the sham of independence was added the indignity of local corruption, inefficiency and poor mismanagement. Also, the International Bauxite Association failed to provide the leverage expected of it and competition within the membership did not enhance its image internationally. The activities within and without the bauxite industry illustrated the continued dependency of the countries on the periphery on those of the center. Foreign trade in all its associations perpetuated what Rodney calls "linkages" between the center and the periphery. That was why the Sierre Leone plan was just an "adjustment" to the conditions that existed from the colonial era, a form of structural dependence. Structural dependencies have been chronicled through the long history of relations between the countries of the center and those of the periphery. Rodney stressed that while there might be many centers and many peripheries and "many permutations and combinations of the ideas of centre and periphery . . . the two form part of a whole." That whole was the international monetary system.

Indeed, domestic underdevelopment, as Gunder Frank has shown in Latin America, was fostered and promoted by foreign trade and finance. To begin with, there was capital flow from the periphery to the center. This transfer of resources naturally weakened domestic resources of the periphery and increased their dependence and made them an integral part of the capitalist system. Also, restrictions of one sort or another were imposed on the internal market, increasing its vulnerability. The outcome was that undue reliance was placed on one or two crops e.g. mining and agriculture and when there was a decline in the one or the other, the internal system became crisis-ridden.

But there was another outcome, perhaps more telling than shaky economic satellite relations. It was how the society of the periphery was affected by these relations. This manifested itself in pronounced divisions of rich and poor: the rich bourgeoisie who could afford to purchase consumer goods imported from abroad, and the poor who lived at or beneath subsistence level. Also, the bourgeoisie at the center countries prospered from the labor and work of the working people on the periphery. This had another consequence viz. that of creating psychological, educational and cultural dependence that militated against the infant nationalism of the periphery. Thus, economic independence and nationalism were severely affected by social and cultural schism. But other forms of dependence were not far behind.

The local bourgeoisie were themselves in a state of perpetual dependence; and perhaps more than the working people who were permanently in a state of need, they were susceptible to winds of change. Seldom could a class of people have been more insecure. Supported by visions of power from the bourgeoisie at the center and sustained by the promise of economic influence, they joined forces to acquire wealth and to exploit the poor. They found themselves—not always reluctantly—in political alliance with the exploiters of their country. Thus, they never were in a position to completely support nationalist movements. They remained on the fringe; frequently also, they actually joined in military alliance with imperialist powers to suppress local uprisings. The familiar divide and rule policy was less strategy than formal policy with precise objectives.

With the continued expansion of imperialism following World War ll,—and this coinciding with the political independence of a number of colonial territories—the stage was set for plans for reconstructing moribund economies, refurbishing tired ones and constructing some anew. The Sierre Leone plan attempted "to industrialize the economy in the manufacturing field." Rodney attacked this as illogical and repugnant to even the usual and accustomed paths to development among progressive governments. His arguments against attempts to industrialize are disarmingly simple. Essentially, he made three points.

First, that industrialization for the sake of it was not productive and could in fact be unproductive. Import substitution, as we have discussed elsewhere, was incomplete because it could place unreal demands on the economy by using up valuable foreign currency for purchase of manufacturing material, expert personnel, technical equipment and so on, which benefitted an elite. Also, the costs of import substitution might be such as to make it difficult for products to be marketed competitively; and finally by concentration on a few manufactures, it rendered the economy vulnerable to external pressures i.e. dependent on the export market.

Second, Rodney argued that industrialization on the basis of local manufactures "was a startling assumption", which "had no basis in the history of any country, in any part of the world under any social system." The history of industrial development indicated that agricultural industries came before industrialization and that the consumer industry was marginal to the process.

Third, by concentrating on industrialization without specifying the strategies for achieving this objective, Rodney believed that these vagaries could only be sustained by foreign and aid about which he had pungent feelings.

Foreign aid could be had only at considerable price and the Sierre Leone plan did specify two sources of international activity : from foreign private interests and from "international lending institutions." Both according to Rodney, "were all representative of the international capitalist class" which is sufficient reason to condemn them. But Rodney was disturbed by their implications. That a plan was friendly to foreign investment dammed it in his eyes because it was an indication of just how strongly fortified these interests were in Sierre Leone—a status generalizeable to much of post—colonial Africa and other places as well. Furthermore, the belief that the International Monetary Fund, the IMF, and other lending bodies such as the World Bank "were not capitalist bodies" was not the least dangerous of its misconceptions. Both the IMF and the World Bank spelled out "sound financial and monetary policies" as conditions for loans. It was incumbent on borrowers to restore if not prop up ailing or weak economies and this often was achieved through disproportional taxation, which fell on the heads of the poor.

Unequal taxation divided societies, further accentuating the differences between rich and poor, with the bulk of its provisions falling on the shoulders of workers and peasants. The post World War ll development plans came out of the same basic mould—international capitalist concerns. For Rodney, a development plan, any development plan should deal with two essentials: what is the future of the society to be be? And what are the means to that end? While the Sierre Leone development plan "posed questions of what kind of future society it envisaged, its answer was less than honest." Rodney did not believe that this was happenstance. That "the seemingly apolitical and technocratic functioning of the planning units or ministries was . . . a cover for the real class interest."

The concept of a development plan as apolitical Rodney ridiculed as specious and barely disguised camouflage for class and sectional interests, which deeply involved and affected Africans at every level. These divisions would have made it very difficult for many countries to organize and sustain national independence efforts and build up intra-African trade and co-operation. The same argument, stated above, was central to the myth of widespread credence that civil servants were apolitical or were supposed to be. Avoidance of political view or attitude was held to be meritorious in itself. That many patently regarded this as crass, was a mixed blessing for colonial territories, some of whose administrators, conscious of or in spite of their burdens, behaved in distinctly political ways to lighten some of the more exacting tasks, or to exert pressure where necessary to obtain obedience and co-operation. But this but tempered the outlines without touching the center of the system.

Rodney himself distinguished between "capitalist elements," and "capitalism as a total social system;" and benign administrators might be considered elements within the capitalist system. The apolitical view of development plans persisted as a holdover from the past and now, social and behavioral scientists of whatever persuasion have taken refuge under this label. It was a flag of convenience that allowed wholesome manipulation of the target without the irritations of close scrutiny, in the same way as a ship, which flew a flag of convenience, escaped watchfulness of its cargo, or its seaworthiness. To this category then, confine all plans, which were so technical, that they laid special claim to the apolitical condition. Rodney mentioned Nicholas Kaldor, whose development plans came down especially hard on the workers and peasants of Pakistan, Ghana, and Guyana, provoking much social discontent and unrest.

Furthermore, some development plans displayed a monumental lack of citizen participation or representation, and fell especially hard on those who could least afford to support changes e.g. workers and peasants who were "not represented in the planning mechanism or elsewhere in the state." In so far as colonialists claimed that they aided colonies in learning the ways of representative government, this was conspicuous in its absence. Rather, the opposite was true: that colonial subjects had to learn about representative institutions in the process of the national struggle towards greater representation. That struggle became increasingly bitter as the contradiction between "growth without development" manifested itself. The growth of consumer goods in post-independence Africa was alarming and "repeated the character of social relations." The bourgeoisie, protected and entrenched behind the military, became the dominant economic group in control of the economy and in league with the international capitalist class.

Gunder Frank shared Rodney's view with regard to the growth and importance of the bourgeoisie in Latin America. This had somewhat more exacting consequences in that their alliance with the center countries i.e. the U.S. and Europe was all the more intimate: proximity to the U.S. imposed ties which were friendly because they could not be otherwise; and Europe, because of perceived and therefore real ties of kinship. This latter was in itself revealing of patterns of power distribution in Latin America since one of the largest ethnic groups, the Indians are indigenous and non European. Control is exercized by the dominant European minority in several countries.

Class analysis

It is in social relations in general, both in Africa and Latin America that one sees clearly the extent to which class divisions are cemented by continued exposure to foreign commercial interests. The concept of class in the sense Marx used it, [and it must be pointed out that there are many interpretations of class] derived from the underpinnings of dialectical materialism. Class cannot be separated from class struggle; and a class society is one in which there is a necessary contradiction between the opposites. When, for example, workers get together they are a class of persons exercizing common interests against capital. But it is in the struggle that these workers become a class. The struggle therefore, the political struggle, is that which transforms. It is the political level that pits the oppressed and exploited against the oppressors. The locus of the struggle is the state within which all the contradictory elements obtain. And it is against the people who rule the state—the ruling class—that the battle is enjoined. In the course of this struggle class consciousness develops depending on the intensity of the political struggle.

That struggle in Africa Rodney depicted as taking place in the particular conditions that adorned life in the colonial empire. Rodney emphasized that the capitalism brought advantages for Europeans and hardly any for Africans. Social services were scarce or non—existent: health, education and communication were administered more in the breach than in the observance. He stressed that the police and the armed forces were "one of the most significant aspects of the colonial educational system" because they were the lifelines of power. Also, whatever social services Africans enjoyed came about because they were a part of the exploitative system and those who were outside of that monetary system suffered deprivation. Those who produced surplus for export "enjoyed" benefits, which were consistent with that status. That status was defined from the beginning, from the very nature of the relations between the capitalist system and what it portended for the rest of the world, for the countries at the center and those on the periphery. Rodney was careful not to make a distinction between the three—the world, the countries at the center, and those on the periphery. This is consistent with orthodox Marxist thought and one finds its echo in some of the more familiar texts for example in Samir Amin and Paul Sweezy. This view bears some repetition since it is crucial to understanding the social class system in the countries of the center and those on the periphery.

They are, of course, part of the same system with some areas strong and others weak. The former tend to be at the center and the latter on the periphery. These relations are, as have been frequently noted, characterized by the domination of the center countries; the location of the conflict is at the level of production and between the bourgeoisie and the working classes. The conflict has ceased to be a local one, i.e. confined to individual countries; it is now a world conflict in which increasingly these classes are pitted the one against the other for survival. The nature of the conflict is between private interests which guard, preserve and defend themselves as they develop and the forces of production.

The system of class has become increasingly complex as capitalism has expanded and monopolies have increased. This is the case because of the uneven development of the bourgeoisie and the working classes at both the countries at the center and those at the periphery. That uneven development is brought about by decline in profits and periodic crises that are an inevitable part of the capitalist system. Decline in profits more severely affects the working classes at the periphery, giving rise to much hardship. Rodney stressed in his lectures on development the importance of viewing the working classes less as a unit or whole than as an assembly comprising groups affected by the world capitalist system. These included the urban unemployed, peasants, casual laborers and other wage earners. Nobody remained unaffected or untouched by the capitalist system.

These groups found common cause in shared oppression and united at certain times in their history; and the history of colonial peoples recorded such examples of unity, however precarious. But such unity became more challenging in the heady days after independence, when it was severely tested by market forces. Rodney discussed how Africans and Indians in Guyana united against the colonial power because it was in their best interests so to do, even though they did not share a common culture. He also emphatically declared that a separate and distinct culture is no barrier to political unity. For Rodney, this was no theoretical exercise, but a belief susceptible to praxis. Indeed, his later work in Guyana with the Working Peoples Alliance illustrated this: a movement harnessing the energies of different racial and social groups is at once capable of political leadership and national salvation. Moreover, belief in the working class must be seen as an antidote to hydra-headed international capitalism and the combined perfidies of both colonial and peripheral bourgeoisie.

The bourgeoisie on the periphery aroused Rodney's gall because of ambitions that were quite distinct: often at the forefront of movements for national independence, they worked ruthlessly and tirelessly in the interests of capitalist nations and pursued no interests but their own. They thus vacillated, now supporting one side, then the other, and remained indecisive. This was not the stuff of independent movements, where a fair measure of commitment was needed to achieve worthwhile objectives; and certainly not what was required to bring about transformations. Also, as a consequence of vacillation, there was a tendency to resist mass action and so abort their rightful place in history. The working class thus left alone, took over the movement—as occurred in Guyana in 1953, when the first resolute working class movement won an electoral majority.

The history of working class movements is incomplete without a corresponding study of the bourgeoisie who in their own ways fueled the working class movement if only by inaction and neglect. The bourgeoisie have no alternative then but to shoulder forces with the metropolitan bourgeoisie, returning to the mother country in spirit if not in flesh. Their remnants remained in the newly independent countries as foot soldiers to the new realities, or appendages to the system that they did not support. Eventually, they became unwilling and uncommitted socialists in order to safeguard what is left of their interests. This left the working classes as the true heirs to national independence.

For example, the political situation in Guyana in 1954 might be seen as reflecting bourgeoisie leadership, the working class and a broad basis for representation and national independence; the forfeiture of that independence by the colonial power because it threatened to overstep permissible limits of national and international conduct; the re-emergence of the bourgeoisie to positions of influence and power with the assistance and support of metropolitan interests; the re-establishment of the bourgeoisie and their tenuous and incomplete hold, based mostly on military presence and police domination; flirtations with images of socialism under the guise of state capitalism and a passive population confused by indecisiveness and ideological fluctuation. Having lost the support of the working class whom they betrayed and comprised, the bourgeoisie lost the constitutional and psychological justification for continued leadership. As a result they are unable to thwart the re-appearance of race as an issue of contention, even as contending political parties mirror the anxieties of social and class conflicts. In Guyana, the state has become powerful and representative institutions have declined.

The factor of race in social conflict deserves analysis. When Guyana was in the throes of the struggle for nationhood, race as active consideration was muted. It reappeared once the national movement collapsed, when the bourgeoisie and foreign capital combined to encourage divisiveness, dissension and rivalry for social position; also, differences in material prosperity contributed to mutual hostility among the Guyanese people. Thus, the result of the marriage of convenience between the bourgeoisie and foreign interests was the split between them and the working class.

The tragedy of present day Guyana is that in an absence of understandable ideology, and social will the country drifts rudderless, unable to satisfy the aspirations of the bourgeoisie completely and an alienated working class which cannot forgive. Working class unity which showed promising though uneven growth in the decade after World War II, became the victim of state repression and ceased to be a dynamic element in the country.

Race and class in development

The concept of class is important in the development of countries and a failure to understand its dimensions can lead to misunderstanding of its history and significantly affect the development process itself, as Shivji has shown with respect to Tanzania. And Cabral erred when he implied that colonialism superceded the indigenous history of Guinea, an unpleasant interlude in the development of Africa. The class struggle was a continuous one during colonial occupation and the independence struggle was itself a culmination of the efforts of a class empowered by the colonial power.

In Guyana, the independence movement was led by the educated intelligentsia who had received training abroad. These constituted a class of their own in the urban areas. The manner of the challenge of the intelligentsia to the state in both Guyana and the other Caribbean territories was decisively in the colonial tradition and a certain orthodoxy informed their methods of operation e.g. peaceful confrontation, debates, discussion, intermittent strikes etc. in the early days of the independence struggle. This changed later on as independence approached and the class struggle became more manifest as racial groups sought to validate their claims as heirs apparent to the departing colonial power. Such claims were based on state power and economic influence to which both predominant racial groups in Guyana aspired (and it must not be forgotten that one political party, the United Force, also had visions of power and was a collage of wealthy individuals with a sprinkling of national bourgeoisie, again a class factor).

Class is more important than race as an element for understanding the development process in those countries in which race and class conflict. Race is the superficial coating that disguised more profound disturbances of class; and class in Guyana meant more of the trappings of economic power which control of the state could ensure. The conflict of Jagan and Burnham and their respective followers was more about the economic control of the kingdom than differences in race, even though civic disturbances tended to support the view that racial considerations were more significant. But concepts of race and class are by no means clear cut or mutually exclusive. They are often interwoven with economic, cultural and historical variables which add to their complexity and meaning. The more formal dimensions of Marx, and Weber are not always complete guides for navigation through the variables imposed by the legacy of history, or for that matter, explanations of their adherents. In Guyana and the Caribbean class is always a significant variable, wherever analysis starts. To class add race, economic determinism and historical legacy, in varying degree and intensity. But all variables are subsumed by political considerations. And national development must be based on a grasp of the importance of all the constituents of the society including race, economics, culture and history.

The extent to which political considerations influence national development can be seen in the independence movement of many countries, where the class which was foremost in the struggle became the class which initially formed the government. Thus, the initial investment into self-rule was contaminated to begin with and development could only be in the breach rather than the observance.

Summative notes on third world development

For Rodney, the abiding issue remained political. That is, the development of the Third World was first and foremost a political task, from which other aspects of the development process, economic, social, and cultural would follow. He did not intend by this to imply that these others were less important or less necessary; it is that he distinguished between priorities and fundamentals. " Nevertheless, we should distinguish between what may be fundamental, (which I think is economic) and what has priority. The latter refers to the question of timing and that is where politics takes precedence."

Underlying the inability to establish priorities, was the fact that many students of the Third World had not carefully investigated their societies, had not made a careful analysis of its constituents, had not in fact, looked behind the glitter of independence. Had they done so, they might have been able to unearth the contradictions which interfered with development, and " . . . locate . . . the forces of change and the forces of reaction." Rodney believed that these shortcomings derived from a fear of power and its responsibilities. But it is the specific use of power, which at once joins the historian to the service of the people and challenges the intellectual to practical endeavor. The role of the intellectual in the Third World has already been reviewed, but the question of power and its proper uses deserves attention. He distinguished between power and the rhetoric that so often attends both the pursuit of power and its application. Political power is prime force for change: in order to wield it in the interests of the working people, it is necessary to carefully analyze the constituents of the society to identify the progressive elements. In fact, he cautioned that internal elements might have played a more significant role in these societies than previously acknowledged, implying that this could be dangerous for future development. While the importance of power and its application to almost any society is common wisdom, it has not been so treated in many Third World countries which have sublimely carried on the development process on the basis of blueprints culled from colonial archives, or the eager application of models, Marxist or otherwise, without pause. Rodney's own experience in East Africa had taught him the importance of social analysis for agenda setting and delineation of development objectives. Research of this kind enabled societies to charter programs on the basis of reasonable expectations; in brief, to predict the extent and form of social participation; and in this respect the role of the petit bourgeoisie in Tanzania was especially noteworthy. Later, his research into the history of the

Guyanese Working People would indicate, to quote George Lamming, " . . . the very great contribution they [the Indians] have made in the struggle for the creative survival of the Guyanese people." But research could also reveal the social class which could not be counted on in national development—the bourgeoisie. He clearly understood the Caribbean bourgeoisie, who "display characteristics such as self-hate, because they are usually black men who have a certain white orientation." Class divisions were a bane of development and he made several observations on this point, notably in Uganda.

There, the Obote regime had come to power under a system which was not "either fish or fowl," but which had usurped the position of socialists by "pre-empting certain Socialist terminology." Rodney believed that political action was an important and necessary move, in fact, it was part of "a strategy of development." Organization was needed to channel the energies of the "leftists" who wished change. But these were hopelessly divided between those who wanted to work within the system and those who did not. This ambivalence carried right through the years of the Obote government to the fulminations of the rule of Idi Amin. Indeed, Rodney was most critical of those who elected to work within both systems; in effect failing to condemn the Amin coup and electing to serve a rightist dictator who was also neo-colonialist. It underlined an inability to analyze the political situation.

The absence of organization, though not the ability to organize, did not cause him to be pessimistic about the chances for development in the Third World. On the contrary, because of the contradictions that daily arose between government and people, promises and performance, poverty and plenty, social repression and status quo, dissatisfaction would mount and the people regain their revolutionary ardors. But Rodney was not blinded by optimism and he was well aware of the resilience of new forms of imperialism; in fact, he anticipated the new techniques which had been devised by international capital—("after all mosquitoes today are able to cope with DDT")—to combat threats to their well-being; for example, nationalization "can just as well be used by the enemy as by progressive Africans, Asians or Latin Americans."

Part of the resilience of imperialism was political maneuvering by imperialist nations for power, a perpetuation of that power and its consequent role in the deterioration of many third world countries. Development was about withstanding this challenge to the constitutional integrity of independent states. "To evade the issue of getting at the political preconditions to economic development is itself a problem of underdevelopment." He cautioned though about how the challenge was to be mounted: the means by which imperial power exploited was as important as the means by which this exploitation should be addressed. Certain familiar signposts illumined the way: unequal trade and capital flows away from the underdeveloped countries, leading to an absence of development; new forms of exploitation such as tourism, which substituted growth rates for development, and do not "add to the well being of the population;" import substitution, and the establishment of "branch plant" industries and the consequent rise in power and prospects of the transnational corporation; limits on the transfer of technology so as to restrict its development to metropolitan areas. The stranglehold on world technology was itself a modern historical development, which enabled the imperialist countries "to adopt radical new strategies in terms of the international division of labor."

Many independent countries in the Third World had opted for disengagement from the "dominant imperial system" and had seriously examined the theoretical and practical implications. But disengagement, as Rodney insisted, was incomplete without disengagement from "historical bonds" and the formation of "linkages with third world economies . . . within Latin America and within Africa." Rodney saw the movement of economic liberation as necessary for all those countries which were and still are subject to imperialist exploitation. The Third World then was victim of the "whole structure of world imperialism." Rodney's attitude to neo-colonial development, which accompanied post-independence in Africa, was that it was not development at all but disastrous for real development. It was, in fact, a conduit for the continuation of imperialist designs and the spread of international capitalism. There was no disengagement from the colonial scene. In consequence the tentacles of international capitalism plunged deeper into Africa. "Restrictions were placed upon African capacity to make the maximum use of its economic potential," and chronic underdevelopment was the result. The failure of national leadership to understand that African economies are very much a part of that of the capitalist world and suffer from its periodic crises, compound the precarious relationship. The ties that bind are cemented by the presence of the national bourgeoisie and their on-going genuflection before the metropolitan bourgeoisie. This could only be divisive of nationalism and unity and sustain underdevelopment. Underdevelopment was not confined to economics but involved culture as well; and the machinations of the Christian Church, for example, have contributed to the extension of "imperialism by other means." Inevitably, assaults of such variety and intensity placed severe demands on fledgling economies and political systems, causing political instability, "a chronic symptom of the underdevelopment phenomena of contemporary reality." Economies on the periphery are vulnerable because they are dependent.

Development was an enormously complex process, as Rodney was aware and he was as critical of neo-colonialist methods as with other forms, including socialism. A static view of the development process he condemned as limiting because it risked attaching too much importance to the part than the whole; besides which, it is "a sociological absurdity." And he had little patience with the premise that "in human history stagnation is the rule and economic development is the exception that requires special explanation." This view implied that Africa was stagnant and required the prowess of Europe to be developed; and also, its derivative, which emphasized how profitable the slave trade was for Africans. Thus, for Rodney, fundamental weaknesses of bourgeois scholarship were betrayed. Central was the tendency "to treat ahistorically embarrassing phenomena of contemporary reality." Western scholarship has suffered from schizophrenia in its analysis of the non-European world. Thus, for instance, because it refused to admit that development is infinite in scope and all societies have infinite capacity for development, it did not have to answer some of the thorny questions. It became easy then to agree that the non-European world has a limited capacity for development; and also, such a view led one to overemphasize one's own role in development (a kind of knight in shining armor who came to assist, or a deus ex machina who performed the same functions); and finally, it provided cold comfort for those who would not wish to seriously consider the root causes of underdevelopment and how it related to exploitation.

But development and its corollary underdevelopment could lead to unfortunate and regrettable social and psychological attitudes. Racism is a response to the failure to explain development and exploitation. A perverse logic held that if Africans were underdeveloped, they must be so because of certain qualities they possessed, or failed to possess. These qualities, generally considered as elements, which facilitated progress, are held by Europeans. Rodney mourned, like Fanon, the effects of racism on how Africans perceived themselves and what this did to their self-image. That this affected development is clear, for development is about how people change their environment and their material circumstances. The Euro-centric view, or to quote Clive Thomas, the Euro-American views of reality have prevailed which are inimical to freedom, solicitous of dependence and destructive of "the liberating potentialities of socialism."

The racist factor was part of the larger canvas of international relations that dominates Africa and the Third World. And dependence was a conspicuous sector that involved economic relations both internally and externally, as conditions that reproduced the international division of labor, continued to persist. And "historical institutionalization of underdevelopment," was the common refrain for the influence of the more pernicious aspects of the reproduction of international capitalism in the internal economy of the dependent country. Indeed, the Third World shared a common frontier in this respect, as the work of scholars from Latin America and the Caribbean showed. But theory was not to be at the expense of practice, as his own later involvement in Guyana demonstrated. "Theory arises out of practice and must confirm to the test of practice." And it was practice that had exposed the bankruptcy of "bourgeois theory." This was marred by inadequate investment, capital outflow, and growth without development, quite apart from other major disasters: hunger, inequality and racism. The capitalist mode of production had failed as a development tool; and the Marxist alternative increasingly beckoned as a philosophy where praxis —the union of theory and practice—appeared as the only beacon.

NOTES

i. A Prime Minister of an island in the Caribbean is said to have warned that any student from that island who studied in Cuba irrespective of study, would not be allowed to work on the island. George Lamming. *Cimarron,* Vol. 1, No. 1, 1985.

ii. Some scholars sought to differentiate between industrialization and modernization. For example, industrialization was considered part of the factory system and modernization as an international standard to which backward nations could aspire. See Nettl, J.P. and R. Robertson. "Industrialisation, Development or Modernization." *British Journal of Sociology.* 1966.

1. Walter Rodney. *"The Role of the University in Developing Africa." Paper.* University of Dar es Salaam, October 7, 1970. Typescript from the collection at the University of Guyana.

2. Ibid.

3. Ibid., p. 1.

4. Ibid, p. 5.

5. Danns. G. K. *"Militarization and Development: an experiment in nation building."* Transition, Vol 1, no. 1, pp. 23-44.

6. Ibid., p. 5.

7. Ibid., p. 6.

9. Eisenstein, Elisabeth.. *The Printing Press as an agent of change.* London: Cambridge University Press, 1979.

10. Rodney, Walter . *"The Role of the University in Developing Africa."* Paper. University of Dar es Salaam, October 7, 1970. Typescript from the collection at the University of Guyana.

11. Ibid.

12. Ibid., p. 7.

13. Lamming, George. *"The Role of the Intellectual in the Caribbean."* In *Cimarron.* Vol. 1, No. 1, 1985, pp. 13—22.

14. Ibid.

15. Ibid., p. 17.

16. C. Wright Mills. *The Power Elite.* London: Oxford University Press, 1956.

17. H. Schiller. *Mass Communications and American Empire.* New York: Augustus M. Kelley, 1969.

18. Harry S. Truman. *Address.* March 1947, Baylor University.

19. Claude Julien. *America's Empire.* New York: Pantheon Books, 1971; and Pierre Jalee. The Pillage of the Third World. New York: Monthly Review Press, 1966 and Pierre Jalee. Imperialism in the Seventies. New York: The Third Press, 1973.

20. Gibbons, *A. Information, Ideology and Communication.* Lanhman. Maryland: University Press of America, 1985.

21. Rodney, Walter. Op. Cit., 1972, p. 3.

22. Rodney, Walter. Op. Cit., 1972, p. 9.

23. Ibid, p. 9.

24. Rodney, Walter. Op. Cit., 1972, p. 11.

25. Ibid., p. 10.

26. Ibid.

27. Rostow, W. *The Stages of Economic Growth.* New York: Oxford University Press, 1960.

28. Rodney, Walter. *A History of the Upper Guinea Coast 1545-1800,* New York: Monthly Review Press, 1970, p. 25.

29. Walter Rodney. Op. Cit., 1972, p. 27.

30. Ibid.

31. W. E. Moore. *Social Change. New Jersey: Prentice Hall, 1973.*

32. Golding, P. *"Mass Media and Development." Journal* of Communication, Summer, Vol. 24:3, 1974.

33. Etzioni, A. *"The Epigenesis of Political Communities at the International Level."* American *Journal of Sociology, 1963.*

34. Amin. Samir. *The Class Struggle in Africa.*

35. Rodney, Walter. Op. Cit., 1 36. *Celso Furtado. Development and Underdevelopment.* Berkeley: University of California Press, 1964,

36. Ibid.

37. Rodney, Walter. Notes. University of Guyana, undated, p. 1.

38. Rey, Pierre. *Colonialisme, neo-Colonialisme et transition au capitalisme. L'experience de la Comilog au Congo, Paris 1971,* quoted in S. Amin. *Unequal Development.* New York: Monthly Review Press, 1976.

39. Thomas, C. Y.. *The Poor and the Powerless.* New York: Monthly Review Press, 1988, p. 103-110.

40. Rodney, Walter. *"One Hundred Years of Development in Africa."* Lectures. Hamburg, University of Hamburg, 1978, p. 50.

41. Walter Rodney. Ibid, p. 113

42. Ibid, p. 114

43. Ibid., p. 115
44. J. Ellul. The Technological Society. New York: Vintage Books, 1964, p. 21
45. Walter Rodney. Op. Cit., 1998, p. 119
46. Ibid, p. 116
47. Ibid, p. 119
48. Ibid.p. 118
49. Ibid, p. 117
50. Ibid, p. 120
51. Ibid, p. 120
52. Ibid, p. 120
53. C. Y. Thomas. " Capitalism in Guyana: An Assessment of Burnham's Cooperative Republic." In F. Ambursley & R. Cohen. *Crisis in the Caribbean.* New York: Monthly Review Press, 1983, pp. 27-48.
54. C. Y. Thomas. *The Poor and the Powerless.* New York: Monthly Review Press, 1988, pp. 214-215
55. Walter Rodney. One Hundred Years of Development in Africa. *Lectures.* University of Hamburg, 1984, pp. 26-27.
56. Ibid., p. 126
57. Ibid., p. 126
58. Ibid., p. 128
59. Ibid., p. 129
60. Ibid., p. 129
62. Ibid., p. 219
63. Ibid., p. 215
64. Ibid., p. 130
65. Ibid.
66. Walter Rodney. *How Europe Underdeveloped Africa.* London: Bogle l'Ouverture, 1974, p. 260
67. Walter Op. Cit, p. 127
68. Ibid, p. 129
69. Walter Rodney. *A History of the Guyanese Working People,* 1881-1905. Baltimore: The Johns Hopkins University Press, 1974.
70. Walter Rodney. *The Groundings with my Brothers.* London: Bogle l'Ouverture, 1969
71. Paul M. Sweezy. *The Theory of Capitalist Development.* New York: Monthly Review Press, 1956, p. 327
72. Clive Y. Thomas. *The Poor and the Powerless.* New York: Monthly Review Press, 1988, pp. 251-265
73. Issa G. Shivji. *Class Struggles in Tanzania.* New York: Monthly Review Press, 1976.
74. A. Cabral. *Revolution in Guinea.* p. 56
75. *Discussion* at the African Studies Center, UCLA., May 30, 1972.
76. Ibid. 1972
77. Ibid., 1972
78. George Lamming, the eminent Caribbean author, wrote this in the Introduction to Walter Rodney. *A History of the Guyanese Working People, 1881-1905.* Baltimore: The John Hopkins University Press, 1981. This work must be seen as a corrective to the generally held view that there was a history of racial animosity between Indians and Africans in Guyana. Social research of this kind can be especially beneficial to those societies where ethnic conflict persists. It forces appraisal, points to past common areas of compatibility and shared destinies and gets rid of convenient stereotypes.

79. Ibid. p. 19
80. Ibid, p. 21
81. Ibid, p. 25
82. Ibid, p. 24
83. Ibid, p. 15
84. Ibid, p. 5
85. Ibid, p. 15
86. Walter Rodney. *How Europe Underdeveloped Africa.* Washington, D.C. Howard University Press, 1972, p. 34.
87. Walter Rodney. "African History and African Development Planning. Paper. University of Dar es Salaam, undated.
88. Ibid., p. 36
89
90. Walter Rodney. "African History and African Development Planning." *Paper.* University of Dares Salaam: undated.
Benjamin Higgins. Economic Development: Principles, Problems and Policies. London: 1959, p. 3. Quoted in Walter Rodney. *African History and African Development Planning.*
91. D. Neumark. Foreign Trade and Economic Development in Africa: a historical perspective. (1964), p. 2. Quoted in Walter Rodney. "African History and African Development Planning." Paper. University of Dar es Salaam. undated.
92. Walter Rodney. "African History and African Development Planning." *Paper.* University of Dar es Salaam, undated.
93. Walter Rodney. "African History and African Development Planning." *Paper.* University of Dar es Salaam: 1973, p. 3
94. Clive Y. Thomas. *Dependence and Transformation. Monthly Review* Press: New York, 1974, p. 307
95. Ibid., p. 4
96. Ibid, p. 5

Chapter Six

The Approach to Armageddon

Rodney 's tenure in Jamaica preceded his African adventure and must be considered in some ways a significant watershed. For it was in Jamaica that he honed the contribution that he would always be renowned for: identification with the masses and political activism. The public intellectual sought always to unite two divergent streams of political life. He brought to the academy an intellectual rigor and to the masses of the people he addressed in Kingston, a sincerity and honesty that many of their leaders could not match.

What Rodney brought to Jamaica was a sophisticated political consciousness that was shorn of middle class pretense that most Jamaicans and West Indians lived by. It was a state of affairs bequeathed from colonial. The middle class was the class that people aspired to and when once they were within grasp of what they wanted were encouraged to forsake the less privileged. Indeed, membership of this class carried an unspoken understanding, namely, that once arrived its members would forsake the under-privileged. The Jamaican situation was typical of the rest of the West Indies varying in degree rather than kind. The middle class was a buffer between working people who had limited aspirations and the rest who were accorded on the basis of education, patronage or dalliance the goods and services that the society could muster.

Rodney had forsaken the middle class, left the rewards of university education, the sophistication of foreign travel and brought a renewed understanding of world affairs gleaned from his work in his earlier experience in Tanzania; and the many seminars he and his fellow sympathizers had with C.L.R. James in London. In fact, one could see the influence of James on Rodney. James' work, emphasized contact with the masses and he believed that there were endless possibilities in the ordinary man if only if his energies could be harnessed.

Rodney inherited a Jamaica whose ambitions were not satisfied in the post independence period. There were reasons for this. Many of the leaders and managers in public office were members of the middle class and many viewed any change in the political landscape as threatening their positions. They could not deal with any left-ward trend, (even though, many affected positions on the left) they could not countenance change in its wider aspect. They subscribed to the myth of a multiracial Jamaica, believed in the inevitability of gradualness in economic terms and valued peace at all costs. But as Carl Stone writes in *Class Race and Political Behavior* there was "growing economic deprivation with increasing levels of racial and class militancy among the poorer classes in Kingston and St. Andrew" which the governing class could not tolerate and its response was heavy handed: the 1960 arrest on treason charges, the trial and imprisonment of Rev. Claudius Henry, a radical evangelist; the 1963 retaliation in Coral Gardens against the Rastafarians, who had taken a stand because of the failure of the government to settle their dispute over land; and this, linked to continued discrimination against the Rastafarians. Inevitably this cauldron of social neglect contributed to a climate of uncertainty on the island and the state visit of Emperor Haile Selassie of Ethiopia in 1966 but furthered the outrage of many of the Rastafarians who even as they saluted him, burned with indignation at the reality of their social condition. That social condition was further exacerbated by measures such as bulldozing houses and their replacement by low cost housing awarded on the basis of party affiliation and increased activity by trade unions and political parties inflamed the situation. The violence of 1967 led to the declaration of emergency in Western Kingston. Rodney was banned from Jamaica on his return from a conference of black writers.

He was considered a dangerous individual whose very presence was considered inflammatory by the government. But the authorities misread the script. Rodney had in his early days at the University appealed to the "young and restless"; those who seemingly felt abandoned and without hope. They were black working people and Rodney was able to share common cause with them. But he wished action, wished that the working class with whom he shared and tried "to find meaning among the mass of the population who are daily performing a miracle . . ." His message carried hope and the strong possibility of unrealized action based on their potential. He embraced the Rastafarians, long considered outsiders and they looked up to him, for he understood their concerns: longing for Africa, their spiritual despair allied to difficulties of living and social neglect.

Rodney made common cause with these, the poor, the working

peoples and such intellectual forces that were interested in change. What Rodney achieved was a unity between them for social action. It was this consummate ability to weld them that created discord in government circles who saw him as a revolutionary bent on destroying the social structure of Jamaica. Rodney did not create a revolutionary movement: multiple dissatisfactions had existed prior to his arrival among the Rastafarians, the left, and the poor. These disparate interests were much influenced by other currents. The Black Power movement that grew out of the civil rights struggles in the U.S., the Garveyites, the Marxists, and disenchanted intellectuals. And intellectuals who did not follow the prescribed script were considered threatening. For example, the Undesirable Publications Law, 1968, outlawed books and magazines that the governing party, the Jamaica Labor Party, JLP, considered inimical. Among such were works of Stokeley Carmichael, Malcolm X and the previous year 1967, the Law was amended to include all English language publications coming from Moscow, Peking and Cuba. And as if this were not enough, the governing party seized the passports of well known intellectuals and banned others from entry. But if the governing party believed that an assault on intellectual opinion would hinder the onward march of progressive forces of change, it was sadly mistaken. The roots of protest ran deep, for above all Black Power touched a particularly sensitive chord among Jamaicans. Rupert Lewis explains (1998,p114)

But let it be understood in this connection that Rodney was no crude black power advocate. His Marxist application to the particular culture of the English-speaking West Indies with their polyglot ethnicity would have considered racism as a contradiction and destructive of the whole.

The history of the ban on Rodney on his return from the conference of Black Writers in 1968 is a well-told tale and never better told than by Ralph Gonsalves, then president of the West Indies Student Union, and now prime minister of St. Vincent. (Gonsalves, Ralph. 1979. The Rodney Affair. Caribbean Quarterly (25) 3: 1-24.) According to Gonsalves, students at the University donned their red academic gowns and walked into Kingston to the office of Prime Minister Shearer and were joined in route by the urban young people many of whom had earlier listened to Rodney's groundings about Africa. To them, it was a great injustice and given their own dissatisfactions with the police, joined common cause with the undergraduates; 13 buses were destroyed , 72 damaged, 90 buildings set on fire, 11 policemen were injured and 23 people were arrested. This spontaneous uprising, harmless in intent, was a sad commentary on the decision making of the Jamaica Labor Party, JLP, in its overzealous pursuit of a distinguished academic. The JLP had mis-read the script, believing that non Jamaican students were threat-ening an assault on the Republic of Jamaica. But this action on its part would not go away and had widespread repercussions not only for Jamaica but for the whole region. Fundamentally what was in-volved was social change from an independent still colonial society that had not dealt with the consequences of change and what this meant to the mass of people who had not benefited from the new arrangements. The repercussions from the dastardly act by the then Jamaican government were huge: many of Rodney's support-ers and sympathizers joined common cause. Rupert Lewis mentions how the radical movements, hitherto muted, gave voice and the rev-olution in Trinidad, 1970, provides example of just one of the pro-gressive movements in the region; also, publications such as *Tapia and Moko* of the New World group in Trinidad, *Abeng*, the Wind-ward Islands, *Outlet*, Antigua and in Guyana the Movement Against Oppression published *Ratoon.*

Rodney left Jamaica in 1968 and did not return until 1976 dur-ing Carifesta, a regional cultural festival that originated in Guyana; 1969-1974 he taught at the University of Dar es Salaam in Tanzania and word of his experiences there, in addition to his pub-lications, preceded him to Guyana. It was not the homecoming that he may have wished. His appointment as professor at the Univer-sity of Guyana was rescinded when pressure was brought to bear by the Board of Governors on the University's appointments commit-tee. It was the first indication of the continuing struggle that was to envelop the historian and pit him against political forces that viewed his return with increasing anxiety.

But Rodney had already been briefed about the affairs of Guyana before his return and arguably, the action to rescind his ap-pointment could have come as no surprise to him. Already in Tan-zania he had corresponded with Moses Bhagwan, a former member of the Peoples Political Party, PPP, about political developments. Bhagwan was himself concerned about the PPP's inability to come to terms with the racial question; and the riots in 1962 reinforced his conviction that he could not continue to remain under its ban-ner. The PPP's Marxist-Leninist position seemed to him too rigid, narrow, and simplistic to make any serious inroads on the social, economic, cultural and political problems facing a country on the verge of independence; and the Peoples National Congress, PNC, lacked any coherent policy for dealing with the social strife. Mired in self-reflection, the PNC saw itself saw itself as a vehicle for the exercise of leadership of the nation. Burnham, its titular leader, promoted both his own dominance and the sovereignty of the party and at times, the distinction between the two remained blurred.

Both political parties either from lack of policy or ineptness did not seriously address the racial polarities that had begun to raise their head in the 60s. In fact, they both might have wished racial considerations to disappear altogether; or perhaps, naively believed that economic and other matters would erase them. But this was disingenuous: for race could not be separated from any other national consideration. Indeed, both Burnham and Jagan could not have failed to realize that from 1953 when they both contested for the leadership of the PPP. Both of them, while not playing the racial card were well aware of its implications. Perhaps because of this, race as a factor in national politics, was muted and not deliberately confronted. It was easier to indulge in the heavy wine of Marxist ideology that they both found beguiling if not intoxicating; and also, too, the struggle for leadership of the party concentrated their energies, leaving them unable to function effectively outside the demands of party loyalties.

Political independence was the main matter under consideration in the 60s. Ethnic rivalry important though it was, quite paled beside the significance of which party was to lead the country into independence. Not for the first time was Guyana let down by its politicians. The riots of 1962 were an important milestone that signaled a frustrated electorate reluctant to wait on leaders "who were neither bold nor flexible to make the necessary bold decisions and concessions that were required in that period with regard to the gravity of the racial question". While ideological questions dominated the two parties, the rank and file sought supremacy in the streets and the occasion was the budget prepared by Nicholas Kaldor, a Cambridge economist whose aim was the introduction of a capital gains tax and a compulsory savings scheme. The budget was labeled "communist" by the opposition UF allied to the Peoples National Congress of Forbes Burnham. The riots destroyed some considerable part of the center of the capital, Georgetown. But more disturbances were to follow: the following year the introduction of a Labor Relations Bill to institute a secret ballot in deliberations between employers and union representatives caused excessive commotion. The longest strike of any union in the country lasted 80 days and caused major industrial disruption. The strike became a trial of strength between the government of Cheddi Jagan's, PPP and the opposition parties of Forbes Burnham's PNC and Peter D'Aguiar's United Force, UF, in which any concessions by the government were renewed occasions for further demands. An investigated report published by the *Times of London, 16 April, 1967,* revealed the most blatant form of vote rigging among Commonwealth countries in which the CIA played a significant part in the activities at the poll which they were indeed to repeat in two subsequent elections. It was a sad commentary on their creativity that their methods were so blatant as not to escape even casual attention.

The U.S. had involved itself in the affairs of the country because of its fears that Jagan, a politician on the left, could not be trusted; also the U.S. viewed with suspicion any administration that flirted or seemed to flirt with Cuba or the Soviet Union. American president Kennedy could not afford another Cuba in the western hemisphere and it certainly seemed that Cheddi Jagan, the leader of the PPP, could be a force in perpetuity, given the demographics of the country that would always favor the Indian vote. Accordingly, U.S. investment in fraudulent elections was extended to include approaches to the British government to change the constitution from first - past - the - post to proportional representation, PR. The primary aim of this election stratagem was that PR would encourage the growth of small parties and bring about the end of Jagan's term in office. The second aim was hopeful: that Burnham, the leader of the PNC, who had already impressed U.S. President Johnson, would replace Jagan as the new leader in Guyana. That the CIA, aided by the British government. excelled at this strategy, led to the ascension to power of Forbes Burnham in the election of 1964, 1968, 1973. (Latin American Bureau, London 1984, p40-42.)The decline of the PPP and the increasing violence of the opposition resulted in the fanning the flames of conflict without any restorative or mitigating factors; and the ascension to power of Burnham's party as a result of the new arithmetic of proportional representation only exacerbated the situation. Seemingly, the country could look forward only to continuing unrest as the fraudulent elections of 1973 illustrated.

Walter Rodney arrived in Guyana in 1975.But Guyana had already been racially polarized under the previous governing administration as the elections of 1964 fought under the system of proportional representation made quite clear. Racial violence, murder, arson dotted the landscape as the PNC and UF joined common cause against the PPP labeling it as communist – a forerunner to later troubles. The PPP won 24 seats, the PNC 22 and the UF 7 seats and the Governor General invited the PNC to form a government in coalition with the UF. British Guiana became Guyana at independence in 1966, with a residue of bitterness that the new administration of the PNC and UF were powerless to prevent. This became all the more so, when massive rigging accompanied the elections of 1968; overseas voting, voting by proxy, faulty counting and other civic hazards including violence were the menu for further disasters. Convincing evidence of the fraud was the documentary produced by Granada television and a British research institute also reported that no more than 15 percent of the people on electoral lists used in Britain were valid. (Guyana: Fraudulent Revolution. Latin American Bureau, London. 1984, p. 49)

Co-operative republic

Once in power without the UF, the PNC lost no time in declaring the country a Co-operative Republic in 1970, replacing the Governor General by a non-executive President. Followed quickly, the nationalization of the bauxite industry, and the nationalization of all major foreign economic interests except banks and insurance companies. In foreign affairs Guyana established diplomatic relations with Cuba and hosted the Non-Aligned Heads of government meeting in 1973. But these external moves could not gloss over unsuccessful domestic economic policies. For example, the nationalization of the sugar company which Booker Brothers controlled for over a century, resulted in decline in production as managerial personnel left the country before the replacements were properly and adequately trained; and to this, add the corporations owned and operated by the state and there was a precipitous decline in the standard of living for persons not affiliated with the party in power. The state was thus encouraged to enlist a cadre of civil servants and bureaucrats who swore allegiance to it and job patronage became very much official policy. To put it bluntly, the standard of living of the middle class did not drop precipitously, but the manual workers were hard put to satisfy their daily needs. There was no noticeable change in economic conditions in the years immediately following independence as reflected in the social and economic disparities. One successful enterprise was the co-operatives of the African Society for Cultural Relations with Independent Africa, AS-CRIA, dedicated to the uplift of black workers who believed they were betrayed by the PNC, or felt their dignity compromised as a result of racial strife. Government-run co-operatives did not benefit workers and became undertakings in which profits were shared among the middle class to the exclusion of those who did not share elite status. Thus, the main objective of the Co-operative Republic was to give government a lion's share in the operation of the economy and this failed.

Import substitution was another brainchild of the PNC. This had much to recommend it if it could fit into the overall scheme of economic policy. But it did not. In the view of C.Y. Thomas and

Percy Hintzen, the PNC was in dreadful hurry to prove itself because it was well aware that there were opposition groups in the wings and the WPA had begun to make exent pressure. Also, too, the nationalizations of the day were not without serious consequences: the departure of overseas managers and their replacement by locals who had yet to learn their trade. Indeed, Guyana on the whole has suffered from a dearth of managers in all phases of industry and the exodus that started in the 1970s has affected the country to the present day. No general plan coordinated the export and import departments and the latter became means for the privileged few to import the products they wished. Thus, in a haphazard fashion a policy designed to encourage the campaign to feed, clothe and house the nation failed to give it the necessary impetus for growth. Nor was this the sole area of challenge. GUYBAU, the state corporation that ran the bauxite industry showed a decline in production even as the wage bill increased. This was a sober example of the limits of state ownership in the absence of management and the presence of a patronage system that demoralized skilled workers driving them away.

But management problems, however troublesome, quite paled beside the various nationalization agreements which, as Clive Thomas points out, incurred large debts; and new contractual agreements were a drain on foreign reserves. The result of which was that there was a decline in per capita income and unemployment in the years 1974-76 reached as high as 40%. The worldwide inflation and the oil crisis did not contribute to the malaise of Guyana's economy; the International Monetary Fund, IMF, came to the country's aid but typically at a time when the country could not meet its debt payments. The upshot of all this financial insecurity was to plunge Guyana into a state of chronic insecurity, what with shortages of food, electricity and transportation; and the inevitable result was suffering among the masses of people. There was another consequence.

The Burnham government which had gained power in 1973 as a result of complicity with Britain, the US and the CIA had doubtful legitimacy, could not muster any public will and what little it did obtain was of a very false kind. It could not govern because it did not have the support of the masses, clever enough to realize that they had been hoodwinked by external powers; and since it could not govern legitimately, it could only rule; and this explains much of "the repressive escalator" of the remaining years of the Burnham regime. At the 1973 elections the PNC won 37 seats, the PPP 14 and the UF two. The elections ended in controversy: two supporters of the PPP were shot when they intervened to protest the removal of ballot boxes to a central establishment by the armed forces. The elections were important too, for they revealed the disillusionment of the PNC stronghold in Georgetown, the capital — two elections 1968 and 1973 were subject to gross violations of fraud. And it was clear that the PNC intended to utilize all power necessary for the enactment of its leaders' will. These elections marked the coalescence of an opposition that began to react to increasing harassment: Ratoon, and MAO, Movement against Oppression, represented leading Marxist intellectuals, WPVP, another Marxist group after the tradition of Communist China, became loosely affiliated with the WPA, explored common cause with the PPP, but later joined forces with the Liberator Party; the Indian Political Revolutionary Associates, IPRA, and the Peoples' Democratic Movement later known as the Vanguard for Liberation and Democracy, DVM. And already the Burnham regime, with the confidence born of inevitability to rule, reacted: for example, the attempted kidnapping of Clive Thomas, an economist at the University of Guyana, the attempted assassination of Dr. Josh Ramsammy, also of the University. Both of these scholars were part of Ratoon and MAO, Movement Against Oppression. And out of the motley crew of assorted Marxists of different persuasion grew the pressure group of the Working Peoples Alliance, WPA.

When Rodney arrived in Guyana, there were already committed activists who were busily formulating the agenda of the WPA; and there was need for extensive work to thwart the machinations of the leader of the PNC. The country was already smarting from his monstrous ego, and certainly, Burnham's doctrine of the "paramountcy" of the party was a barely disguised method of maintaining absolute control of the country, through the agency of his party, the PNC: authoritarianism by legislation. Burnham had failed to honor the recommendations of the International Commission of Jurists and ignored the report on racial justice; and further, his government passed the National Security Act that allowed it to suspend the writ of Habeas Corpus, and detain persons whom it considered dangerous or threatening; and the free press suffered throughout his regime. A free press, so central to a democratic state, was threatened with extinction as the party took over the dissemination of information. The state usurped all the functions normally associated with the socialist state it pretended to be; indeed socialism was dishonored in the affairs of Guyana by a party that shouted its adherence from the roof tops. It failed the cardinal test of socialism; that is, socialism could only be built as a consequence of free elections and the system of top down mechanism did not do justice to the frustrated masses below, who were ready and willing to emancipate themselves. It was a tragedy, not unknown in post colonial countries whose leaders have stifled the masses, imprisoning their energies, and frustrating their abilities; and the Declaration of Sophia, a pompous statement of principle, acknowledged that the Co-operative Republic of Guyana had come into being determined to bring about such changes that the PNC had already dismally failed to implement.

According to Clive Thomas (1983) Its main constituents were four: the growth of state capitalism; control of the economy and that included production and the right to dispose of human resources; the growth of a strong military sector as both a threat to prevent untoward activity; and active in the pursuance of activity it perceives as inimical to the state.

The state is now very much on the way and from here on, the government, through state-manipulation, propaganda and force, makes it unmistakably clear that it cannot be changed by legal or constitutional means.

There was immediate evidence of this: local government elections constitutionally due every two years since 1970 were never held. The ideological apparatus of the state was extended to include private schools which were abolished in 1975; all media became part of the state including newspapers and two radio stations and newsprint curtailed for all media not supported by the state.. A country of 700,000 people was made to feel the persistent arm of the state in all spheres of human activity. A new constitution making "Comrade" Burnham, Executive President for life, ensured his inviolability from arrest, criminal or civil proceedings during his term of office or thereafter. He was head of state, supreme executive authority, commander-in-chief, affected a General's uniform and occasionally mounted a white horse, reminding of the buffoonery of Emperor Bokassa of the Central African Republic. Burnham made sure that his every whim was obeyed. Guyana Human Rights Association report 1980-81 declared:

The courts have been used as an instrument of political harassment on a widespread scale. This has been made possible by the subordination of the Judiciary to the political executive in a number of ways

And the Organization of Commonwealth Bar Associations condemned the regime's Criminal Law Bill and the Administration of Justice Bill and utterly disapproved of the former because of 'its infringement of the citizens' right to trial by jury' and also because of its 'retrospective effect on pending criminal proceedings to annul decisions of Court of Justice and to abrogate the civil liberties of the citizens of Guyana'. The 'repressive escalator' that had gradually begun to envelop the country had an unanticipated effect: agricultural and factory workers achieved a tenuous class solidarity which, as Clive Y. Thomas suggests, cut across traditional racial boundaries; as evidenced by the 1977, 1978 and 1979 strikes by the bauxite and sugar workers.

In the 70s too, the country experienced a productivity crisis that contributed to the worsening human rights situation, exacerbated by the increasing use of violence by armed gangs in the capital; and the depredations of Rabbi Washington and the House of Israel, who were in the pay of the PNC, contributed to national insecurity. The referendum of 1978 was a significant watershed that defined the wider limits of public disgust with the state. *Dayclean*, the two page mimeograph of the WPA was to chortle.

But the single most important fact about the referendum of July 10 was the silence in the street. The people of Guyana boycotted the referendum and stayed home The absence of voters at the 1978 referendum pointed to two elements: an electorate that had grown weary of the continued spurious claims by the government about co-operative socialism, in the face of massive evidence to the contrary; and second, the decline in standard of living among the workers as a consequence of state ownership. Unemployment between 1975-80 was 40 percent and house, feed, and clothe yourself campaign was an embarrassment. Also, the laws, previously mentioned, seemed designed to prevent if not control the emergence of progressive forces within the country; and trade unions could not strike without the permission of the government.

The plight of the worker in a Guyana faced with the debilitating fortunes from the rising price of oil, non-productivity in the main industries, bauxite, and sugar, was pitiable. Both of the main political parties, the PNC and the PPP appeared bankrupt of ideas with which to stem polarization and economic hardship. In a bid to strengthen its own waning power, the PPP in 1977 called a strike in the sugar industry, traditionally a strong point and a strike that lasted 135 days. But this came to no avail and nothing much was gained as the governing party utilized the armed forces and the House of Israel to replace the striking workers in estates close to the capital. The strike failed. If its aims were to embarrass the government or to resuscitate the fortunes of the PPP, it signally failed to do. Indeed, the PPP was seriously compromised, for its hold on the Trades Union Congress, TUC, appeared shaky at best, in as much as the PNC was prepared to go to any lengths to frustrate any opposition.

The failure of the sugar strike was significant in other ways. The strike revealed the ineffectiveness of the opposition party, PPP; and

to the governing party, PNC, it provided a certain deceptive infalli-
bility about its ability to rule without challenge – a challenge that
had already begun to appear with the Working Peoples Alliance,
WPA. For example, *Dayclean,* the party organ was sued because it
had not placed a bond and Eusi Quayana, one of the defendants,
asked the court to declare itself free of political influence; and the
case was postponed indefinitely and afterwards dropped completely. Media control was central to a government flirting with totalitarianism and *Dayclean,* a single page mimeographed sheet of
the WPA, challenged the ruling party and two of its members were
carted off to prison. When in 1974, Arnold Rampersaud, a PPP activist, was charged with shooting a policeman at a toll stop on the
Courentyne, his trial assumed political dimensions. Rodney and the
WPA opposed the transfer of the trial from a predominantly Indian
area to the capital, a predominantly black area, in which, given the
racial strife, Rampersaud might well have been found guilty and
pay the ultimate price. Rodney and the WPA marshalled a team of
lawyers from the Caribbean and after three attempts to reach a verdict, eventually the case was dismissed on a legal technicality. The
Rampersaud defense allowed Rodney to claim the moral high
ground as far as race relations were concerned. Rodney put this in
context:
    "The whole history of the 1960s was a history in which our polit-
ical choices were fundamentally dictated, not by any class position
but by the on-going race conflict..." Lewis (1998).
    With the PPP moribund, the PNC incapable of progressive vi-
sion, both seemed unable to take Guyana beyond the racial agenda
that had dictated policy for much of the violent 60s. The country
was dispirited and resigned to the leadership of Forbes Burnham
whose PNC won the 1965 elections and two subsequent elections,
1968 and 1973, both massively rigged. The effect of this was to accentuate racial divisions that drove each group behind irreconcil-
able positions. The country had attained what Donald Horowitz
called "racial census," meaning elections results determined by voting along racial lines. But within parties, however, there was evidence of a schizoid manifesto: while denying a racial agenda, each
group did not hesitate to encourage precisely such at the grassroots
level. And Cheddi Jagan insisted that his followers in the PPP vote
on Marxist-Leninist lines that eschewed race.
    Guyanese might have been confused but they were not blind to
party political machinations and it was this that paved the way for
the appearance of the WPA as a pressure group in 1974. Similar
protests against the inadequacies of government power occurred at
the same time in the region. In the Caribbean as a whole the post-

war generation was coming to terms with the imbalances that accompanied decolonization and political independence. Many realized that new rulers did not guarantee better living conditions for the masses. The New World Group of the 60s comprised a group of middle class intellectuals, including Miles Fitzpatrick, David de Caires, C.Y. Thomas (Guyana), George Beckford, (Jamaica) and Lloyd Best (Trinidad). But while they were able people cognizant of the problems of the region, none of them was convinced of the need for self-emancipation of the working people.

The WPA had addressed the main issue in Guyana from which all else related. No economic progress could be made in the country as long as it remained racially divided and progress of any kind was held up in consequence. Indeed, "Bread and Justice," an article by Clive Y. Thomas and "Racial Insecurity and the Political System" of Eusi Quayana became the central foci of WPA's objectives as a political party in 1979. Both captured the essence of the problems facing the country: corruption and racial polarity. And the overarching question of ethnic identity dominated the lives of most people and became the platform of the future development of the WPA. It was a platform with which Walter Rodney could sympathize. Race and racial concerns were a contradiction, working against the national unity. Speaking to Jamaican writer Andrew Salkey he said:

Rodney's vision of Guyana was of a multiracial society where each individual counts equally. "Because the moment that power is equitably distributed among the various ethnic groups then the very relevance of making the distinction between groups will be lost." This was a challenge to the PNC; for so much of their power depended on playing the race card, a position shared by the PPP, the opposition party. Rodney's position was a threat. Guyana which had endured the multiple infusions of race politics did not gladly welcome a philosopher whose vision did not accord with its own. Rodney was a hero even before he arrived home as news of his expulsion from Jamaica had preceded him and his books had given him currency among intellectuals in the country. The PPP, IPRA, Ratoon, ASCRIA and MAO, joined in denouncing the decision to deny him the professorship of history at the University of Guyana; protest meetings were held in the capital; readings from his essay, *Groundings with My Brothers*, adorned some of the speeches. "Black power is not racially intolerant. It is the hope of the black man that, he should have power over his own destinies. This is not incompatible with a multiracial society..." Black power was not exclusive; for him it included all the oppressed Blacks and Indians in the West Indies for whom power was denied. And it was these very groups that joined in the protests against the regime that denied him the right to teach at the University of Guyana. The various ethnic groups had begun to have confidence in what he had to say and expectations began to grow in what he could accomplish. His speeches inspired confidence both within the capital and beyond and he treated the whole country very much as his oyster. And it became clear that this man who aspired to be a Marxist Leninist had a profound message: the self-emancipation of the working class. To illustrate his meaning he told the story of lions at an art exhibition who were truly astonished at the claims on canvas made by hunters. After a while, a lion shook his head with resignation and said "If only lions could paint!" If the hunted, Rodney implied, could free themselves of their limitations they might tell another story, record another history. To that end Rodney became part of the outreach programs of the WPA organized by the Organization of the Working People and together with Clive Y. Thomas conducted classes in political economy and labor economics respectively. Rodney concentrated on the bauxite communities of Linden, Kwakwani, and Everton.

The political and educational activities of the WPA affected a moribund political culture: the PNC was galvanized into activity; and the PPP which had worker support in the sugar industry increased its commitment. As Rodney continued his public lectures on nonracial politics, the PPP in 1977 proposed the National Patriotic Front whose principle objective was a political solution: which ever party won a fair and free election, it would stand unopposed should the other decide to accede to the Presidency. An unwritten assumption of this attempt at national reconciliation was that the PNC, the governing regime, was without credence; it lacked support, legitimacy; and its will to govern was defended by an increasing militarization of the armed forces and the police. In any case the PNC ridiculed the power sharing arrangement. The government's moral fibre was further weakened by the Jonestown mass suicide of 914 people in November 1978. According to the Human Rights Report "collusion by the Guyana government, of at least a passive nature, with the Jonestown leadership requires that they accept part of the responsibility for what occurred." (January 1980-June 1981) And the total ignorance of the people about the details of the suicide, which had been reported on the BBC 24 hours previously, pointed to the existence of tight controls over the media. Rodney was no doubt about the government's collusion in the Jonestown disaster.

If we were to draw attention to the horrendous events of Jonestown, we would see that what occurred through neglect on the part of both the US and the Guyanese governments. The US Government had admitted in its reports that it had done far less than it should have done for US citizens who were at Jonestown and some type of intervention on behalf of those citizens might well have avoided the holocaust. . . .

Scolding the US.

The point is if the US is going to be allowed to get away with making a lot of pious statements about human rights when, in fact, in this region, it proceeds indirectly to bolster a tyrant whose quality is no different than any dictator who arose in any other part of the world. (Rodney 1983, p3, Guyana Forum, 1980, 3.)

The government became further embroiled even as Rodney and his cohorts in the WPA stimulated public awareness about the state of oppression under which they lived. And the time could hardly have been more propitious. A bauxite strike in July 1979 against the wage freeze was joined by the sugar workers acting in sympathy. 42 bauxite workers were arrested and subjected to tear gas in their cells; scabs were employed to break the strike of sugar workers. In the meantime, public education and agitation by the WPA continued amidst the full glare of the unsavory conduct and activities of the PNC; and the failed referendum of 1978 perpetuated conditions for national uncertainty and disequilibrium. Rodney was arrested September 13 in Leonora a village on West Coast Demerara. Dr. Rupert Roopnaraine hid from killers all night amid the stalks in a cane field, but managed to make his escape under cover of an early dawn. Rodney was again arrested at Linden, a town that was the center of the bauxite industry, on October 3; released within 24 hours, he returned to a ransacked home where quantities of books were seized. He slept in a different home each night but managed to leave Guyana illegally to attend the independence celebrations of Zimbabwe which Burnham also attended. The shock of the meeting has not been recorded!

The government was under pressure, not least from the opposition parties, PPP and WPA and the referendum campaign of 1978 designed to change the constitution failed to raise public hopes. Even a casual nod in the direction of democracy was not taken; indeed, the administration frustrated the very socialism that it claimed to believe in by denying political democracy. Lack of representation was often a pretext for the imposition of autocracy and repression and it was this that Guyana was on the verge of although the governing regime was at pains to camouflage its intents through questionable legality.

And having succeeded in controlling the country through social and political networking, threats, violence and corruption, the PNC proceeded to effect controls of the main areas of civic society; e.g. parliament, the courts, civil service and local government. And while controlling domestic affairs Burnham established friendly relations with Cuba and the Soviet Union. Strict party control was very much in the tradition of Soviet leadership and the party flag and not the national flag adorned public buildings on important occasions, symbolizing the supremacy of the PNC.

The management of the state by a narrow elite cast serious doubts on the entire democratic process and also on the much heralded socialism trumpeted by regime spokespersons and media apologists – and the nationalization of the private media would have facilitated the propaganda of the state. Indeed, the lack of democracy was the antithesis of socialism.

The PNC consistently and as a matter of policy abrogated the freedom that was an important part of democratic thinking. Indeed, the party seemed to celebrate policies that were more in keeping with those of totalitarian countries. For example, the "paramountcy" doctrine identified three areas: establishing a linkage between the party and the ministry of national development, extension of the armed forces and control of the economy through the dissemination of state funds. The first area gave the party control over funds allocated for national development; the second ensured that the armed forces would be subject to party discipline and by ensuring that the military was not bypassed, made scholarships to secondary institutions dependent on national service; finally, control of the press facilitated the manipulation of the ideological apparatus of the state.

But the curbing of any semblance of independent criticism that did not stem from the party press resulted in an information gap and the country was robbed of news which could assist the development process; and even the radio stations fell under this umbrella as Radio Demerara, acquired from Rediffusion in 1976, joined Guyana Broadcasting Corporation as a second channel. The state's control of information was therefore complete. And Guyanese from all walks of life had gradually grown accustomed to a pattern of conduct on the part of governing authorities: social, political repression that mocked their humble attempts at representation in their daily lives as economic policies seemed irrelevant to their standard of living: slow rates of growth and diminished productivity led to the inability of government to control the national economy; shortage of foreign currency affected trade; state corporations were bywords of corruption, elitism; and the military apparatus, including paramilitary groups, stifled any perceived opposition and violence became part of the menu of power. And through its ministrations

the Peoples Temple had insinuated itself in the life if not the conduct of government.

The year of the turn

The Guyana government began to appear vulnerable as a result of
the consequence of its brutality. Hardly a section of the Caribbean,
or the world press, be it socialist or capitalist which did not know
that Guyana now has a petty dictatorship comparable to any of the
old banana republics. (*Caribbean Contact,* 1979)

A brittle economy, dissatisfied citizens, tiresome relations with
the World Bank and the International Monetary Fund contributed
to the general malaise. It was the Year of the Turn, "a bad year for
dictators", as Rodney described it, and popular movements had
taken place in Nicaragua and closer home in Grenada; and the
killing of Vincent Teekah, a minister for Education and Social Development, and the murder of Ohene Koama, a WPA supporter, indicated that the ruling regime had begun to panic. The supporters
of the opposition were under increased stress. "Prepare your wills,"
Burnham threatened. But Rodney and the 14 member executive of
the WPA began to take steps for the removal of the dictatorship.

(The decade of the 70s was marked by more violence than the
country had ever seen. Rabbi Washington, an American wanted for
blackmail, larceny and tax evasion was responsible for much of the
organized violence that took place in the capital, Georgetown.
Washington headed the House of Israel which had no claim to Israel, but believed that it had. This cult was used by government to
break up strikes and disrupt public meetings of groups opposed to
the government. Observers claimed that members of the cult allegedly prevented delegates from entering the annual meeting of
the Guyana Council of Churches in Georgetown. A member of the
cult, Bilal Ato, murdered Father Darke, a journalist for *The
Catholic Standard,* a weekly, on July 1979. Father Darke had been
taking photos of anti government demonstrations. The incident was
filmed by other journalists but the government took 3 years to bring
the case to trial. The judge reduced the charge to manslaughter and
sentenced him to 8 years in prison. When President Desmond
Hoyte took power in 1985, the House of Israel fell out of favor and
other key cult members were arrested and charged with murder.
Rabbi Washington pleaded guilty to manslaughter and received a
15 year sentence.)

The WPA's campaign, was in the main devoted to organization,
speeches and dealing with the results of its own success when hun-
dreds of young people, and unemployed and volunteers joined the

party, thereby creating problems of self-definition. Also, their plans to unseat the dictator were embellished by the general dissatisfaction that existed. Dr.Wazir Mohamed, former co-leader of the WPA described it graphically:

The PNC became the paramount institution in the country. To gain employment from a government who controlled 80% of the economy, a Guyanese had to be a card-carrying member of the ruling party. In many instances, even to get food the PNC party card was necessary. Guyana had become in the words of Walter Rodney "one large prison".

Suppression, repression and the wholesale commandeering of trade unions became the order of the day. Everything and everyone were to be under the heel of the ruling party. This included the suppression of long-established collective bargaining and grievance procedures. Not surprisingly, by 1979 Guyanese workers in general, but more especially African Guyanese workers in the Bauxite belt and Indian Guyanese sugar workers became restive especially as nationalization had not brought the promised economic prosperity. Nationalization had only replaced expatriate managers and management practices with local political elites who were tasked with enforcing rules in keeping with the imported "socialist" principle that the ruling party is god and master over all national affairs.

Walter's call for "self-emancipation" was formed, defined and redefined in the context of these attacks by the state on the trade unions, on the people and the peoples' institutions. His rallying call of "peoples' power, no dictator" not only resonated, but became the catalyst for self-mobilization and self-organization in the workplace and among communities across the country. Spontaneous organization and mobilization accompanied Rodney's every word with the blossoming of grassroots movements within trade unions, such as the Organization of Working People (OWP) among the predominant Afro-Guyanese bauxite work-force, and the creation of the four union grouping within the Guyana Trades Union Congress (GTUC).

In Guyana Walter Rodney became a living legend and a growing threat to the government. For this he had to be silenced.

Events were soon to precipitate a crisis between the state and the WPA. On July 10, 1979, the office of the General Secretary of the PNC and deputy Prime Minister, Ptolemy Reid was razed to the ground. The following day security agents raided the homes of several prominent Guyanese and five persons were arrested. Among those were Walter Rodney, Rupert Roopnarine, Omawale, Kwame Apata, and Karen DeSouza. They were accused of arson and unlawful possession of arms, theft and larceny. Predictably, the government's case was that the suspects were arrested in connection with

the fire which it alleged was started by men in army uniforms who
had arms and wore gasmasks. The men allegedly abducted the security guards and set fire to the building. The guards, bound and
gagged were later found some distance from the capital, according
to a communiqué from the government.

When the five, the "Referendum Five", appeared in court three
days later fighting broke out between the rival demonstrations esti-
mated at over one thousand. Rodney's lawyers applied for bail but
the prosecution claimed that this would prejudice the state's case,
but in the opinion of the presiding magistrate the state's case was
weak. The trial of the "Referendum Five" reflected the manipulative tendency of the government that would tolerate no dissent and
then there was crush it with the forces of the state. To add to the
decline in public morale was a reported purge of the army after the
fires and arrests of persons the state considered dangerous. Unrest
in the Armed Forces was emblematic of the political insecurity in
the country since the July 10 referendum. The WPA was quick to
capitalize on what it saw as the government's weak moral fibre — it
had failed to call national elections and twice failed to hold local
government elections. The WPA noted the increasing tendency for
dictatorial rule and accused the government of "clinging to power illegally at the same time as plotting to drive fear in its opponents
and suppress all articulate opposition." (Africa. No. 97, September
1979)

The affairs of Guyana, Britain's former colony on the mainland
of South America, did not go unnoticed in Britain, the former colonial master. Guyanese nationals living in Britain, organized a Committee Against Repression in Guyana and demanded that the
spurious charges against Rodney be dismissed. Also, the Pan-
African Union of Writers and Journalists, PWJ, which wired the
government to release Rodney and his cohorts. Guyanese in London
organized a picket at the Guyana High Commission. But not to be
outdone, the High Commission also paraded its own counter
demonstration and published a leaflet that urged Guyanese in
Britain to 'support attempts to remove from our midst those criminal dissidents who wish to retard the growth and prosperity of our
people and mete out just penalties to those murderers and sabo-
teurs when found guilty.' (Africa, No. 97, September 1979).

The PNC stepped up its repressive index and with the armed
forces, the violence of Rabbi Washington's House of Israel, it can be
said that Guyana reached its lowest point since independence in
1966. The "civil rebellion" had grown and the masses seemed well
informed about the untoward state of the country. The government
provided the occasion for public unrest and disillusion. The WPA

mobilized public opinion around the trial of the 'Referendum Five' and other unjust and illegal acts committed by the ruling party, PNC.

The referendum of 1978 replaced the national elections that were to be held that year. The purpose of the referendum was to make it possible, legitimately, for the ruling party to change the constitution and establish an executive presidency. And this same new constitution "marks the formal stage of the restructuring of the state as the process of totalitarianism proceeds." op-cit, Thomas , 1983,p 40 The national elections that followed did not enhance the credibility of the ruling party, indeed, it made it worse for it to establish legitimacy of any kind when a group of concerned citizens declared that the maximum turnout was 14.1 per cent though the government claimed 71.41 per cent of the voters, winning 97.7 per cent. Also, the ruling party was subjected to a damning report by the International Team of Observers.

We came to Guyana aware of the serious doubts expressed about the conduct of previous elections there, but determined to judge these elections on their own merit and hoping that we should be able to say that the result was fair. We deeply regret that, on the contrary, we were obliged to conclude, on the basis of abundant and clear evidence, that the election was rigged massively and flagrantly. Fortunately, however, the scale of the fraud made it impossible to conceal either from the Guyanese public or the outside world. ('Something to Remember.'International Team of Observers, 1980:28)

The excesses of the ruling party - and certainly the rigged elections in which neither the media nor public protest groups had much of a say in their deliberations - ensured that for the foreseeable future the ruling party would share equal billing with a restive population; moreover, one which had come to realize that "the ruling class is being plagued by symptoms of lunacy – losing touch with reality". Rodney had thrown down the gauntlet and he could expect an equal if not disproportionate response: GS70 million were spent on the armed forces; thugs dressed as police patrolled the streets and broke up many of the public meetings of the WPA. At one of them Rodney had to escape with his life. In November 1979, he addressed a meeting at the corner of Lamaha Street and Vlissengen Road in Georgetown and goons wielding greenheart truncheons chased him through the nearby streets of Kitty, a suburb. Rodney ran into a yard and found himself in a trench of excreta that he waded through and ran to safety, turning up at the home of his friend Colin Chlomondeley: "smelling like an unwashed ram goat". The goons, meanwhile, discouraged by the mess, turned back.

Burnham identified Rodney as the *eminence grise* of the opposition. It was a struggle for the soul of the nation.

During this period, the WPA grew in stature as the dominant political force in the country; the PPP had run out of constructive ideas and Dr. Jagan, the main figure had glued himself to the formula of holding free and fair elections that Burnham wasn't going to allow and even though Burnham had established a legal framework for ends that were entirely illegal and unfair. In fact, Burnham had subjected both his party, PNC and the country to his private machinations that it appeared inconceivable that matters could change.

Rodney presented a different picture. He was unafraid of Burnham and matched wits with him in the public spaces whenever Burnham managed to appear. He ridiculed Burnham, calling him "King Kong". This explains why goons of the House of Israel, at the behest of Burnham, pursued Rodney wherever and whenever he appeared. Rodney's public meetings were never publicized, but amazingly word would spread and he would turn up seemingly unannounced, hold them enthralled and then disappear just as the Burnham gangs appeared. Rodney's activities were not confined to street meetings. Political education took place in bottom houses, in private homes and unscheduled appearances wherever needed. Much concerned about youth he made efforts to formulate plans for young people who had been left out of the political process and represented the future of the nation. Rodney's agenda for citizenship affected the WPA which up until that time had been a pressure group seeking to build ties with leading opposition groups and to establish some unity. But the need to merge its old responsibilities with the new directions caused it to declare itself a full fledged political party. The change in status was not without attending controversy as Nigel Westmaas writes (Small Axe. 15. (63-81) p. 75

And to move from pressure group to political party required not only an understanding of the wider limits of power but also a great deal of public education. As a pressure group, the WPA was concerned with public criticism of keeping tabs on the ruling party and explaining what it did but intended to do. Meetings were held dealing with certain foci of interests such as the meaning of socialism in a developing country, the organization of the working class and race relations. The party manifesto was *Dayclean*, the party newssheet.

Also, the ruling regime had begun to retaliate in kind, circulating rumors that the WPA had assembled "hit lists" of those persons the party intended to assassinate. Rodney in his strongest statement about the role of political assassination declared:

And we say further that we do not want those who have been re-

sponsible for crimes against the Guyanese people to be assassinated...And there is another reason why assassination is not within
our political textbook. And that is because assassination is the act
of one man – any one man can assassinate a leader. But only the
people can cause a revolution. And the day has to come when the
real revolution will begin. (Rodney. Guyana Under Siege: the struggle goes on. P. 9)

Events led up to the new political status of the WPA. It could
function best in an enlarged role where the removal of the Burnham regime assumed priority "by all means necessary". In fact after
the burning down of the PNC's party headquarters, and the trial of
the "Referendum Five", the party could operate best if it bringing
about the desired change it needed. Public opinion was on its side:
the draconian measures imposed on the Guyanese people as a result of the conditions for a loan by the International Monetary
Fund, IMF, had brought increasing misery. The WPA organized a
demonstration to mark the rigged Referendum of 1978; a major
army purge created conditions of political instability, conveying the
impression that the government had lost the ability to govern. Rodney who had by this time had become a popular hero was just one of
those who led the opposition to the governing regime. Eusi
Quayana, an ardent member of the WPA, had published a seminal
piece "Racial Insecurity and the Political System", that explained
even as it provided a philosophical justification for the party's existence. Dr. Clive Y. Thomas's text, "Bread and Justice – the Struggle
for Socialism in Guyana" examined Dr. Rupert Roopnarine had produced and directed a film, *Terror and the Times*, Andaiye, a stal-
wart party activist, edited *Dayclean* and also assisted Rodney with
his book *The History of the Guyanese Working People 1885-1905*.
The party drew on committed supporters and many sympathizers
who had fallen foul of the government and many who had lost their
jobs for one transgression or another joined ranks with the WPA.
Indeed, persons of different racial origins rallied behind the banner
of the party and influenced its constitution. The party had subscribed to the Leninist brand of socialism; that is a strong central
leadership but with a rejection of the cult status that attended socialist organizations. Indeed, according to Nigel Westmaas, Rupert
Roopnarine had rejected the cult of personality on the grounds that
a more flexible response was necessary, given the challenge of such
a party in Guyana; and a revolving chairmanship ensured that
there would be no romantic or other attachment to power. Clive
Thomas had himself written about the necessity for socialism to be
built from the bottom upwards and the workers enlisted as prime

movers in the process.

And the enthusiastic following in 1979, particularly after the WPA had declared itself a full-fledged political party, led the leaders of the party to accommodate the demands of young people who wished to participate in its work, and rules for membership were relaxed. The WPA had become a victim of its own success. It had become in the seventies the main opposition to the ruling regime. The PPP had seriously compromised itself by insisting on 'critical support' for the government and Burnham knew that he could outwit that party because the PPP was rather less concerned with violence than with electoral morality; and to its cost it did not realize the extent to which Burnham wanted to hold on to power by any means. Burnham could out wit the PPP but could not Walter Rodney and the WPA. He was supported internationally by the US, the Soviet Union, Cuba and generally by the rest of the Anglo-phone West Indies which were themselves toiling against leftwing movements. Burnham did not have to raise the spectre of Communism to enlist the support of the US. Jagan did that for him and an entire constitutional system, proportional representation, enabled him to deal frightening blows against the opposition. But he couldn't against the WPA which had succeeded in less than 5 years to utilize public dissatisfaction and turn it against him. The WPA did not rival him ideologically, (that was never a problem) for with his majority he could change the constitution at will and did so on two separate occasions in a 5 year period. But the WPA had managed to challenge him in an area that he could not reach, —at one stage he did — that was with the people. Burnham had disassociated himself from the people and the WPA had managed to strive for racial unity when Burnham preferred divisiveness to remain in power. And he was faced in 1979, the 'Year of the Turn' with the problem of what to do about his nemesis.

Violence became the one area that Burnham held supreme and murder his preferred means either under state power or by private assassins. This explains why the violence was stepped up in the period 1978-80. In Rodney's opinion: a dictatorship feels threatened by anyone else claiming to offer some direction. To offer even to assist in the formulation of direction in Guyana today is considered as an act of hostility – is considered in the words of their press as "the counter revolution." (Interview with Wordsworth MacAndrew) (*Caribbean Contact* September 1979.)

Rodney did more than "to assist in the formulation of direction in Guyana". He and his party had wanted to formulate an entirely new direction and for that he had incurred the hostility of Burnham, the president, "whose government had heaped so much contempt on the people of the country".

Rodney understood the tragic consequences of his actions; he could not have been more prophetic. Seldom could a character have foretold his death with such accuracy. It was truly a chronicle of death foretold.

Chapter Seven

The Assassination of Walter Rodney

On the evening of June 13, 1980 at about 7.30 p.m. Rodney and his younger brother Donald collected a walkie-talkie set from Gregory Smith, a former member of the Guyana Defense Force, and received instructions about how the set was to be operated. Donald Rodney was informed that the test was to be carried out in two positions and Smith demonstrated the first position when he turned the knob on the set clockwise.

The two men then synchronized their watches at 7.50 p.m Donald was informed the first test should take place at 8.00 p.m. and the second in the vicinity of the prison. Donald then left Smith's home and joined his brother Walter who had remained in the motor car.

At 8 o'clock by my watch Walter looked down at the package which he held in his lap. The signal light flashed Walter remarked that was very good I then reminded him to turn the knob which he immediately did. I then drove off north along John Street across D'Urban St., and passed the prison. I parked on the western side of John St approximately 20 yards from Hadfield St. and turned off the ignition and all the lights. We waited for a signal from the package. There was no signal. Within a minute from the time. I parked the vehicle, Walter started saying something in reference to Gregory. I turned slightly to look through the driver's window which was open. Suddenly, I heard a loud noise and at the same time I felt my body twisted against the driver's door which flew open. (Rupert Lewis, Walter Rodney's Political Thought. Detroit: Wayne State University Press, 1998, p. 245)

The assassination of Walter Rodney shocked the region, and all over the world his friends in academia and beyond could not comprehend it. Most knew of his activism both in Jamaica and in Guyana, but could not translate his efforts to establish a union between the academic world and the working people, to energize them both, could bring about such an untimely death. But Guyana had become as George Lamming was later to say, a "dangerous land" and there was some evidence and warning about what could be, what things the government had planned for those daring to undermine its program or lack of it. The home of his mother was searched even as the government launched a propaganda campaign that boldly suggested first, that the body of an unknown man whose face was unrecognizable was found in a car next to the prison. This proved to be far from the truth, for Rodney's face had been untouched by the explosion; later, while admitting the death of Rodney, it declared he had been killed as he went to try out an explosive device near the Georgetown prison with the aim of allowing prisoners to escape Radio Demerara broadcast a news bulletin the very evening of the assassination, reinforcing government propaganda. The attempted cover-up was disingenuous and showed the complicity of the government in a sordid affair.

Georgetown, the capital, was in a state of great anxiety as news of the Rodney assassination spread; armed forces from the Guyana Defense Force roamed the streets to forestall the possibility of civil unrest. The fall out from the Rodney assassination electrified a region that would later in the decade encounter troubles of its own e.g. the execution of Maurice Bishop, the Grenada Prime Minister, the economic difficulties in Cuba and the uncertain destiny of the region in the face of the election of Ronald Reagan in the U.S.

Rodney's funeral service was befitting that of a national hero defined as such by the popular imagination and the working class that he strove to unify. The funeral procession marched for 12 miles from Buxton on the east coast to the Church of the Immaculate Conception where it lay in state. That the Burnham government vainly attempted to discourage civil servants from participating in the procession was another indictment of its cowardice. Tributes poured in from Europe, Africa and the Americas for a person who had been the driving force of a working class movement that sought to enrich understanding of the dominant elements that were an essential part of West Indian history; and to break down barriers between Blacks and Indians in Guyana. To professors at Ahmadu Bello University in Nigeria, he was a "heat storm across the tropical consciousness of an oppressed Caribbean."

The persecution of Rodney followed his burial. His brother Donald had signed an affidavit identifying Gregory Smith as the person who had handed him the walkie-talkie. But he was nevertheless charged with possession of an explosive device. The government hypocritically sought to determine the whereabouts of Gregory Smith, even as it denied that the man was a member of the GDF and vigorously tried to erase his name from the record books Rodney's brother was sentenced to 18 months in prison, but he never served his sentence and was granted asylum in Britain. Lord Avebury, chairman of the British Human Rights Group announced that "it can now be proved" that the man directly linked with the death of Walter Rodney was trained in Britain: Ministry of Defense records acknowledged that Gregory Smith of the GDF had attended a radio and electronics course in Fareham, Hampshire from February 1 to July 9, 1976 (*Guyana Chronicle*, February 12, 1981)

The Guyana government could not claim ignorance; indeed Gregory Smith, the man who knew most about the assassination of Walter Rodney was last seen June 17th, four days after Rodney's assassination boarding an aircraft with a GDF insignia at Kwakwani, a bauxite mining town, destination unknown; and his wife, children and an associate were spirited out of the country as well.

The Guyana government had succeeded in constructing the perfect crime. Burnham had previously warned Walter Rodney to prepare his will and there had been previous attempts on his life after June 1979 when Ohene Kohama, a WPA member had been killed. The steel band of the Guyana Police Force composed and played a piece "Run, Rodney, Run," and small posters of the same title were posted around Georgetown. There was a meeting to finalize plans for Rodney's elimination, a day before June 12, 1980 and at that meeting it was decided that Walter Rodney would be assassinated on June 12; and Walter Rodney was killed on June 13, 1980.

Inevitably, Rodney's assassination created an unbelievable shock in Guyana, and the region, judging from reactions in Africa, Europe, and around the world. And the attempts of the Burnham government to deny that the alleged assassin, Gregory Smith, was ever a member of the GDF, but served to exacerbate an already tense situation. Calls for an inquest at first met with little reaction. The government might indeed have wished the foul deed to be swept under the carpet and there is evidence that it badly underestimated Rodney's international importance even as it overestimated its own capacity for deception. But its machinations were not lost internationally. The US State Department Human Rights (1980) declared that from available evidence the government was involved in the assassination of Walter Rodney and the removal of key witnesses to the tragedy. And a conference of Caribbean lawyers and US conference of black lawyers meeting in Grenada called for an international tribunal to be set up to investigate state violence in Guyana and the circumstances surrounding the death of Walter Rodney.

In Guyana, the WPA was unrelenting in its pursuit of justice and *Dayclean,* the party newspaper, exposed inconsistencies in the government's interpretation of events leading up to and following Rodney's assassination Further, the party sought to damn in the eyes of the Caribbean the image of Burnham, the president of Guyana.

All citizens of the Caribbean community cannot lose this opportunity to condemn the assault, by a 'Death-squad' party, on the home of Walter Rodney, on the night of his murder The manner of the searches was quite unlike that of professional policemen, even in a fascist country.

(*WPA release* to Press and Public Walter Rodney's assassination a cold-blodded plot by the PNC state! July 13, 1980.)

Efforts by Walter Rodney's wife, and others succeeded in unearthing Gregory Smith, living in Cayenne, French Guiana, under the assumed name of Cyril Johnson since the assassination Eusi Kwayana, a party elder, petitioned the magistrate court in Guyana to bring a charge of murder against Gregory Smith, but this was denied because of lack of evidence. In addition, there was an another obstacle: the French government did not extradite persons to countries that maintained the death penalty. Gregory Smith contacted by Hugh Crosskill, of the BBC Caribbean Service, declined an invitation to return to Guyana because his safety could not be guaranteed; also he referred to Rodney's death as an "accident;" and insisted that Donald Rodney take a lie detector test Smith's grievance was that he had worked with the WPA to manufacture explosives to get rid of President Burnham and he himself was not involved in a plot to kill Walter Rodney.

The inquest into the death of the historian which took place in 1988, eight years after his death, further revealed the quagmire in which the government found itself. The main witness, Donald Rodney, was in the U.K and other witnesses were reluctant to come forward or too cowed to do so, including persons who lived in the immediate vicinity of the explosion. Documents crucial to the inquest could not be found and two forensic experts commissioned from the U.K. did not testify and their reports were not divulged. The result of the inquest was predictable. The coroner directed the jury to return a verdict of death by accident or misadventure.

But the controversy surrounding the death of Walter Rodney would not go away. On President Burnham's death in 1985, Desmond Hoyte assumed the presidency Hoyte eased the burdens suffered by the country as a result of Burnham's failed socialist experiment and opened up the economy to foreign investment—as well he should—for the country was in ruins, its infrastructure all but irretrievably damaged and shortages of foodstuff and medical supplies abounded. He permitted newsprint to be imported and allowed and encouraged a semblance of a free press. Hoyte also made overtures to the WPA seemingly to diffuse the racial situation exacerbated by the assassination of Rodney. Also, to his credit, in 1992, in response to outside pressures he called for elections which were supervised by former US president Jimmy Carter (Burnham, it will be remembered, had presided over fraudulent elections.) As far as these matters could be known, the US brought pressure to bear on Hoyte to investigate other killings that had taken place under the previous presidency: the murder of Vincent Teekah, a former minister of education remained a mystery and also that of Edward Dublin, a bodyguard of the slain historian.

Fifteen years after Rodney's assassination, in 1995, a three-member International Commission of Jurists, ICJ, held hearings among a wide cross-section of persons of civic interests and reported its findings Unsurprisingly, the ICJ, noted:

Several official files critical to the June 1980 death of Walter Rodney were missing;

Gregory Smith was a member of the GDF; Government and judicial officers of the day made no serious effort to identify people involved in the Rodney death; they could not trace police files relating to the case; and recommended that:

A full fledged commission should be mounted into the case

The ICJ also recommended that a full and comprehensive and thorough inquiry into the circumstances surrounding the death should be held; also that the inquiry should be entrusted to an impartial and independent international commission with the sufficient powers to summon and examine witnesses and gain access to relevant governmental and judicial files; and further, that the criminal case of Donald Rodney pending since 1982, should be speedily brought to an end

The matter of an inquiry posed a problem. There was understandable fear of what could be revealed. And as Horace Campbell wrote, quoting Fidel Castro, "the intellectual authors" of the crime were still at large. Finally in January 2005, the Guyana parliament met to consider a motion:

That this National Assembly, in paying tribute to the memory of this illustrious son of Guyana and on the occasion of the 25th Anniversary of his untimely and tragic death, support an international enquiry being conducted into the circumstances surrounding the death of Dr. Rodney.

After much deliberation, the motion was passed by the whole

House with four amendments to its clauses proposed by the WPA. That enquiry is yet to take place.

But even as uncertainty still surrounds the assassination of Walter Rodney, his work and contribution to local and regional politics continues. Neither the assassination of Rodney nor the stalled enquiry can submerge the problems in Guyana: deep seated racial cleavages remain and curtail progress. He was as much concerned with the plight of the working classes as with the uneven development that they were victims of. He argued that "the transformation and true human development can only be achieved through the common struggle of all peoples to recognize the necessity for a single humanity." Here was a man not imprisoned by the orthodoxy of Marxism nor by the compulsions of dogma. He supported grass roots democracy formerly embraced by Pablo Friere and according to Wazir Mohamed, chair of the WPA, now professor of African American studies at Indiana University.

Walter anticipated the movements that are now flowering all over Latin America, the fusion of the struggles for collective land rights with the struggle for women's equality and human rights— represented by the horizontal and unemployed workers movement in Argentina, the struggles of indigenous and black people, landless workers and trade union movements to Brazil, the indigenous Amerindian and water justice movements in Bolivia, Ecuador, Colombia and Peru, the Zapatistas of Mexico, and of course Chavez's Bolivarian revolution in Venezuela. These movements like Rodney's, are a rejection of the traditional party politics that have failed the peoples of the region Instead, people are moving to take power in their own hands.

In Guyana, the ethnic struggle between Africans and Indians had its roots in the old racist forms between white and black people. It was a form that was promoted in the plantation society that existed after slavery was abolished and in which both Africans and Indians were victims; and both groups used convenient stereotypes to define each other. But Rodney insists that capitalism was responsible for racism and grew out of productive relations in the 17th century and to the extent that capitalism was alien to the region it was promoted by forces outside of Guyana v.i.z Europe. But the production of rice and sugar caused the division of the two ethnic groups to go further Indians who were imported under a system of indenture for the express purpose of creating a labor surplus confined themselves generally to the estates and Africans who were not encouraged to work on the plantations because the wages were so low applied their talents to establishing villages and later to the safe ranks of civil services and professions of law and medicine.

Thus a schism was created with both groups vying for political power.

Thus we have in Guyana the beginnings of a class struggle based on occupation and race. And these colonial relations could only be maintained by intra class relations between Indians and Africans. And both groups as they competed for such power as they were allowed to have, were not reluctant to use racial symbols as a means of pursuing their interests. The consequence of this was that each hid behind race and both exploited the working class Guyana has suffered over the years because of racial rivalry.

Rodney was adamant that the ideology that supported racism had to be confronted before any progress towards a rapprochement could take place. The historical roots of racism were central to the discourse and the effect of capitalism on it. Only when there was debate on the ideology of what was to succeed capitalism could social transformation be effective. And socialism grew out of productive relations.

Chapter Eight

Garvey and Rodney

The circumstances of Garvey's involvement in the world of oppression and the uplifting message he propagated came about as a result of many factors. The continued racial oppression practised by white people against black people the world over was the main one; but others contributed in no small measure. The U.S. was experiencing industrial changes e.g. increased urbanization and the war economy pushed the need for increased manufactures on railroads, steel mills and other industries; and the movement of African Americans from the South in search of jobs after the failure of the Restoration period 1875-1900. Competition from European immigrants, who arrived in the cities and fought to establish themselves at the same time as blacks came from the South. It was a time of great importance and the American dream was vigorously pursued with casual attention paid to scruples of any kind. And the dignity of blacks, new arrivals, was the least of the society's concern; and people who had been brought in slavery from Africa, given the opportunity to participate in state matters, served in the U.S. army in World War 1 would be right in feeling that they had lost that most precious of possessions—one of identity. Just who were they? Beaten from pillar to post African Americans were ready for precisely the kind of message that Marcus Garvey preached.

Garvey himself had honed his philosophical attitudes in Jamaica where he apprenticed as a printer. His early years showed dedication to knowledge and he read widely. But it was his early experiences of racism and the colonial presence that imbued him with a passion to activity that was to last his entire life. Garvey like many others who came from the country areas of Jamaica understood better than town folk the indignity of colonialism. In fact, the Morant Bay rebellion of 1865 and the execution of Paul Bogle was imprinted in the minds of small land owners. The struggle was over land and how it was distributed; and those who earned their living as small farmers understood well enough the unfairness of it all.

Indeed, Garvey's father was a victim of great unfairness when he lost his land and his chief means of survival through the unfairness of the courts.

The sense of oppression was widespread among the farmers who were denied land and could not depend on the courts for justice. Inevitably, the union of racism allied to class warfare radicalized many and produced leaders and spokes men like Dr. Robert Love, one of the early influences on Garvey, who came from the Bahamas, settled in Jamaica after working with the Haitian government as an army doctor. He quickly established himself as a radical, championing the rights of the poor and downtrodden who had no representatives in the legislative council, composed for the most part of English planters and their lackeys. His message was clear: race and class dominated Jamaica, both as a consequence of colonialism. And the antidote: a race consciousness among those who were deprived of their rights. Love produced a newspaper, the Jamaica Advocate which even as it excoriated the powers that be for their cruelties warned blacks of the chicanery of the planter class.

"Let no Negro allow any man to deceive him by saying there is no class feeling against him. That is a falsehood." (Rupert Lewis *Marcus Garvey*, Trenton. N.J. African World Press, 1988, p.26) The oppression he felt was not only in Jamaica but throughout the Caribbean and later he was to carry his message and his organization the United Negro Improvement Association, UNIA, to all the territories that comprised the Caribbean and beyond.

The young Garvey (he would have been in his teens) absorbed the pronouncements of Dr. Love and more so since his father was a victim of that oppression. Racial oppression and colonialism were the two causes that drove Garvey and there was convincing evidence of both in Jamaica and later in the United States. Indeed , the pervasive character of the symbols of oppression were more evident in the latter country. They became the driving force of Garvey. The United Negro Improvement Association (UNIA) founded in 1914, was a consequence of the dire conditions existing for black people in the Central Americas, the U.S. and the United Kingdom. Its aims were not at first radical but became increasingly so. But the deplorable conditions for black people in general left it no alternative and the UNIA soon led the initiatives aimed at restoring some of the pride that generations of oppression had weeded out and especially in the generation following World War 1. It coincided as shown elsewhere with the arrival of blacks from the South remarkably chronicled by Nicholas Lemann in his excellent book, The Promised Land: The Great Black Migration and How It Changed America. And the failure of Reconstruction left no doubt in the minds of those subjected to the continued and repeated wrongs, that they could not trust either the good wishes, or the philanthropy of their oppressors. Also, they had become impatient with the shifting patterns of leadership that depended in large part on making alliances of doubtful validity with white people. Garvey and the UNIA identified with the new scheme of things. Henceforth, the philosophy of the New Negro was self-reliance and personal responsibility. Many other persons of prominence in the affairs of black people were of like mind; and certainly Malcolm X, Walter Rodney, Kwame Nkrumah, and Sekou Toure are beacons that illumine the landscape.

Garvey's philosophy embodied in the UNIA was to give the black masses a sense of mission. Repatriation to Africa was only part of it; and certainly many later realized that that was a dream deferred. But it was important to give black people wherever they were a sense of themselves, that they mattered, that they too had a kingdom to return to; when constructed that kingdom would be s harbinger of their hopes for a future away from the inequalities and cruelties of racism. It was a message whose simplicity was all the more powerful because it touched the well springs of kindness and compassion and united workers wherever they were.

In the Caribbean, a homegrown nationalism fed principally by Garvey's American adventures sprung up. Branches of the UNIA were established in most of the Caribbean islands and Panama and Costa Rica in Central America. The former territory was important on account of the 30,000 workers on the Panama Canal who were subjected to often inhumane conditions of service. In Guyana, then British Guiana, the main irritant of the local white bourgeoisie was Garvey's newspaper, *The New World*. And attempts to declare it a seditious publication met with mixed results. The heyday of imperialism was undoubtedly the partition of Africa at the Congress of Berlin, 1875, where Africa was carved up at the behest of the European powers. Enormous riches accrued to Britain, France, Belgium directly, but such was the expansive effect of trade that Europe benefited enormously from colonial trade in many different areas. Much of the investment in the colonies in Canada, New Zealand, Australia, Ceylon, India, Burma contributed immensely to British coffers; and profits ensued from loans at huge rates of interest. Jingoism, the nationalist fervor that accompanied the industrial revolution, owed so much to colonial expansion. A music hall ditty boasted of a Britain triumphant in all its dealings. "We've got the ships, we've got the men, and we've got the money too."

The prosperity left most of the Caribbean territories impoverished. From British Guiana on the mainland of South America to Jamaica, the northernmost of the territories; and the competition

that came from an expanding United States in Central America ensured the triumph if temporary of monopoly capitalism. What
Garvey brought to Jamaica was a program that would unite farmers, working class and petite bourgeoisie into a movement. He recognized the suffering among the strata of the country that could least
afford and the agricultural workers on whom the country depended
were destitute. But his vision was all-embracing, encompassed economic measures such as the protection of the workers by insurance
against accident and other hazards, a guarantee of labor; a political
program touching on representation and responsibility at the local
government level and also representation for self-government. On
the social and cultural levels, Garvey called for a Jamaican university and other institutions of higher education and entertainment
including an opera house and he would bestow on Montego Bay and
Port Antonio, the rights of cities (Lewis and Lewis, 1986, p. 91)

But Garvey's vision was broader than Jamaica. Wherever black
people were disempowered his watchful presence was always there
as a witness first, then as an instigator of change. He went beyond
the barriers of nationalism into the turbulent waters of internationalism. He wrote letters to the League of Nations vainly trying to establish the legitimacy of the UNIA which he saw the nucleus of a
Black government. He was involved in the anti-colonial struggles in
India, was admired by Mahatma Ghandi, (Rajmohan Ghandi.
Ghandi: The Man, His People And The Empire. University of
California Press, Berkeley, California, 2007, p. 403) and dared to
raise his pen against similar outrages in Ireland, Egypt and China.
Rupert Lewis. ("The Question of Imperialism and Aspects of
Garvey's Poltiical Activities in Jamaica 1929-30." In Garvey, Europe
and the Americas. (ed.) Rupert Lewis and Maureen Warner-Lewis.
Africa World Press. Trenton, New Jersey, 1986, p. 84.) The view that
the beleaguered working classes everywhere were natural allies in
the anti-colonial struggle was shared by many of other writers who
did not openly support Garvey (James R. Hooker. Black
Revolutionary: George Padmore's Path from Communism to Pan
Africanism. London. Pall Mall Press, 1967.) Indeed, the strength of
the UNIA and its ultimate demise had much to do with the lack of
support of many prominent Africanists such as DuBois and such
African American supporters who felt estranged from the movement. But there were other reasons why the UNIA went into eclipse.

Garvey's was a people's movement rather than a movement of
intelle ctuals . . . Its weakness lay in its demagogic leadership, poor
finance, intemperate propaganda, and the natural apprehension it
aroused among the colonial powers. (W. E. DuBois. The World in
Africa, p.226.)

That was one view and an important one and arguably DuBois either did not understand the significance of this worldwide movement or found Garvey's methodology personally offensive. Garvey was non-U and there certainly would have been a silent reproach by people of DuBois' background at the upstart from Jamaica. Garvey's ebullience was welcomed in the streets of Harlem and other cities across the US he visited. Overseas, his message in the early 20th century (1917-1937) reflected a supremely confident man who was determined to organize a black nation with the most comprehensive plan that would be the envy now of many independent nations . This man who had read the bible, Shakespeare and Plutarch wrote.

Like the Great Church of Rome, Negroes the world over must practice one faith, that of confidence in themselves, with one God, one Aim, one Destiny . . . the founding of a Racial Empire where only natural, spiritual and political limits shall be God and Africa, at home and abroad.

(M. Garvey, Philosophy and Opinions, Vol.11. cited in George Padmore. *Pan-Africanism or Communism*. London. Dennis Dobson, 19555, pp. 415-416.)

A constitution governed the objectives and the activities of the UNIA and the ACL, the African Communities League. It is a remarkable document that dictated social, economic and political behaviors; and the First Convention of Negro Peoples of the World was held in New York City in 1920, proclaimed that Garvey's vision had taken its proper place among nations.

Unfortunately that vision did not last long. Jealousies among the New Negro groups subverted Garvey's attempts to make his organization count for more than it did; he strove to enlarge it because it was the only way for him to counter the many challenges. Also, it had become evident that the UNIA had succeeded in getting the aspirations of black people known around the world, quite apart from instilling new confidence in their ability to succeed. The organization had empowered black people and given them a sense of dignity that had been lost in the years of oppression. The Garvey movement had repercussions to the present day and its effects on America and more importantly on the creative impulses of African American scholarship and the Harlem Renaissance. But the movement also provoked chasms: the Caribbean contribution to national liberation has never been fully acknowledged; indeed, it has been attacked by Harold Cruse, (*The Crisis of the Negro Intellectual*, William Morrow, 1967) drawing an equally eloquent if pungent response. (William James. *Holding Aloft the Banner of Ethiopia: Caribbean Radicalism in Early Twentieth Century America*. Verso Press: New York, 1998)

And the unity that Marcus Garvey fought for had been breached by lack of understanding and trust.

Again, the movement was controversial and its ideas, radical as they were, did not sit well with officialdom in any way. The left wing seemingly supported Garvey, but racial emancipation did not appeal to them and unity among people of African descent conjured up sinister images. Freedom, suggesting something more than abstraction, was an unthinkable proposition. And social justice appeared distant. Garvey was a threat to all their preoccupations. His philosophy about black control of their lives threatened the integrity of the communists, socialists and others who sought involvement in the affairs of black people. It was a social philosophy that would encompass the world and Black Nationalism was the panacea that would triumph over all obstacles. "No race is free unless it has a strong nation of its own and its own system of government and its own order of society." (Tony Martin. *Marcus Garvey. Message to the People: The Course of African Philosophy*. Dover, Mass. 1986, p. 34) Clearly such a strong statement of beliefs appeared to threaten the western powers which had just carved up Africa and the communists who were busily trying to establish beachheads in the West. Garvey did not approve of communists, and said so.

Communism is a white man's creation to solve his own political and economic problems...It was never conceived and originally intended for the economic or political emancipation of the Blacks, but rather to raise the earning capacity of the lowest class of white workers.

But on the death of Lenin he sent a telegram to Moscow to express his condolences. (Lewis and Lewis, 1986, p. 171)

Significant about Garvey's views about communism was that he was the first Caribbean leader who understood the methodology of oppression and was prepared to deal with it on his own terms. He understood that race had no place in a Marxist scheme of things and class differences he saw as evidence of bourgeois ideology. But he was rather more concerned with rooting out the bourgeois taint from his mass movement so that he could concentrate and be consistent with his original beliefs. He was the first philosopher of the Caribbean who marshaled the masses together based on the knowledge of the situation about them, the terms of their oppression. Other philosophers were to follow but none quite succeeded in developing such a movement.

Walter Rodney, for example, was a Marxist, but well did he understand that in Guyana, Marxism had to be applied in a particular way; indeed any foreign ideology needed to take cognizance of the society in which it found itself. In Guyana, ethnicity was an important element that Rodney had to visit.

But ethnicity in and of itself was not by means the central issue though both the PNC and the PPP made it so. For Rodney, the new politics that he spoke about was larger than the challenge of Guyana, though it came to be tested there. His vision was twofold: the rights of scholars, and intellectuals and activists of every shade of opinion to voice their views in the marketplace of ideas. But working class and working class unity could not be achieved uniquely by that class alone. It had to take a nation to build a nation. And the career of Rodney in the six years he spent in Guyana was replete with public meetings (some held under conditions of great duress), discussions under bottom houses, sessions at street corners; and he would go anywhere in the country to share ideas with people, especially those who disagreed with him. He shared this facility with Marcus Garvey who actually made reasonable argument an important part of his Course on African philosophy; and Rodney was a skilled debater known for his prowess in language at the University of the West Indies and in later jousts with Ali Mazrui in televised encounters at the University College of Dar es Salaam.

The academy was never far from the working people; indeed their interests and concerns informed his work as a historian. The public intellectual became more than praiseworthy acknowledgment. Rodney sought to mobilize the working people of the two ethnic groups in Guyana, made them see that the animosity that was encouraged by both opposition political parties, reflected the interpretation of yesteryear i.e. how Britain defined each of them. The perception of economic injustice, of unfair development, held them in check, paralyzing social relations and preventing long term political development. In fact, political development achieved for the most part in fits and starts, followed no coherent plan and Guyana could only move forward if the nation as a whole defined the terms and conditions that it wished to live by: economic equality and an end to working class isolation; only then, with the working class, freed from the stifling currents of inhibition, could the country move in the direction of a democratic future.

This then was the message of Walter Rodney, what he set out to achieve. And he was encouraged by the support of his party, WPA, first of all, then by the increasing numbers of people in the country areas and finally by the silent minority in the capital, Georgetown, and Linden, the bauxite community. It was a gathering consensus that the Burnham regime had to go and many had agreed with it, but agreement is not the same as action. The same persons who vociferously agreed would not have taken to the streets in public protest, given the strength of the police and the armed forces. There was no evidence of any precipitous action on Rodney's part. He certainly did not seek the overthrow of the government by violent means, whatever remarks may have been accredited to him.

His murder set back Guyana, the country he loved so well. But it also was a setback for the progressive forces within the country and arguably in the rest of the Caribbean. Three years after Rodney's assassination, Maurice Bishop, the prime minister of Grenada also came to a dreadful end, forced to stand against a wall and executed by firing squad.

Rodney's assassination brought a temporary end to the people movement in Guyana and the problems that he addressed still remain. It is often the place that those who lead do not live to see the results of their vision. Guyana is still a divided nation unable to deal effectively with the corruption endemic to modern government, the proliferation of drugs which stream across its borders, the dissatisfactions among ethic groups, and the high cost of oil importation.

Above all, the liberation of working people from the oppressions of race and class, — the special forte of Marcus Garvey; the unity of scholarship and action on behalf of the masses where power was centered of CLR. James; Eric Williams and the destruction of imperial myths, specifically the claims that emancipation of slavery was due to the goodwill of Her Majesty's government and not economic thinking; Franz Fanon and the false claims of the French Empire and the role of violence in national liberation; and Walter Rodney seeking changes in the self-perception of the working people in Guyana through education and unity, even as he tried to bring about revolutionary change; and Bob Marley, "a smiling revolutionary", a poet of song whose lyrics reached a world tired of cant and humbug. This radicalism that adorned the history of the 20th century will forever endure.i

NOTES

i. Rodney's concern with liberation and working class unity had already been the focus of attention in Peru in the 1970s when Gustavo Gutierrez, a Peruvian priest and theologian, defended the liberation theology movement in his book *A Theology of Liberation* wherein he pointed out that " liberation theology derives most significantly from unjust suffering, not from abstract arguments." (Gutierrez, G. A Theology of Liberation: History, Politics and Salvation. Sister Caridad India and John Eagleston (Eds.) and Trans. Maryknoll, NY: Orbis Books.)

1. Lewis, Rupert. *Marcus Garvey*. Africa World Press Trenton, N.J . 1988, p. 26

2. Ghandi Rajmohan. *Ghandi: The Man, His People and the Empire*, University of California Press Berkeley, California. 2007, p. 403

3. Lewis, Rupert. Warner-Lewis, Maureen. ed. *"The Question of Imperialism and aspects of Garvey's Political Activities in Jamaica"* 1929-30 *"In Garvey, Europe and the Americas."* (ed).Trenton, NJ, 1986. p. 84

4. Hooker, James R *Black Revolutionary: George Padmore's Path from Communism to Pan Africanism*. London Pall Mall Press, 1967

5. Padmore, G. M. *Garvey Philosophy and Opinions Vol 11*. London: Dennis Dobson, 1955, pp. 415-416

6. Martin, Tony. *Marcus Garvey Message to the People*. The Majority Press, Dover. 1986, p. 171

Chapter Nine

C. L. R. James, Rodney and the Taking of Power

Rodney had not studied the cauldron in Guyana. To attain power required an understanding of the limitations of those opposed to him and his party, knowledge of the people on whom he would depend and just how far they were prepared to go in order to overthrow Burnham and establish a government more in harmony with the perceived needs of the country. Rodney's tragedy was that he had not come to understand the lengths to which this alien power would seek to dispose him, to eliminate him in the desire to continue to maintain control. James was clear about the need for supportive elements in the revolutionary armory: first was the support of the masses ready for revolutionary activity, second was the advanced class of people who were ready for change, and third, when the rulers vacillated from their purpose, showed signs of instability, the time would be ripe; or put another way, when the rulers appeared vulnerable. Timing was the uniting factor. Revolutionary upsurges are caused when the classes feel dissatisfaction with the government, then they are best able to join common cause with the masses. In the Caribbean, there were times when these upsurges coincided with general dissatisfaction with the government in 1937 and 1938, in Trinidad.

The point is well taken and in his brilliant assessment of the Russian Revolution in 1917 when the revolution came "like a thief in the night." He underscored preparedness, for nobody could foretell when the people would be ready for revolutionary activity. It was one of the great mistakes of Walter Rodney not to wait for signs of general activity, not to wait until the Guyanese workers were ready to topple the ruling regime. He also did not reckon on the viciousness of the regime: it would take no prisoners. And yet as James points out, there are actions Rodney could have taken: enlist to his cause sections of the armed forces, disaffected members of the police and the workers who had more than a passing idea of what was in store. But in a country of 700,000 people, the bulk of whom lived on the coastlands Georgetown, the capital, and New Amsterdam, the governing regime was able to keep a sharp eye on all protest movements and disaffection; and with media, limited to two government owned and controlled radio stations and a newspaper, main channels of information were immediately suspect, and censorship, intrinsic or open, frustrated any meaningful communication. Rumor ran amok, providing the ruling regime with excuses for petty harassment.

Rodney was little prepared for this activity when he returned to Guyana. Schooled like most Caribbean people, especially politicians who were trained in jurisprudence at various universities in Britain, the Westminster model became the *lingua franca* of their social, economic and political activities. Rodney was part of that generation and hadn't realized the depths to which that model could be perverted in the interests of the maintenance of power. The governing regime was prepared to use arms to remain in power. The tragedy of the situation was that the regime understood the Guyanese people better than Rodney, who could capitalize on their dissatisfaction, but could offer them nothing tangible in return; and though they agreed with his theoretical positions, were not ready to take the ultimate step; and well they knew what that would be: the regime had succeeded since independence in seizing and holding the commanding heights of the economy; it had been guilty of falsifying elections; several unexplained deaths took place on its watch and a climate of uncertainty pervaded the land. No wonder the man in the street was fearful for his job, for the hand of the regime was long indeed, touching all sections of the country. Workers too were part of the Westminster model of reasoned protest and the inevitability of gradualness in affairs of state. Unaccustomed as they were to rapid changes in their life style, successive governing administrations before and after independence had made promises but betrayed them. Many who could afford to leave the country left for what they believed were greener pastures. Although sympathetic with Rodney for his daring, they would wait for the dawn of another day. There was little need to hurry. For radical ideas to spread among the people, wrote Jacques Ellul, in *Propaganda* much preparation is needed and this was conspicuously absent in Guyana. Not that they were ignorant of political activity; indeed, in the middle years of the 20th century, the trade union movement was central to worker participation in the sugar industry and the contribution of Hubert Nathaniel Critchlow reflected the growth of trade unionism in Guyana and similar activities in the rest of the Caribbean: Uriah Butler, Trinidad and Tobago and Alexander Bustamante, Jamaica. But Guyana lagged behind both

Trinidad and Jamaica in this respect. Consequently, Rodney was unable if indeed, he thought of it, of marshalling workers for an assault on the governing regime. The time was not propitious. C. L. R. James put it admirably: "A revolution is made with arms, but a revolution is made by the revolutionary spirit of the great mass of the population." (C. L. R. James. Walter Rodney and the Question of Power. *Race*. Race Today Publications. London, 1983, p. 8)

It was not just the workers who were not ready for revolutionary activity: their leaders were in the same category. While they lectured up and down the country and followed Rodney's inspiring presence as he sought to end the divisiveness between Blacks and Indians and pierced holes in the surviving myths of class and other distinctions. That they were not ready points to a fundamental error within the ranks of the Working Peoples Alliance, WPA. Revolutionary activity is incomplete without organizational skills; and given their ambitions, care should have been taken to shield their leaders from untoward possibilities. It was because of this lapse that violence was done to Rodney and with his untimely assassination a new chapter dawned in the history of Guyana.

What Rodney left was a country that was dispirited. His idealism that had touched so many, seemingly was put out and the flame that burned brightly for a time, the flame of racial togetherness, was no more.

The governing regime had succeeded in quelling a challenge to it. Opinions differ as to whether Rodney contemplated violence, that is, sought a violent overthrow of the government. That he spent his time at the forefront of change, of lecturing on the possibility of a better country if the governing regime could be cast out, denies the validity of the violence argument. His party, the WPA, had no arms. Rodney himself carried none. The argument about violence is revisionist and seeks to disenfranchise his significance as a public figure of some importance. Let us not forget the consummate abilities of the governing regime to restore the status quo ante, following Rodney's assassination. Less than three years after his assassination, his name had vanished from public memory and only the efforts of the comrades, who spoke in whispers of the wrongs done, kept alive his name until recently when on his 25th anniversary of his assassination, the memory came alive again, supported by the presence of representatives from over 100 countries who knew and admired his work.

The violence argument is without foundation. Decidedly so. Rodney was too much a scholar in the constitutional sense not to have realized that violence could not have succeeded in Guyana. His was the electoral alternative. No country among the former

British territories in the Caribbean has succeeded in bringing about violent change. The class system, that most reliable barometer of British exports, would have prevented this, and seen to it that there were enough divisions to thwart any such development among the locals. Riots there were galore in all of them and public protests as well. But revolution, no, such was the exciting fate of Haiti, Cuba and Suriname but not Guyana.

While there was no record of successful revolution in the English-speaking- Caribbean, there was certainly revolutionary activity, which is to say, the masses and others discussed alternatives to the ruling regimes. They might even have plotted what they wanted to do to bring to an end the conditions of work, labor and other iniquities. Such had become so deplorable that the British government sent Professor MacMillan to do a report in 1937 and his book, *Warning from the West Indies*, summarized the shocking state of affairs. It so frightened Whitehall that they didn't immediately release the report because, coming as it did on the verge of World War II, its publication might just conceivably have affected the morale of colonial troops whom they wanted to serve in the British army.

Rodney was very much aware of the conditions of poverty that prevailed and which independence had done little to alleviate. He knew of it from his experience in Tanzania, where despite Ujamaa, and Nyerere's attempts at Socialism, corruption marched hand in hand with economic development. The plight of the workers in Guyana was hardly better and in the absence of coherent national policy what remained was middle class machinations. In fact, part of such chicanery was to conceive of a new name for state deception and to underline the differences that existed between the two leaders Linden Burnham and Cheddi Jagan: the Cooperative Socialist Republic of Guyana was the brainchild of the former while the latter preached the usual Marxist rhetoric, promising much but delivering little of substance. (C. L. R. James, *Race*, 1993 p.7) It was an interesting footnote to the use of names to define a new reality. The Cooperative Socialist Republic of Guyana, was neither cooperative nor socialist. It was a resplendent means of deceiving the masses, giving them a semblance of importance but at the same time disguising the emptiness beneath it. The country was at the time run by a governing elite that used words to cloak the shabbiness beneath the words and an opposition, minority party that shielded itself behind the fabric of Marxism. They were men of large but distorted vision, seeking personal glory from narrow premises and derivative intelligence.

It was in this state of affairs that Rodney returned to Guyana. He was determined to do something about it. Denied a position in the department of history at the University of Guyana, he had little choice but to take to the streets via the ministrations of the Working Peoples Alliance. WPA. According to James, (1993, p.7) Rodney approached Cheddi Jagan with a view to establishing a coalition of the Peoples Progressive Party, PPP, against Burnham, and in the process lessen tensions between Blacks and Indians. Jagan demurred, citing the need to include Burnham in the coalition. Thus, the first serious attempt of Rodney to establish a working opposition to the Burnham party, PNC, was aborted by Jagan who wished to include in the opposition, the very party they were opposed to. This illogical premise could only be attributed to Jagan's confused perception that a national movement including the PNC and all dissident activity was a more desirable objective. James suggests that the reason for Jagan's failure to join an anti-Burnham movement was because he could not abide the notion of "living without conflict," with Burnham, with whom he had shared the halcyon days of 1953 when the first universal adult suffrage resulted in the formation of a national government. The present author thinks otherwise. It might well have been that, concerned about his own role in an anti-Burnham movement, Jagan did not see himself as central to it, especially with Rodney who was already beginning to appear as the people's champion. It was safer from Jagan's point of view to bring his party and Rodney into an alliance with Burnham in a national movement. There might also have been an element of wishful thinking on his part — within a national movement of the PPP and the PNC, there would be a resurgence of his own waning influence. At any rate his support for Rodney's endeavors was lukewarm at best. Rodney was left *with* his party to confront the ruling regime.

But there was little organization and the party discipline that was customary among Marxists parties absent. The people were not prepared, though they opposed many of the initiatives, or lack thereof, that came from the government. And the lack of preparation corroborated the absence of party discipline, making the leaders of the opposition, and Rodney in particular, vulnerable.

In his stellar address to the University of California at Los Angeles in 1981, on "Walter Rodney, Revolutionary and Scholar: A Tribute," C. L. R. James underlined the importance of preparation for the seizure of power and one that was totally lacking in Guyana. That preparation also included the protection of the leadership from the possibility of assassination, the very fate that would befall Rodney. It was a circumstance that Rodney and his party should have been aware of. But how does one anticipate and take steps to guard against one's own assassination! There were particular circumstances that exist in Guyana that made it difficult. Leaders who opposed the government could not hide and still retain their influence among the workers and others. They would have had to remain in the capital, Georgetown, and the two principal towns, New Amsterdam and Linden. Rodney and those who opposed the government had not begun preparing for alternative possibilities e.g. purchase of arms, — he would have been opposed to this — infiltration of the armed forces and the police and the recruitment of sympathetic elements in the country to their cause and many of the latter existed. Rodney, in the course of his lectures, had galvanized widespread support among Blacks and Indians who would readily have rallied to him.

The entire Rodney episode from his arrival in the country, his political activism, and challenge to the governing regime, establishing a consensus among disparate citizens, and events leading to his assassination, revealed both the strengths and limitations of revolutionary activity in the Caribbean.

To get crowds of people listening to the social and political roots of their oppression: no problem; to get them to identify with speakers who were opposed to those that prevented the exercise of their rights as citizens: no problem. But to get them to move to overthrow challenging regimes, posed insuperable difficulties. Rhetoric alone could not obtain the desired effect. The mass media, such as existed, could not reach all of the people, and in any case, were inadequate to reach even some of the people. Discussion and debate were confined to intellectuals who possessed an ascribed status in the Caribbean, attaching to themselves the currency of wisdom and knowledge that separated them from the bulk of the people; and in most cases they benefited from the adulation of those who had not pursued higher study. In fact, one of the criticisms ascribed to our societies has been the emphasis on book learning as the panacea for knowledge, to the exclusion of other forms of social and cultural activities. George Lamming, the noted writer, said that Caribbean intellectuals "are so bright they remained dazzled by their brightness." The prominence of book learning, analysis of fact and opinion, essentially a theoretical basis for knowledge and activity, divorced from the concerns of the masses, tended to make intellectuals poor revolutionaries. They could think radically, of revolutionary situations, of the application of theory to practice and the pitfalls that attended improper and faulty application. Many like Rodney were scholars of many disciplines, who held great sympathy for the people who held them in esteem. But they were not revolutionaries, not capable of overturning a corrupt government, though they might indeed have wished it, perhaps even have thought about it. That they were doubtless men of the people, and their integrity

could not be doubted, but as C.L.R. James states, colonial administrations had trained them "in terms of a leading figure." Essentially, this limited their ability to reach out to the people and
curtailed any aggressive intentions. But it was the people who
should reach out and anoint them leaders. It was a one-way communication process with all the inconsistencies of such a process:
when once a leader had been identified, people were ready to follow
him without challenging his authority, or the efficacy of his agenda.
This affected the free exchange of ideas, limited where it did not
compromise the making of policy and covered over differences of
opinion.

In Guyana, the Constitution, enshrined voting patterns that
are divisive of a national polity: the Indian majority is all but guaranteed victory at the polls. And that was where Rodney challenged
the Burnham regime: he had the ability to get along with Indians
without self-consciousness, sharing their frustrations and planning
with them the future of the country. And he said pointedly . . .
"some fear that Black Power is aimed against the Indian. This
would be a flagrant denial of both the historical experience of the
West Indies and the reality of the contemporary scene." (The
Groundings with my Brothers. Bogle L'Ouverture. London, (1969).
It was a future recognized by those who knew him of electoral politics. Rodney was a radical who supported revolutionary change but
didn't realize the extent to which those opposed to any change
would go towards frustrating him; and he knew what he wanted to
do in Guyana was to rid the country of that imperial mindset that
separated the intellectual from the masses, that prevailed against
unity by fomenting questions of race and class. "The black intellectual, the black academic must attach himself to the activity of the
black masses" (Rodney 1990 [1969], p.63. It was indeed because he
attached himself to the fate of the masses that the governing
regime went after him. He was out of sync with the regime, the
Westminster-educated, who believed that their education entitled
them to rule; and with an electoral system that facilitated if it did-
n't ensure their leadership.

Rodney continued in Guyana what he had begun in Jamaica.
He had bridged the gap between scholarship and the masses and
made of intellectual activity a universal within reach of the man in
the street. Put another way, the man in the street, the "barefoot
man" had as much intelligence as the university graduate, un-
schooled but active and alert. Public education and by that we mean
the modern equivalent of continuous or adult education, which sets
out a defined curriculum for persons, who had not been previously
exposed to higher study or training, has been a feature of

Caribbean societies; and in particular, in political science. Eric Williams, an eminent scholar, and later prime minister of Trinidad and Tobago, delivered a series of public lectures in Woodford Square in Port of Spain, and so also had the Manleys, Bustamantes, Adams, Burnhams in their respective territories. In fact, public speaking was a highly publicized art among West Indian politicians and such oratory a more than convenient vehicle for public education; and public gatherings were part of the classroom for philosophical thinking. So it was that Eric Williams, the first public intellectual, was able to capture the minds of his people. These public lectures were important not only for education and communication of ideas but also means by which leaders obtained feedback from the audience.

C.L.R. James and African Americans

James was to speak about learning from the audience at the Apollo Theatre in Harlem. "But the audience at the Apollo shaped James's thinking on the African-American struggle as much, in its way, as Lenin's theses on the national question." Scott McLemee, 1996, p. 245 ed. C.L.R. James. *On the Negro* Question. "All the power is hidden in them there. It's waiting to come out. And the day . . . it takes political form, it is going to shake this nation as nothing before has shaken it."

The discourse on the question of African-Americans was central to James's ideas of what was to be done about economic exploitation and racial discrimination in the United States. That the persistent inhumanity derived from slavery still existed was a perpetual stain on the affairs of the nation. Radicalization was inevitable. That was to be achieved with the help of the Socialist Workers Party. But this attempt at organization was not to be exclusive to African Americans. James discussed John Steinbeck's book, *The Grapes of Wrath,* underlining the fact of poverty among whites provided an excellent opportunity for cohesion. But the key to any social and political advance was in African American leadership in an organization devoted to wider social purposes e.g. membership and participation in trade unions and in all unions. No ethnic chauvinism was to rule the day and self-sacrifice, already demonstrated by adherence to the church; and Marcus Garvey had proved that African Americans had the necessary qualities to sustain a movement based on socialism. It was a tall order, but James was uncompromising. The mass movement of African Americans should embrace similar movements overseas e.g. Ethiopian resistance against the invasion of Italy, and difficulties encountered by other peoples and organizations in the daily conduct of affairs. James had confidence in the masses of people, who could formulate an organization without the help of intellectuals or the machinations of the Communist, Republican or Democratic parties.

He saw organization as the key to a new society that promised to make an assault against the racial discrimination and inequality that exuded the society — voting rights, discrimination in schools and universities, and exorbitant rents, to say nothing of jobs. Without such an organization socialism could not thrive.

Eric Williams did not derive his analysis from Marxism, but from historical method. His reading of history emphasized the role of imperialism in the poverty of the colonies over which Britain ruled: uneven development, commercial capitalism, poverty and its stepchild, misery, and a class system that supported the dominance of the rulers. Williams saw through the hypocrisy of the British historians who, while subscribing to the concept of Empire wrote trenchantly about the inability of the West Indies to go it alone and achieve some form of self-government or dominion status— purely on racial grounds. And at a time when as a result of the cultivation of beet sugar, the future of these islands was in much doubt. But the prosperity of the sugar islands had long since began to diminish and Williams pointed to the high costs of slavery that led to its emancipation and not as was trumpeted the result of humanitarianism.

It was an important position to adopt in view of the bigotry and destructive arguments of many British historians, among them, Thomas Carlyle and others of the Pro-Slavery faction, including Anthony Trollope. Carlyle was in the first rank of these fascists and his infamous essay, *The Nigger Question* reflected his views. In fact, Carlyle views were elitist: he supported a militaristic society of the "Best and the Bravest", an aristocracy of talent, and was thoroughly opposed to the reform movement in currency in England at that time. He considered slaves inhuman and deserving of their fates.

To place Carlyle and the notable intellectuals of the day in context: they were governed by the dominant economic philosophy of the 18th century. Mercantilism advocated increased trade as a means of bridging the gap between exports and imports. A search for markets, control of such as were obtained and a vigorous defense of them. The ensuing wealth would create a favorable balance of trade. Thus, the 18th century was noteworthy for the growth of imperialism when Spain, France and England fought for exclusive control of their colonial possessions. Slavery became important in large part because slaves provided free labor and cut down on expenses in the production of sugar; and at the same time slaves contributed to the industrial revolution, and growth in other areas in their respective metropoles.

The degrading conditions of slavery in the New World have been recorded extensively and their contribution to the welfare of European peoples also documented. But the effects of slavery on black people is the ongoing saga of the past and the present. Eric Williams puts it context.

[The effects] must be seen against the background of the economic degradation, political disabilities and racial discrimination which are and have been the lot of the masses of Negroes in the New World. (Eric Williams. *British Historians and the West Indies.* A and B Publishers, N.Y. 1994, p. 176.)

There was convincing example of these degradations: the end of the First World War had exposed the underbelly of a racist system that had exploited African Americans and having done so, continued that exploitation on their return home from war. And the special plea of W.E. DuBois in *Crisis Magazine,* 1918. "Let us, while this war lasts, forget our special grievances and close ranks shoulder to shoulder with out fellow citizens . . . " seemed the stuff of myth. The war's end brought no substantive change in their conditions; and those whites who had supported civil rights had grown discouraged as lynching and cumulative distress, including disenfranchisement of black voters grew apace. Leadership in the black community was in transition and the imperialism that was so much a part of the 19th century reached its apotheosis at the Treaty of Berlin 1885, when Africa was partitioned among European powers; and the same century that had witnessed the beginnings of imperialism found common cause with the ideology of racism in the United States. The failure of the Reconstruction period 1875-1900 had already exposed the contradictions of a society that preached one thing and acted in another direction. And as far as the working classes were concerned there was almost an abandonment of hope. Indeed, riots had broken out in Chicago and elsewhere and over half a million African Americans left the South for the doubtful certainty of jobs in industry and better schools for their children. Social and economic circumstances were ripe for Marcus Garvey and the new sojourners to the North found that racism that continuous bane in American life had not deserted them.

Bibliography

Ambursley, F and Cohen, R. *Crisis in the Caribbean.* New York: Monthly Review Press, 1983.

Amin, Samir. *Unequal Development.* New York: Monthly Review Press, 1983.

Burnham, Linden. *A Destiny to Mould.* Georgetown: Guyana Publishers, 1973.

————."Declaration of Sophia."*Address.* Georgetown: Guyana, 1975

Best, Lloyd. "A Model of Pure Plantation Economy.: *Social and Economic Studies.* Vol. 17, No, 3 Sept. 17, 1968.

Burn, \W.L. *Emancipation and Apprenticeship in the British West Indies, 1838-42.* London, quoted in Alan H. Adamson. *Sugar Without Slaves.* New Haven. Conn: Yale University Press, 1979.

Cabral, A. *Unity and Struggle. Speeches and Writings.* New York: Monthly Review Press, 1979.

Caute, David. *Fanon.* London: Fontana, 1970.

Chase, A. 133 Days Towards Freedom in Guiana. Georgetown: Government Printers, 1953.

Clementi, A. *A History of British Guiana.* London: MacMillan, 1937.

————. *Report on the Condition of the Colony of British Guiana during the Great European War and the Chief Local Problems Awaiting Solution.* Combined Court, No. 21.

Cruse, H. *The Crisis of the Negro Intellectual.* New York: William Morrow, 1967.

————. *Plural but Equal.* New York: William Morrow, 1967.

Dalton, H. G. A History of British Guiana. Vol 11. London: Faber and Faber, 1955.

Danns. G. K. *Militarization and Development: an experiment in nation-building.* Transition, vol 1, 1978.

Davidson, B. *Black Mother: Africa and the Atlantic Slave Trade.* London: Penguin, 1961.

Despres, L, *Cultural Pluralism and Nationalist Politics in British Guiana.* Chicago: Rand McNally, 1967.

Eisenstein, E. *The Printing Press as an agent of change.* London:

Cambridge University Press, 1978.

Ellul, J. The Technological Society. New York: Grove Press, 1967.

Fanon, F. *The Wretched of the Earth.* London: Penguin Books, 1967.

———. *Black Skins, White Masks.* New York New York: Grove Press, 1967.

Frank, A. Gunder. *Capitalism and Underdevelopment in Latin America.* New York: Monthly Review Press, 1967.

Frucht, R. "A Caribbean Social Type: Neither Peasant Nor Proletariat." In Horowitz, M. (eds.) *Peoples and Cultures in the Caribbean.* New York: Natural History Press, 1971.

Gibbons, A. *Information, Ideology and Communication.* Lanham, Maryland: University Press of America, 1985.

Goveia, E. V, *A Study on the Historiography of the British West Indies to the end of the Nineteenth Century.* Mexico City: Instituto Panamericano de Geographia e. Historica, 1956.

Grant, Colin. *Negro With A Hat. The Rise and Fall of Marcus Garvey.* Oxford University Press, 2008.

Hall, Douglas. "The Flight from the Estates Reconsidered: the British West Indies 1838-42."*Journal of Caribbean History. Vol. 10, 1978.*

Hall, Stuart. "Pluralism, Race and Class in Caribbean Society." In *UNESCO Race and Class in Post Colonial Society: A Study of Ethnic Group Relations in the English-speaking Caribbean, Bolivia, Chile and Mexico.* UNESCO, Paris, 1967.

Hoetink, H. *Two Variants in Caribbean Race Relations: A Contribution to the Sociology of Segmented Societies.* London: Oxford University Press, 1967.

Horowitz, D. *Ethnic Groups in Conflict.* Berkeley. University of California Press, 1985, p. 326.

Irele, Abiola. "Negritude – Literature and Ideology." *Journal of Modern African Studies,* 1965.

Jagan, Cheddi. *The West on Trial.* Berlin: Seven Seas Publications, 1972.

Jahn, J. *Muntu.* London: Faber and Faber, 1961.

Jalee, P. *The Pillage of the Third World.* New York: Monthly Review Pess, 1972.

James, C.L.R. *Spheres of Influence.* Westport. Conn.: Lawrence Hill,1980.

———. Selected Speeches. Westport. Conn.: Lawrence Hill, 1980.

———. Nkrumah and the Ghana Revolution.: Lawrence Hill, 1980.

———. "Walter Rodney and the Question of Power." *Race Today.* London: 1983, p.8.

————. C,L.R. James Reader (eds) Anna Grimshaw. Blackwell, Oxford: 1992.

————. American Civilization.(eds.) Anna Grimshaw and Keith Hart.
Blackwell: Oxford,1993.

Kestleloot, L. *Les Ecrivains noire de langue francaise:naissance d'une litterature.* Editions de l'Institut de Sociologue de l'Universite de Brusselles, 1965.

Lamming, G. *The Pleasures of Exile.* London: Michael Joseph, 1956.

————. "The Role of the Intellectual in the Caribbean." *Cimarron. Vol. 1, No. 1,* Spring, 1985.

Lewis, G.K. *Main Currents in Caribbean Thought: The Historical Evolution of Caribbean Society in its Ideological Aspects.* Baltimore. Maryland: The Johns Hopkins University Press, 1983.

Lewis, R. *Walter Rodney's Intellectual and Political Thought.* Detroit, Michigan: State University Press, 1998, p. 114.

Lowenthal, D. *West Indian Societies.* Oxford University Press: Oxford University Press, 1972.

Lutchman, H. *From Colonialism to Co-operative Republic.* Institute of Caribbean Studies, Rio Piedras. University of Puerto Rico: Puerto Rico, 1974.

————. *An Imperial Presidency,* unpublished paper, 1983.

Magdoff, H. Foreword. In Pierre Jalee. *Imperialism in the Seventies.* New York: Third Press, 1973.

Martin, T. *Marcus Garvey, Hero.* Dover: Massachusetts: The Majority Press, 1983.

McLewin, P. *Power and Economic Changes: the Response to Emancipation in Jamaica and British Guiana.* Unpublished dissertation. Cornell University, 1971.

McMillan, F. *Warning from the West Indies.* London: Faber and Faber, 1936.

Mintz, Sidney, W. "The Question of Caribbean Peasantries: A Comment." *Caribbean Studies, 1961.*

Monroe, Trevor. *The Politics of Constitutional Decolonization 1944-62.* Jamaica. University of the West Indies: Institute of Social and Economic Research, 1972.

Nath, Dwarka. *A History of Indians in British Guiana.* London: Nelson, 1950.

Nettleford, Rex. *Mirror, Mirror: Identity, Race and Protest in Jamaica.* Jamaica: Sangsters, 1976.

Othman, H. (eds.) *The State in Tanzania: Who Controls It and*

Whose Interest does it Serve. Dar es Salaam: Dar es Salaam University Press, 180.

Owens. J. *Dread: The Rastafarians of Jamaica.* Kingston, Jamaica: Sangsters, 1976.

Quamina. O.T. *Mineworkers of Guyana.* London: Zed Books, 1987.
Rodney, Walter. "African History and African Development Planning." *Paper.* University of Dar es Salaam, undated.

———. *The Groundings with my Brothers.* London. Bogle l'Ouverture Press, 1969.

———. *How Europe Underdeveloped Africa.* Washington, D.C.: Howard University Press, 1974.

———. *A History of the Guyanese Working People.* Baltimore. Maryland: The Johns Hopkins University Press, 1985.

———. "Marxism as Third World Ideology." *Paper.* Undated. Collection at the University of Guyana.

———. *A Tribute to Walter Rodney. Paper.* Hamburg: University of Hamburg, 1972.

———. "C.L.R. James and the African Revolution." *Paper.* University of Michigan. March 3, 1972.

———. *Talk.* African Studies Center, University of California at Los Angeles, May 30, 1972.

Ruhoman, Peter. *Centenary History of the East Indians in British Guiana, 1838-1938.* Georgetown: Chronicle Publishers, 1947.

Said, Edward. *The Word, the Text and the Critic.* Cambridge. Massachusetts: Harvard University Press, 1983.

Shivji, I.G. *Class Struggle in Tanzania.* New York: Monthly Review Press. New York: 1976.

Smith, M.G. *Culture, Race and Class in the Commonwealth Caribbean.* Jamaica: Department of Extra-Mural Studies, University of the West Indies, 1984.

Smith, R.T. *British Guiana.* London: Oxford University Press, 1962.

Thomas, Clive, Y. "State Capitalism in Guyana: An assessment of Burnham's Co-operative Socialist Republic." In Ambursley, C. and Roy Cohen, *Crisis in the Caribbean.* New York: Monthly Review Press, 1956.

———. *Dependence and Transformation.* New York: Monthlyh Review Press, 1956.

———. *The Poor and the Powerless. Economic Policy ad Change in the Caribbean.* Monthly Review Press, 1988.

———. *Plantation, Peasants and State.* Jamaica: Institute for Social and Economic Research. University of the West Indies. Jamaica: 1984.

Williams, Eric. *Capitalism and Slavery.* London: Andre Deutsch, 1964.

Summary

The Legacy of Walter Rodney in Guyana and the Caribbean

Walter Rodney asked two questions in his writings:one, the reasons for poverty and two, what were some of the circumstances that prevented its elimination. He claimed that developing countries were heirs to factors such as uneven development and ethnic disequilibrium, to say nothing of continued forms of oppression both from the capitalist countries and from their own leaders. In Guyana, his home, ethnic chauvinism persisted both before, and after independence from their leaders. In Guyana, his home, ethnic chauvinism persisted both before and after independence from Britain; and a false reading of history allowed the two ethnic groups to distort the contributions of the other and thereby frustrate nationalism. He made his position clear in How Europe Under developed Africa in which he argued that Europe arrested the development of Africa and prevented their institutions from pursuing their own economic and directions. As a Marxist he was wary of theoretical solutions to [problems because these were Euro-centric and did not apply to individual states. He could see the difficulties of a doctrinaire approach to Marx; and as a close observer of the African scene he saw at close hand the attempts of Nyerere to establish a workable socialism; and as a critic of Europe in Africa, he would not have committed the error of applying Marx undiluted in Guyana and would have been saddened by the absolute application of Marx to Grenada.

As a Caribbean person he was disturbed by the inability of intellectuals to share common cause with the masses of the population; and in failing to do so ensured that these would be unable to contribute either to the uplift of their talents or participate in the growth of the nation. The Caribbean intellectual was like most of those from former British colonies; brought up in the tradition where book knowledge was valued for its own sake and totally unrelated to the needs of the local population. This a created a wedge among the citizenry: thye middle classes were caught between the masses and the upper class, variously described as planter class, colonial upper class, professional class; and education provided the mobility for those fortunate to be exposed to it. C.L.R. James, Rodney's mentor, declaimed that "the Caribbean middle class is like no other in history:" it aspired upward, and while critical of colonial power, was itself an example of that power in operation, and pursu-

ing its own class interests. The middle class believed itself heir to
British interests and these could be enhanced by education.

Walter avoided these temptations. The son of a tailor, he gained
a scholarship to Queens College, then to the University of the West
Indies and the University of London. Rodney could have pursued
the upward mobility syndrome, but did not. The unity of the working class against entrenched interests was his objective and in pursuing it he emphasized the role of the intellectual in the politics of
developing countries. The intellectual in a developing country must
assume a number of roles, according to Edward Said. Each of these
deals with knowledge and how it is used and applied in social, political, historical and institutional matters. Rodney as an intellectual
was both a part of the dominant culture and outside it. His formative work had been in history, yet it is precisely this that enabled
him to go beyond the historical perspective and distance himself
from the dominant culture. And this was his challenge to the political culture in

Guyana. His appointment as professor history at the University
of Guyana was rescinded, leaving him limited options to earn a
livelihood. He studied the political situation and sought out like-
minded individuals with whom he could interact. Guyana like the
Caribbean were both subject to the traffic in sugar and slaves that
constituted cheap labor for the plantations and buttressed the
capitalist-industrial system. One of the significant by-products of
that system was the master-slave relationship; A no-less iniquitous
consequence was an active racism. Thus, social inequality promoted
by a class system, that had been part of the capitalist-industrial
system, became the heritage of Guyanese and Caribbean history.

These two social evils have influenced all the social, economic
and political institutions in Guyana since then. And the admission
of indentured Indians, Chinese and Portuguese in the nineteenth
century to work on the sugar plantations provided additional opportunities for class differences. Fledgling political parties emerged
after World War II, building on reform movements in the early 20th-
century. In Guyana, race, class nd color became the determinants of
social value and how the various racial groups responded to them is
both the triumph and the tragedy of Guyanese nationalism.
Elections in 1953 saw the emergence of the Peoples Progressive
Party, PPP, a party in which most elements of the nation were represented. It was short-lived for the Constitution was suspended
because Britain suspected communist influence and was disturbed
by Jagan's radicalism. This divided the leadership and L.F.S.
Burnham formed the Peoples National Congress, PNC. Thus the
halcyon days ended in division, some members followed Burnham,

others remained with Jagan; and by 1961, another party, the United Force, UF, entered the fray. Racial divisions muffled for a time, reappeared in full force when Rodney appeared on the scene and he joined the Working Peoples Alliance, WPA., an organization of several different groups. From the outset, Rodney's party challenged the PNC, by then in office, through gerrymandering and violence. For example there were twobungled assassination , attempts, one on Clive Thomas, an internationally respected economist and Joshua Ramsammy, a university professor; in 1979 Rodney himself and four party members were put on trial, charged with setting fire to a government building and the headquarters of the PNC and denied trial by jury; two of Rodney's colleagues were killed and one week after Rodney's trial began, he came to a tragic end. His death was mourned throughout the region and around the world.

Evaluating his work, many of yesteryear recalled Marcus Garvey, the more recent saw similarities with Franz Fanon and C.L.R. James. The present writer is full of admiration for Bob Marley whose universal theme of compassion underlined the need for understanding and wisdom throughout the world. The Caribbean needs them all.

Walter Rodney belongs in that pantheon of philosophers whose names adorn the history of the Caribbean and elsewhere and who have carved a niche in the imagination of any who has studied them: C.L.R. James, Eric Williams, Marcus Garvey, Franz Fanon and Bob Marley. Each has understood the Caribbean people nd made a personal contribution, seeking always to uplift them from the victimization of history and the poverty of material circumstance. C.L.R. James puts it nicely in Party Politics in the West Indies.

People of the West Indies, you do not know your own power. No one dares to tell you. You are a unique combination of the greatest driving force in the world today, the underdeveloped formerly colonial,colored peoples;and more than any of them by education, way of life and language,you are completely part of Western Civilization. Alone above all people in the world you began our historical existence in a highly developed modern society —the sugar plantation.

Index

Breinigsville, PA USA
03 December 2010
250651BV00002B/3/P